Touching Incidents

and

Remarkable Answers to Prayer

by
S. B. Shaw

Schmul Publishing Co.
Schmul's Wesleyan Book Club   Salem, Ohio

Copyright © 1997 by Schmul Publishing Co.
All rights reserved. No part of this publication may be reproduced or used in any form or by any means—graphic, electronic, or mechanical, including photocopying, recording, taping, or information storage or retrieval systems—without prior written permission of the publisher.

Published by Schmul Publishing Co.
PO Box 716
Salem, Ohio 44460

Printed in the United States of America

Printed by Old Paths Tract Society
RR2, Box 43
Shoals, Indiana 47581

ISBN 0-88019-365-4

Contents

Preface 9
Introduction 11

1 .... **13**
    The child-heroine of New Brunswick 13
    The influence of a mother's prayers 14
    Death of a Soul-Sleeper 16
    A man who lacked moral courage 17
    A rich man's death scene 19
    The widow's wood and flour—the unbelieving ones made speechless 20
    They who trust the Lord shall not want 22

2 .... **24**
    Annie and Vanie's first real prayer 24
    She was a good wife to me 26
    Prevailing prayer for a revival 27
    And dying is but going home. 28
    I'll never steal again—if father kills me for it. 31
    Charlie Coulson, the Christian drummer boy. 32
    God's care for the widow and orphans. 36
    A would-be murderer's arm paralyzed. 36
    Dying children and youth. 37
    Does this railroad lead to Heaven? 39
    The sequel. 40

3 .... **42**
    For His sake 42
    Experience of a minister's wife on the frontier 46
    Superhuman control of the locomotive, in answer to prayer 49
    Married to a drunkard 50
    Kicked for Christ's sake 52
    An effectual prayer 53
    Bishop Simpson's recovery 55
    Healed of diphtheria 56
    A widow's wonderful deliverance 57
    The conversion of Hudson Taylor 58
    Awful providences 59

4 62

- John Byers' prevailing prayer 62
- A vision of Heaven. 63
- Miracle of healing. 65
- Remarkable healing of Mrs. Susan E. Miller 67
- Instantly healed of rupture 67
- The young martyr 68
- Revivals vs. fairs—wonders of prayer 70
- An army miraculously delivered 71
- Little mother 72
- The Quaker who refused to fight 73
- A child's prayer answered 74
- Send food to John. 75
- Kiss me, mama 77

5 79

- The converted infidel 79
- The stowaway 85
- The midnight conflict 86
- Healed through faith. I am the Lord that healeth thee. —Exodus 15:26 88
- Translation of Bishop Haven 91
- Jessie finding Jesus 93
- A mob quieted in answer to prayer 94
- Show me the doctor 95
- She died for him 95
- Praying for wood 96
- Miraculously healed 96

6 98

- Carletta and the merchant 98
- The Golden Rule exemplified 102
- How the prayer of faith reached a family 103
- The stone chair 104
- They are not strangers, mamma 107
- A cancer healed, and a withered arm restored 108
- Only a vote 108
- Waiting for the angelic convoy 109
- How a little girl utilized the telephone 110
- Dying in despair 111
- A wonderful visitor 112
- The lame healed 115

REMARKABLE ANSWERS TO PRAYER

7 .... **118**
Prayer for the preacher 118
Prevailing prayer of a child 118
Visions of heaven and hell 119
Visit to heaven 121
A view of hell 122
The wonderful cure of Mrs. Sherman 126
The dying newsboy 128
The dying babe 129
Little Jennie's sickness and death 131

8 .... **134**
There is no rest in hell 134
The bridal wine cup 139
A mother's faith–the life of Beate Paulus 141
Dying words of Miss Mary Willard 144
A cyclone of power and glory in answer to prayer 146
Only a tallow dip 147
A manifestation of parental love 148
There's the Lord's answer 150
A lesson for mothers 151
I'm so glad you have come! 152

9 .... **153**
A mother's prayer answered 153
The prodigal 154
A great revival in answer to prevailing prayer 155
Ship's crew saved in answer to prayer 156
A most miraculous escape 157
Remarkable experience of C. H. Spurgeon 157
Kate Shelly's bravery 159
He blesses God for the faith of his little girl 160
The greatest revival of the Christian era 162
The widow and the judge 162
Saved from the flames and waves, and shall be from sins 165
The famous Praying Johnny 165
How three Sunday school children met their fate 167
The dying child's prayer for her drunken father 168
A prevailing prayer of Mrs. Van Cott 169
A great revival in a single night 170

10 171

William Clowes, the spiritual mountaineer 171
How Carvosso prevailed with God for his children 173
New England saved in answer to prayer 173
The escape of the Spree 174
The sailor and the picture of Christ 175
A persecutor's awful end 176
Revival at Harvey, Illinois 177
George Müller, of Bristol, England 178
John Wesley healed in answer to prayer 180
Prayer answered for a debt of ninety dollars 180
Corn the frost could not kill 181
The dying boy 182
Instances of the power of prayer 182
Edward Payson, a man who prayed without ceasing 183
The angel of mercy 184
Ivy poison suddenly healed 185
Revelations from God in dreams 187

11 190

The wonderful results of a little praying band 190
Triumphant death of three children 192
A guiding voice 193
A wonderful answer to prayer 194
Miss Carrie Webb's story of her restoration to health by prayer 196
Remarkable prayer of missionary Cox and his brother, for their brother 197
The heaven-built wall 199
A wonderful experience 200
Instances of divine power 202
Persecutors put to silence, and converted 204
John Knox's prevailing prayer for Scotland 206

12 207

The blind restored to sight 207
Special answers to prayer 208
The secret of James Caughey's wonderful success 209
Let them abide till the morrow 212
Behold, I send you forth as sheep among wolves 213
The secret of John Smith's success 214
How William Tennent defeated the powers of darkness 215
In India—in answer to prayer 216
Can I be saved? 219
The widow's prayer answered 220

12 (continued)
Prayers answered for rain 221
The widow's shoes 223
Instantaneously healed 224
The Lord's way of sending help 224
Redfield in a hard place 225

13 227
Prayer answered for one hundred missionaries and money to support them 227
Testimony of a saved infidel 228
I don't love you now, mother 229
How a blacksmith prevailed with God for a revival 231
Result of Rev. John S. Inskip's prayer 231
The winds controlled in answer to John Wesley's prayer 232
The clouds stayed in answer to prayer 233
Results of a life of prevailing prayer 234
Protected by angels 235
Dr. Charles Cullis—the man that believed God 236
The Lord will provide 238

Preface

IT IS NEEDLESS TO say much by way of preface to this book. It will speak for itself. From the writer's standpoint, none but those "given over to hardness of heart" can read these *Touching Incidents* without having their souls wondrously stirred within them; and none but the willfully unbelieving can say, in view of the *Remarkable Answers to Prayer* herein recorded, that God does not hear and regard the cries of his faithful children.

But let it be remembered that "prayer rises far above a mere form of good words. These, of themselves, are nothing, and may be much worse than nothing. The soul of the reader or utterer must be in them to give them life and power. God hears not my words, He hears me. I rise to Him upon the wings of prayer. I might recite good words forever, but unless my spirit is in them, they are nothing." Yea, nothing but idle words, and mockery before God. The prayer of faith is always prompted by the Holy Spirit, and always receives an answer from the living Father whose Spirit moved its utterance in harmony with His own blessed will.

In these pages no place is given to anything that did not appear to be reliable, as well as calculated to do good. Some of the accounts narrated have come within our personal knowledge. Others have been written or furnished expressly for this work. Still others have been selected from the works of well-known authors, or gleaned from the large number of periodicals which came regularly to our office in connection with the periodical that was under our control. Nor has the supply of material by any means been exhausted. We have felt, rather, as did Paul, when, after referring to many of the mighty works wrought through faith in olden times, he said, "And what shall I say more? For the time would fail to tell me of Gideon, and of Barak, and of Samson, and of Jephthae; of David also, and Samuel, and of the prophets; who through faith subdued kingdoms, wrought righteousness, obtained promises, stopped the mouths of lions."

We pray that through the perusal of these pages, precious souls may be led to the cross and the Savior, and God's children encouraged to trust Him in every hour of need.

Your brother, true to God and man,
S. B. Shaw

Introduction

TRUE PRAYER IS THE language of an earnest soul breathing after God, and a knowledge of his will. The praying spirit is a search for the presence of God, and a continued craving for a conscious blessing from Him, "Give ear to my prayer, Oh God, and hide not thyself from my supplication."

"Oh Lord God of my salvation, I have cried day and night before thee; let my prayer come before thee; incline thine ear unto my cry; for my soul is full of troubles." "Hear me when I call, Oh God of my righteousness; thou hast enlarged me, when I was in distress; have mercy upon me, and hear my prayer." These are the cries of a dependent, trusting, and enriched heart. They show the natural disposition of troubled man to fly to God for succor and relief.

Man has always prayed. He cannot help it. He is made so. His prayers may not always be prompted by the right motive, nor couched in acceptable phraseology, nor offered in the proper spirit. "Ye ask and receive not because ye ask amiss." But man will pray. He must pray. The very nature of his earthly life demands prayer. He may rebel against his environments, scoff at the necessity for supplication, for years neglect his duty, yet sooner or later, secretly or openly, he will call upon a higher power for that aid which earthly help cannot render.

There is no substitute for prayer. Praise is excellent, and good works are noble, but prayer is indispensable. "Ask and ye shall receive," has its counterpart in, "ask not and ye shall receive not." The prayerless life is a barren life. Jesus said, "Men ought always to pray." He set a glorious example—"Sit ye here while I go and pray yonder." His human life was the grandest life ever lived, yet it was a life at conscious dependence upon God, and constant supplication for His aid and blessing.

Prayer is successful when offered in faith and with obedience. No man can expect God to bless him while conscious of willful and unrepented sin. "He that turneth away his ear from hearing the law, even his prayer shall be abomination." "If I regard (*cherish*) iniquity in my heart, the Lord will not hear me." Man knows that his heart must be emptied of Satan, if it is to be filled with God. Just in proportion as his life is straight and pure will his trust take hold upon the Infinite. "The effectual, fervent prayer of a righteous mail availeth much." Mark you, "*a righteous* man." An unrighteous man may pray much and avail little.

Whatever tends to encourage the praying habit should be itself encouraged. That a carefully selected list of incidents and statements, showing the beauty, power and success of prayer, will in itself encourage further devotion, we most candidly believe. Such a list is to be found in the following pages. Every incident may not be in complete harmony with the exact facts. Scientific accuracy is impossible in gleaning so large a fund of matter from so many and varied sources. Yet the collection as a whole is both creditable and incredible. It shows diligence and painstaking care on the part of the author, and illustrates unmistakably the efficacy and utility of true prayer. Let the book be widely read, and let us hope that every reader may receive an abundant blessing while he peruses these attractive pages.

—James H. Potts
The Michigan Christian Advocate
Detroit, Michigan

REMARKABLE ANSWERS TO PRAYER

1

The child-heroine of New Brunswick

WE HAVE READ A touching incident about three little children, who, last autumn, late in the season, wandered alone in a dreary region of New Brunswick. The sun had already sunk in the west, and the gloom of evening was spreading itself over the surrounding country.

The night came on fast; and feeling sure that they could not get home before daybreak, the eldest, a girl of only six years, quietly placed the two little ones in a sheltered nook on the sea-beach; and fearing the cold, chilly night for the younger children, Mary stripped off most of her own clothing to keep them warm.

She then started off to gather dry seaweed, and whatever else she could find, to cover them with. Having tenderly in this way wrought for some time to make them a nest, she at last fell down exhausted with the cold, and half bare to the cold inclement night.

That evening the loving father and tender mother sat up wondering at their children's long absence; the hours dragged slowly past with anxious watching, and silent listening for the well-known little pattering feet. In vain the fond parents' eyes pierced through the darkness. At length they roused the neighbors with their anxious inquiries after their lost ones. All that night was passed in searching and in tears, till early in the morning, lying fast asleep, and somewhat numbed with cold, were found little Johnny and Lizzie. But, oh, a touching spectacle lay near them; their young savior was stiff, cold and dead on the seaweed which the poor little child-heroine had not strength to drag into the nook, where those she so deeply loved, and died to save, were sleeping. Thus this little New Brunswick girl died in her successful and self-sacrificing endeavor to save her brother and sister.

Does not this recall the love of the Lord Jesus Christ to you who read? Mary went to the full extent of human love in dying for her little brother and sister. "Greater love hath no man than this, that a man lay down his life for his friends." Yet the Lord Jesus laid down his life for his enemies; for "scarcely for a righteous man will one die; yet peradventure for a good man some would even dare to die; but God commendeth His love toward us..." He makes no mistakes. Yet how many listen to this story with more emotion and interest than they do to the story of the cross, where the love of Jesus, the Son of God, is told in letters of blood!—*Dawn of the Morning*

The influence of a mother's prayers

More than thirty years ago, one lovely Sabbath morning, about eight young men, students in a law school, were walking along the banks of a stream that flows into the Potomac river, not far from the city of Washington. They were going to a grove, in a secluded place, to spend the hours of that holy day in playing cards. Each of them had a flask of wine in his pocket. They were the sons of praying mothers.

As they were walking along amusing each other with idle jests, the bell of a church in a little village not two miles off began to ring. It sounded in the ears of those thoughtless young men as plainly as though it were only on the other side of the little stream along which they were walking.

Presently one of their number, whose name was George, stopped, and said to the friend nearest him that he would go no farther, but would return to the village and go to church. His friend called out to their companions, who were a little ahead of them, "Boys! Boys! Come back here, George is getting religious; we must help him. Come on, and let us baptize him by immersion in the water." In a moment they formed a circle around him. They told him that the only way he could save himself from having a cold bath was by going with them.

In a calm, quiet, but earnest way, he said, "I know very well that you have power enough to put me in the water, and hold me there till I am drowned; and, if you choose, you can do so, and I will make no resistance; but listen to what I have to say, and then do as you think best.

"You all know that I am two hundred miles away from home; but you do not know that my mother is a helpless, bedridden invalid. I never remember seeing her out of bed. I am her youngest child. My father could not afford to pay for my schooling; but our teacher is a warm friend of my father, and offered to take me without any charge. He was very anxious for me to come; but mother would not consent. The struggle almost cost her what little life was left to her. At length, after many prayers on the subject, she yielded and said I might go. The preparations for my leaving home were soon made. My mother never said a word to we on the subject till the morning when I was about to leave. After I had eaten my breakfast she sent for me, and asked me if everything was ready. I told her all was ready, and I was only waiting for the stage. At her request I kneeled beside her bed. With her loving hand upon my head, she prayed for her youngest child. Many and many a night I have dreamed that whole scene over. It is the happiest recollection of my life, I believe, till the day of my death, I shall be able to repeat every word of that prayer. Then she spoke to me thus:

"'My precious boy, you do not know, you never can know, the agony of a mother's heart, in parting, for the last time, from her youngest child. When you leave home, you will have looked, for the last time, this side of the grave, on the face of her who loves you as no other mortal does or can. Your father cannot afford the expense of your making us visits during the two years that your studies will occupy. I cannot possibly live as long as that. The sand in the hourglass of my life has nearly run out. In the far off strange place to which you are going, there will be no loving mother to give counsel in time of trouble. Seek counsel and help from God. Every Sabbath morning, from ten to eleven o'clock, I will spend the hour in prayer for you. Wherever you may be during this sacred hour, when you ear the church bells ringing, let your thoughts come back to this chamber, where your dying mother will be agonizing in prayer for you. But I hear the stage coming. Kiss me farewell!'

"Boys, I never expect to see my mother again on earth. But by God's help, I mean to meet her in heaven."

As George stopped speaking the tears were streaming down his cheeks. He looked at his companions. Their eyes were filled with tears.

In a moment the ring which they had formed about him was opened. He passed out and went to church. He had stood up for the right against great odds.

They admired him for doing what they had not the courage to do. They all followed him to church. On their way there, each of them quietly threw away his cards and his wine flask. Never again did these young men play cards on the Sabbath.

From that day they all became changed men. Six of them died Christians, and are now in heaven. George is an able Christian lawyer in Iowa; and his friend, who wrote this account, has been for many years an earnest, active member of the church. Here were eight men converted by the prayers of that good Christian woman. And, if we only knew all the results of their examples and their labors, we should have good illustration of a mother's prayers.—*Bible Models*

TOUCHING INCIDENTS AND

Death of a Soul-Sleeper

Mrs. Mattie Campbell relates the happy death of her sister, a soul-sleeper, which occurred last May. It seems that her views were changed just before she entered heaven.

"In Sabbath-school this afternoon a message came: 'Emma is dying. Come quickly if you want to see her alive.' My dear sister. We had played together, and more than all, we dreamed dreams of the fairy future, wherein we saw everything but care and temptation crowning the golden pathway for our jubilant feet. She was plump and rosy, full of laughter and frolic, which life's stern realities had not subdued. Strong and well I had seen her, but five days before. Yet, Ah! In such an hour as ye think not the Son of Man cometh. On our way the sad face of our family physician confirmed the truth. 'She may linger until sundown,' he said; and all the way I prayed, and felt it would be answered, 'Lord, dear Lord, only let me have one word to know how it is with her soul.'

Mother met me at the door. This was a heavy grief. 'Ask how it is with her soul,' said she. I entered the room filled with weeping friends. I pressed the damp, damp, cold brow. She knew me, and spoke in the old sweet way. Soon I commenced slow and low the hymn we used to sing together, *Jesus, Lover of My Soul*, while I anxiously watched to catch a mark of grace upon her fast changing features. A happy, peaceful smile broke over her face. I bent down and she spoke, 'God was always good to us, sister. He has not given me one harsh word since I came down to my bed.' How the praise rushed to my lips. 'He giveth and upbraideth not.' Glory be to His name!

"Divinely assured that she was dying, she spoke of a long, sweet sleep, the sleep of the soul and body, until the general resurrection—for this was her belief. She called for one and another of her friends and neighbors, and exhorted them in burning words to meet her in heaven, charging them to bring their families for whom they were also responsible.

"With mind clear and composed, she then lay, waiting to pass into an unconscious slumber, only to awaken at the last trump. 'Hark,' said she, listening intently; 'I hear music; don't you hear it? And mother, I see a door.'

'Is it open?' Asked her mother. And we held our breath as she answered. 'Yes, it is open.'

'Do you see inside?' Her face grew radiant as she answered, 'Yes, I see inside. It is a beautiful place. It is heaven. I see forms clothed in white, many, yes, a multitude of beautiful beings, their hands upraised, while they are waving something in their hands.' And then in wonder and astonishment, 'Why, there's Pa!' Then she very intelligently gave orders for her burial. Good-byes were said, and in childlike pleading tones she called, 'Come, dear Lord, I am ready; come now, and take my breath, it hurts me so.' An effort on her part to close the dear eyes and mouth, a few more agonizing moments, and the open door received her gentle spirit. We led the bereaved mother from the room, all that was left of my happy childhood days."–*Earnest Christian*.

A man who lacked moral courage

A few years ago I went to close a meeting, and said, "Are there any here who would like to have me remember them in prayer? I would like to have them rise!" And there was a man rose, and when I saw him stand up, my heart leaped in me with joy. I had been anxious for him a long time. I went to him as soon as the meeting was over, and took him by the hand, and said, "You are coming out for God, are you not?"

He said, "I want to, and have made up my mind to be a Christian; only there is one thing standing in my way."

"What is that?" I asked.

"Well," he replied, "I lack moral courage." Naming a friend of his, he added, "If he had been here tonight I should not have risen; I am afraid when he hears I have risen for prayer he will begin to laugh at me, and I won't have moral courage to stand up for Christ."

I said, "If Christ is what he is represented in the Bible, he is worth standing up for; and if heaven is what we are told it is in the Bible, it is worth living for."

"I lack moral courage," he answered, and the man was trembling from head to foot. I thought he was just at the very threshold of heaven, and that one step more was going to take him in, and that he would take the step that night. I talked and prayed with him, and the Spirit seemed to be striving mightily with him, but he did not get the light. Night after night he came, and the Spirit strove with him; but just one thing kept him back—he lacked moral courage. At last the Spirit of God, which had striven so mightily with him, seemed to leave him, and there were no more strivings. He left off coming to church, was off among his old companions, and would not meet me in the street; he was ashamed to do so.

About six months afterward 1 got a message from him, and found him on what he thought was his dying bed. He wanted to know if there was hope for him at the eleventh hour. I tried to tell him that there was hope for any man that would accept Christ. I prayed for him, and day after day, I visited him.

Contrary to all expectations, he began to recover; and when he was convalescent, finding him one day sitting in front of his house, I sat by his side, and said, "You will soon be well enough to come up to the church, and when you are, you will come up; and you are just going to confess Christ boldly, are you not?"

"Well," said he, "I promised God when I was on what I thought to be my dying bed I would serve Him, and I made up my mind to be a Christian; but I am not going to be one just now. Next spring I am going over to Lake Michigan, and I am going to buy a farm and settle down, and then I am going to be a Christian."

I said, "How dare you talk that way! How do you know that you are going to live till next spring? Have you a lease of your life?"

"I was never better than I am now; I am a little weak, but I will soon have my strength. I have a fresh lease of my life, and will be well for a good many years yet," he answered.

I said, "It seems to me you are tempting God," and I pleaded with him to come out boldly.

"No," he said; "the fact is I have not the courage to face my old companions, and I cannot serve God in Chicago."

I said, "If God has not grace enough to keep you in Chicago, He has not in Michigan." I urged him then and there to surrender his soul and body to the Lord Jesus; but the more I urged him the more irritated he got, till at last he said, "Well, you need not trouble yourself any more about my soul; I will attend to that. If I am lost it will be my own fault. I will take the risk."

I left him, and in about a week I got a message from his wife. Going to the house, I met her at the door weeping. I said "What is the trouble?"

"Oh, sir! I have just had a council of physicians here, and they have all given my husband up to die; they say he cannot live."

I said, "Does he want to see me?"

She replied, "No."

"Why did you send?"

"Why," she said, "I cannot bear to see him die in this terrible state of mind."

"What is his state of mind?"

"Why, he says that his damnation is sealed, and he will be in hell in a little while."

I went into the room, but he turned his head away. I said, "How is it with you?" Not a word; he was as silent as death. I spoke the second time, but he made no response. I looked him in the face, and called him by name, and said, "Will you not tell me how it is with you?"

He turned and fixed that awful, deathly took upon me, and, pointing to the stove, he said, "My heart is as hard as the iron in that stove; it is too late, my damnation is sealed, and I shall be in hell in a little while."

I said, "Don't talk so; you can be saved now if you will."

He replied, "Don't mock me; I know better." I talked with him, and quoted promise after promise, but he said not one was for him.

"Christ has come knocking at the door of my heart many a time, and the last time He came I promised to let Him in; and when I got well I turned away again, and now I have to perish without Him."

I talked, but I saw I was doing no good, and so I threw myself on my knees. He said, "You can pray for my wife and children, you need not pray for me; it is a waste of your time, it is too late." I tried to pray, but it seemed as if what he said was true—it seemed as if the heavens were brass over me. I rose and took his hand, and it seemed to me as if I were bidding farewell to a friend that I never was to see again in time or eternity. He lingered till the sun went down. His wife told me that his end was terrible. All that he was heard to say were these fearful words: "The harvest is past, the summer is ended, and I am not saved." There he lay, and every little while he would take up the awful lamentation, "The harvest is past, the summer is ended, and I am not saved." And just as the sun was sinking behind those western prairies he was going into the arms of death.

As he was expiring, his wife noticed that his lips were quivering, he was trying to say something, and she reached over her ear, and all she could hear was, "The harvest is past, the summer is ended, and I am not saved;" and the angels bore him to the judgment. He lived a Christless life, he died a Christless death, we wrapped him in a Christless shroud, nailed him in a Christless coffin, and bore him to a Christless grave. Oh, how dark! Oh, how sad! I may be speaking to someone today, and the harvest may be passing with you, the summer may be ending. Oh, be wise now, and accept the Lord Jesus Christ! May God's blessing rest upon us all, and may we meet in glory, is the prayer of my heart!—D. L. Moody

A rich man's death scene

A striking incident was communicated to the *New York Press* a few years ago, by a deeply humble minister. One of the leading members of his church was greatly distressed in his last sickness, on reviewing his mode of living and reflecting upon his family and the comparatively small sum he had given to the Lord's cause. In every way the pastor endeavored to comfort him. He spoke of his having given cheerfully, and as much as others did. He reminded him that the best of us are unprofitable servants, and must look to the mercy of God in Christ as out only hope. The troubled man found no peace or comfort, but grew more and more uneasy, distressed and agonized as his end drew near.

At last, taking the hand of his pastor, he said, "Brother, I am going to the judge unprepared to meet Him, because you have been unfaithful to me. For years I have lived, and taught my family to live largely for this world. We have denied ourselves nothing, but spent thousands on personal comforts. When I gave hundreds to Christ and His church it should have been thousands. My business energy and time and money have been mostly devoted to self-pleasing and gratification, and how can I meet my judge and give an account of my stewardship? I am beyond recovery. Do what you can to save other professors who are in the current of worldly self-indulgence and extravagance, which is sweeping them to destruction."—Matlock

The widow's wood and flour—the unbelieving ones made speechless
The following instance is known to *The Christian* as true, and to a remarkable degree indicates how thoroughly God knows our minutest needs, and how effectively He makes those who ever reproach His name ashamed of their unbelief.

"A friend and relative of the one who was 'a widow indeed,' one who trusted in God, and continued in supplications and prayers day and night, was once brought into circumstances of peculiar straightness and trial. She had two daughters, who exerted themselves with their needles to earn a livelihood; and at that time they were so busily engaged in trying to finish some work that had long been on their hands, they had neglected to make provision for their ordinary wants, until they found themselves one winter's day in the midst of a New England snowstorm, with food and fuel almost exhausted, at a distance from neighbors, and without any means of procuring needful sustenance.

"The daughters began to be alarmed, and were full of anxiety at the dismal prospect; but the good old mother said, 'Don't worry, girls, the Lord will provide; we have enough for to day, and tomorrow may be pleasant;' and in this hope the girls settled down again to their labor.

"Another morning came, and with it no sunshine, but wind and snow in abundance. The storm still raged, but no one came near the house, and all was dark and dismal without.

"Noon came, and the last morsel of food was eaten, the wood was almost gone, and there was no token of any relief for their necessities. The girls became much distressed, and talked anxiously of their condition, but the good mother said, 'Don't worry, the Lord will provide.'

"But they had heard that story the day before, and they knew not the strong foundation upon which that mother's' trust was builded, and could not share the confidence she felt.

REMARKABLE ANSWERS TO PRAYER

"'If we get anything today the Lord will have to bring it Himself, for nobody can get here if he tries,' said one of the daughters, impatiently; but the mother said, 'Don't worry.' And so they sat down again to their sewing, the daughters to muse upon their necessitous condition, and the mother to roll her burden on the Everlasting Arms.

"Now mark the way in which the Lord came to their rescue, and just at this moment of extremity, put it into the heart of one of His children to go and carry relief. Human nature at such a time would never have ventured out in such a storm, but waited for a pleasant day. But Divine Wisdom and power made him carry just what was needed, in the face of adverse circumstances, and just at the time it was needed.

"Mr. M. sat at his fireside about a mile away, surrounded by every bounty and comfort needed to cheer his heart, with his only daughter sitting by his side.

"For a long time not a word had been spoken, and he had seemed lost in silent meditation, till at length he said, 'Mary, I want you to go and order the cattle yoked, and then get me a bag. I must go and carry some wood and flour to Sister C.'

"'Why, father, it is impossible for you to go. There is no track, and it is all of a mile up there. You would almost perish.'

"The old man sat in silence a few moments, and said, 'Mary, I must go.' She knew her father too well to suppose that words would detain him, and so complied with his wishes. While she held the bag for him, she felt perhaps a little uneasiness to see the flour so liberally disposed of, and said, 'I wish you would remember that I want to give a poor woman some flour if it ever clears off.' The old man understood the intimation, and said, 'Mary, give all you feel it duty to, and when the Lord says stop, I will do so.'

"Soon all things were ready, and the patient oxen took their way to the widow's home, wallowing through the drifted snow, and dragging the sled with its load of wood and flour. About four o'clock in the afternoon, the mother had arisen from her work to fix the fire, and looking out of the window she saw the oxen at the door, and she knew that the Lord had heard her cry.

"She said not a word—why should she? She was not surprised, but presently, a heavy step at the threshold caused the daughters to look up with astonishment, as Mr. M. strode unceremoniously into the room, saying, 'The Lord told me, Sister C., that you wanted some wood and flour.'

"'He told you the truth,' said the widow, 'and I will praise Him forever.'

"'What think you now, girls?' She continued, as she turned in solemn joy to her unbelieving daughters.

"They were speechless; not a word escaped their lips; but they pondered that new revelation of the providential mercy of the Lord, until it made upon their minds an impression never to be effaced.

"From that hour they learned to trust in Him who cares for His needy in the hour of distress, and who, from His boundless stores, supplies the wants of those who trust in Him."—*Answers to Prayer*

They who trust the Lord shall not want

Mrs. Mary Grant Cramer, whose husband is a member of the Cincinnati Conference of the Methodist Episcopal Church, who was for many years U. S. Minister to Denmark, and afterwards to Switzerland, and has also filled the chair of Systematic Theology in Boston University, has related for us, by letter, several accounts of answers to prayer, among which are the following:

"When Dr. George E. Shipman and wife, of Chicago, came to see us in Copenhagen, I was much impressed with the striking and interesting incidents Mrs. Shipman told us, in connection with their faith-work in the Foundlings' Home. For instance, when they had put all they had in the Home, and there was a payment of six hundred dollars to be made, and it could no longer be postponed, for the man to whom it was due said, 'Business is business, and I must have my money, and I will send my son for it in the morning.' They betook themselves to prayer, hoping the postman would bring them a letter containing the required amount, but he did not. Soon after he passed, a man rang the bell, and left an envelope containing a check for six hundred dollars, as a present from the mayor of the city, who was not a religious man; but his wife, who was then in Europe, was interested in the Home, and he sent the money on her account. Directly after it came they handed the check for the amount to the man who was expected to call for it. In a similar way, Dr. Shipman on another occasion received four hundred dollars a little while before it was needed, and often got smaller sums in answer to prayer.

"Mrs. Shipman told me of Mrs. Pithey, an invalid saint she knew in Chicago, who was supported by voluntary gifts in answer to prayer. This made the closing years of her life a marvelous proof of God's care for His helpless children who trust Him.

"I might add another incident: Recently a saintly woman, who has consecrated all she has to the Lord, and who lives by faith, giving her services gratuitously to His cause, felt that after the fatiguing labors of the summer, a change would be beneficial to her; she kept this to herself. Soon after a lady sent for her to call upon her, her object being to inform Miss M. that she felt impressed that she ought to go away from home for awhile, and gave her fifty dollars. One day a co-worker of this good sister, told me that she asked a token of the Lord in money, and the same day she found it in anenvelope on the table, directed to her, from one who had never before made her a present, and who at first intended this sum for some one else.

"I am acquainted with a minister in New York city, who gave up his church and a salary of five thousand a year, to establish a church where he could reach the masses. He met with much opposition, but has met also with great success in his work. He said that on various occasions he felt it his duty to give all he had away, and before be could reach his home it would be replaced fourfold. His wife was greatly opposed to his giving up a certainty for what she thought an uncertainty, especially as they had five children; but be told me that since they depend upon the Lord for their support, his wife has less solicitude about how they will be provided for, than she had when his salary was five thousand dollars a year.

"Truly they who trust the Lord shall not want."

TOUCHING INCIDENTS AND

2

Annie and Vanie's first real prayer

TWO SISTERS, ONE ABOUT five years of age, the other next older, were accustomed to go each Saturday morning, some distance from home, to get chips and shavings from a cooper shop.

One morning, with basket well filled, they were returning home; when the older one was taken suddenly sick with cramps or cholera. She was in great pain, and unable to proceed, much less to bear the basket home. She sat down on the basket, and the younger one held her from falling.

The street was a lonely one, occupied by workshops, factories, etc. Every one was busy within; not a person was seen on the street.

The little girls were at a loss what to do. Too timid to go into any workshop, they sat a while, as silent and quiet as the distressing pains would allow.

Soon the elder girl said, "You know, Annie, that a good while ago mother told us that if we ever got into trouble, we should pray, and God would help us. Now you help me to get down upon my knees, and hold me up, and we will pray."

There, on the sidewalk, did these two little children ask God to send some one to help them home.

The simple and brief prayer being ended, the sick girl was again helped up, and sat on the basket, waiting the answer to their prayers,

Presently Annie. Saw, far down the street on the opposite side, a man come out from a factory, look around him, up and down the street, and go back into the factory.

"Oh sister, he has gone in again," said Annie. "Well," said Vanie, "perhaps he is not the one God is going to send. If he is, he will come back again.

"There he comes again," said Annie. He walks this way. He seems looking for something. He walks slow, and is without his hat. He puts his hand to his head, as if he did not know what to do. Oh sister, he has gone in again; what shall we do?"

"That may not be the one whom God will send to help us," said Vanie. "If he is, he will come out again."

Oh yes, there he is; this time with his hat on," said Annie. "He comes this way; he walks slowly, looking around on every side. He does not see us; perhaps the trees hide us. Now he sees us, and is coming quickly."

A brawny German in broken accents, asks, "Oh children, what is the matter?"

"Oh sir," said Annie, "sister here is so sick she cannot, walk, and we cannot get home."

"Where do you live, my dear?"

"At the end of this street; you can see the house from here."

"Never mind," said the man, "I takes you home." So the strong man gathered the sick child in his arms, and with her head pillowed upon his shoulder, carried her to the place pointed out by the younger girl. Annie ran round the house to tell her mother that there was a man at the front door wishing to see her. The astonished mother, with a mixture of surprise and joy, took charge of the precious burden, and the child was laid upon a bed.

After thanking the man, she expected him to withdraw, but instead, he stood turning his hat in his hands, as one who wishes to say something, but knows not how to begin.

The mother, observing this, repeated her thanks, and finally said, "Would you like me to pay you for bringing my child home?"

"Oh no," said he with tears, "God pays me! God pays me! I would like to tell you something, but I speak English so poorly that I fear you will not understand."

The mother assured him that she was used to the German, and could understand him very well.

"I am the proprietor of an ink factory," said he. "My men work by the piece. I have to keep separate accounts with each. I pay them every Saturday. At twelve o'clock they will be at my desk, for their money. This week I have had many hindrances, and was behind with my books. I was working hard at them with the sweat on my face, in my great anxiety to be ready in time. Suddenly I could not see the figures; the words in the book all ran together, and I had a plain impression on my mind that some one in the street wished to see me. I went out, looked up and down the street, but seeing no one, went back to my desk, and wrote a little. Presently the darkness was greater than before, and the impression stronger than before, that some one in the street needed me.

"Again I went out, looked up and down the street, walked a little way, puzzled to know what it meant. Was my hard work, and were the cares of business driving me out of my wits? Unable to solve the mystery I turned again into my shop and to my desk."

"This time my fingers refused to grasp the pen. I found myself unable to write a word, or make a figure; but the Impression was stronger than ever on my mind, that some one needed my help. A voice seemed to say, 'Why don't you go out as I tell you? There is need of your help.' This time I took my hat on going out, resolved to stay till I found out whether I was losing my senses, or there was a duty for me to do. I walked some distance without seeing any one, and was more and more puzzled, till I came opposite the children, and found that there was indeed need of my help. I cannot understand it, madam.'"

As the noble German was about leaving the house, the younger girl had the courage to say, "Oh mother, we prayed."

Thus the mystery was solved, and with tear-stained cheeks, a heaving breast, and a humble, grateful heart, the kind man went back to his accounts.

I have enjoyed many a happy hour in conversation with Annie in her own house since she has a home of her own. The last I knew of Annie and Vanie, they were living in the same city, earnest Christian women. Their children were growing up around them, who, I hope, will have like confidence in mother, and faith in God.—*Jeigh Arrh.*

Annie was the wife of James A. Clayton, of San Jose, California. I have enjoyed their hospitality, and esteem both very highly.—*James Rogers, Of Alabama Conference, M. E. Church*

She was a good wife to me

"She—was—good—wife—to—me. A good wife, God bless her!" The words were spoken in trembling accents over a coffin-lid. The woman asleep there had borne the heat and burden of life's long day, and no one had ever heard her murmur; her hand was quick to reach out a helping grasp to those who fell by the wayside; and her feet are swift on errands of mercy. The heart of her husband had trusted in her; he had left her to long hours of solitude, while he amused himself in scenes in which she had no part. When boon companions deserted him, when fickle affection selfishly departed, when pleasure palled, he went home and found her waiting for him.

> Come from your long, long roving,
>   On life's sea so bleak and rough;
> Come to me tender and loving,
>   And I shall be blessed enough.

That had been her love song always on her lips or in her heart. Children had been born to them. She had reared them almost alone, they were gone! Her hand had led them to the uttermost edge of the morning that had no noon. Then she had comforted him, and sent him out strong and wholehearted, while she stayed at home and cried. What can a woman do but cry and trust? Well, she is at rest now. But she could not die until he had promised to "bear up" not to fret, but to remember how happy they had been. They? Yes, it is even so. For she was blest in giving, and he in receiving. It was an equal partnership after all! "She—was—a—good—wife—to—me." Oh man! Man! Why not have told her so, when her ears were not dulled by death? Why wait to say these words over a coffin wherein lies a wasted, weary, gray-haired woman, whose eyes have so long held that pathetic story—of loss and suffering and patient yearning which so many women's eyes reveal—to those who read. Why not have made the wilderness in her heart blossom like the rose with the prodigality of your love? Now you would give worlds—were they yours to give—to see the tears of joy your words would have once caused, bejeweling the closed windows of her soul. It is too late.

> We have careful thoughts for the stranger,
>   And smiles for the sometimes guest;
> But oft for our own, the bitter tone,
>   Though we love our own the best. —Selected

Prevailing prayer for a revival

We know a preacher, still living, who was appointed to the charge of a church in Springfield, Illinois. The church seemed very much depressed. Its life was at a low ebb. It was in the midst of the harvest, in the hot weather when things seemed most depressed. The pastor, a holy man of God, announced on Sabbath evening to a small congregation of a score or two of persons, "There will be a prayermeeting in this church tomorrow morning at sunrise for the revival of the work of God and for the conversion of sinners." The people wondered at the notice, and went home.

The pastor went up into his study, which was in the parsonage by the side of the church, and gave that night to prayer. Just as the East began to lighten up a little with the coming day he had the assurance that his prayer was answered, and cast himself down on a sofa for a little rest. Presently he awoke suddenly to see the sun shining on the wall over his head. He sprang up and looked out of the window to see how late it was, when he saw the sun just rising above the horizon. Looking down into the yard by the church, he was overjoyed to see the church crowded with people, and the yard full, and teams crowding into the street for a long distance. God had heard his prayer, and had sent out his Spirit into the community, and there had been no sleeping in Springfield that night. People in the country who knew nothing of the appointment got up in the night, hitched up their teams, and drove into town and to the church to find out what the matter was. A good man had taken hold of God.

The prayermeeting began, and was closed that night at eleven o'clock. Several souls were converted. A gracious work broke out, and the community was greatly blessed. The foregoing we certify to on the highest authority, having it from the lips of the man himself, whom every body knowing him believes as soon as any thing outside of the Bible. We greatly need earnest, persevering, believing prayer. One night of such prayer kept by all the Church would startle the nation We sorely need a mighty baptism of power. We have all the other elements of success. We lack no machinery. We have truth, and the experience of its saving power and the appliances. What we now need is the outpouring of the Spirit upon us as a people. We must rekindle our fires. We must make our churches centers of saving power. One hour a day spent by the church in earnest prayer for the revival of God's work would make the coming year the most memorable in the history of the church. If you do not feel burdened, ask for the spirit of prayer, and that shall be given you. Forsake your sins and leave yourself with God, and give yourself to prayer, and all over the land God will hear and answer, and pour out his Spirit, and bestow his power, and make this year a revival year.—*Bishop C. H. Fowler.*

And dying is but going home.

Wending her way every Sabbath to a school in the west end of London, might have been seen a young girl, named Mary Jane Howes. Attached in no common degree to both her teachers and fellow scholars, nothing but sickness ever kept her away from school. Naturally of an obedient and kind disposition, she was, never known to tell a lie; but with all this natural amiability, the great change which alone fits the soul for an entrance into the kingdom of heaven had never taken place in that young heart. She had often been touched, awakened by the Holy Spirit to feel her need of this great salvation, but had neglected to seek it with all her heart. Her last sickness was brought on by what appeared at first to be only a slight cold.

As other symptoms followed, her mother took her to a doctor who pronounced her case to be dangerous, advising that she should keep her bed. She became rapidly worse, and being alarmed, her parents sent for one of the agents of the Mission, Mr. Garland. By her bedside he prayed for her with great fervor, and early on the following morning repeated his visit. At night she had become so much worse that they had sent for him, for they feared she was dying. No one had told her of her danger, and Mr. Garland requested all except her mother to leave the room. He then asked her if she thought her end was near, and if she felt prepared to meet her God. When the awful danger of her case dawned upon her, she exclaimed, "No, I am not prepared to meet my God, but I am not dying. I hope soon to recover, and be a help to my dear mother." Mr. Garland then told her that to all appearance, she would be in the world of spirits before many hours had passed, and urged her to seek the mercy of God through Jesus Christ our Lord.

"Oh!" She exclaimed," I am not fit to die; I am not converted; I can't die!" Seeing her great distress, her visitor kept pointing her to Jesus, praying with her most earnestly, the expression all the time deepening of her awful danger, repeating to her the gracious invitation, "Him that cometh unto Me, I will in nowise cast out." He left her for a little while.

When he departed she looked at him with a look of agony and despair, and exclaimed, "Oh Mr. Garland! My soul, my poor soul! I am unprepared for death and judgment."

Despair seemed to have settled on her soul, and was depicted on her countenance. It was heart-rending to hear her groans and see her tears. After a while she asked those present to sing the hymn beginning,

> *Rescue the perishing, care for the dying,*
>   *Snatch them in pity from sin and the grave;*
> *Weep o'er the erring one, lift up the fallen,*
>   *Tell them of Jesus the mighty to save.*

When they had sung the whole through she said, "Oh, sing it again!" While they were singing the second verse ,

> *Though they are slighting Him still He is waiting,*
>   *Waiting the penitent child to receive;*
> *Plead with them earnestly, plead with them gently,*
>   *He will forgive if they only believe.*

Despair yielded to faith, and with a joyful smile she exclaimed, "Jesus loves me; I can believe; I am saved! Saved through the blood of the Lamb!

My burden is all gone, my sins are all forgiven. I can die now. Jesus is mine, I am his. Hallelujah."

She now desired all present to join in singing,
> Safe in the arms of Jesus,
>   Safe on His gentle breast;
> There by His love o'ershaded,
>   Sweetly my soul shall rest.
> Hark, 'tis the voice of angels,
>   Borne in a song to me,
> Over the fields of glory
>   Over the jasper sea.

Each of her family, father, mother and two brothers, were called, and with tears and earnest entreaties she plead with them to meet her in heaven. Being now quite exhausted she laid down for a few minutes, and appeared to be in a calm sleep, when suddenly starting up she said, "Sing another hymn, for I feel so happy I must sing."

A friend commenced singing, "Jesus of Nazareth passeth by."

"No! No! Not that!" She exclaimed, "Jesus is not passing by; He is here in my room—in my soul. Sing, 'Ring the bells of heaven, there is joy today.'"

And on she talked, breathing forth words of rapturous joy and thanksgiving. After a while her mother said, "Are you not tired, my dear Mary?"

"Oh no!" She replied. "I am crossing the river, but the water is not deep. I can feel the bottom, and like David, I can walk through the valley of the shadow of death. It in the way home to my Father's house above."

A little while after, she said to her mother, "Hark, mother! Hark! They're singing. Oh! Such singing! I see angels. They all have long white robes, and golden crowns on their heads. Dear mother, this must be the valley of death. It seems dark and long, but I do not fear. Jesus is holding my hand, and I see a light at the other end, and the angels with outstretched arms to receive me, and I shall have a harp, a golden harp and, oh! Won't I strike it loud when I reach the other side!"

The enemy was suffered to tempt and distress her for a little while, and when he was overcome, with a sweet smile she cried out, "He is gone now; I only see Jesus."

Her sight now began to fail, but she was conscious to the last. "Can you see me, Mary?" Said her mother. "No," she replied, "I cannot see you, but I do see Jesus I'm nearly home now. All sing,
> Who, who are these beside the chilly wave,
>   Just on the borders of the silent grave;
> Shouting Jesus' power to save,
>   Washed in the blood of the Lamb?

REMARKABLE ANSWERS TO PRAYER

She joined in the singing, and when it was all over said, "Mother, one more kiss." Shortly after she exclaimed; "Jesus! Jesus! My–precious–Jesus." Her last words, and in a few moments another soul had joined the innumerable company around the throne.—*Selected by Sarah A. Cooke.*

I'll never steal again—if father kills me for it.

A friend of mine, seeking for objects of charity, got into the room of a tenement house. It was vacant. He saw a ladder pushed through the ceiling. Thinking that perhaps some poor creature had crept up there, he climbed the ladder, drew himself up through the hole, and found himself under the rafters. There was no light but that which came through a bull's-eye in the place of a tile. Soon he saw a heap of chips and shavings, and on them a boy about ten years old.

"Boy, what are you doing there?"

"Hush! Don't tell anybody please, sir."

"What are you doing here?"

"Don't tell anybody, sir; I'm hiding."?

"What are you hiding from?"

"Don't tell anybody, if you please, sir."

"Where's your mother?"

"Mother is dead."

"Where's your father?"

"Hush! Don't tell him! Don't tell him! But look here!" He turned himself on his face, and through the rags of his jacket and shirt, my friend saw the boy's flesh was bruised, and the skin broken.

"Why, my boy, who beat you like that?"

"Father did, sir."

"What did your father beat you like that for?"

"Father got drunk, sir, and beat me 'cos I wouldn't steal."

"Did you ever steal?"

"Yes, sir. I was a street thief once."

"And why don't you steal any more?"

"Please, sir, I went to the mission school, and they told me there of God, and of heaven, and of Jesus; and they taught me, 'Thou shalt not steal;' and I'll never steal again, if father kills me for it. But, please, sir, don't tell him."

"My boy, you must not stay here; you will die. Now, you wait patiently here for a little time; I'm going away to see a lady. We will get a better place for you than this."

"Thank you, sir; but please, sir, would you like to hear me sing a little hymn?" Bruised, battered, forlorn, friendless, motherless, hiding away from an infuriated father, he had a little hymn to sing.

"Yes I will hear you sing your little hymn."

He raised himself on his elbow and then sang,
> Gentle Jesus, meek and mild,
> Look upon a little child;
> > Suffer me to come to Thee.
> Fain would I to Thee be brought,
> Gracious Lord, forbid it not;
> > In the kingdom of Thy grace,
> > Give a little child a place.

"That's the little hymn, sir, Good-bye."

The gentleman went away, came back again in less than two hours, and climbed the ladder. There were the chips, and there was the little boy with one hand by his side, and the other tucked in his bosom, underneath the little ragged shirt—dead.—*John B. Gough.*

Charlie Coulson, the Christian drummer boy.

Two or three times in my life God in His mercy touched my heart, and twice before my conversion I was under deep conviction,

During the American war, I was surgeon in the United States army, and after the battle of Gettysburg there were many hundred wounded soldiers in my hospital, amongst whom were twenty-eight who had been wounded so severely that they required my service at once. Some whose legs had to be amputated, some their arms, and others both their arm and leg. One of the latter was a boy who had been but three months in the service, and being too young for a soldier had enlisted as a drummer.

When my assistant surgeon and one of my stewards wished to administer chloroform, previous to the amputation, he turned his head aside and positively refused to receive it. When the steward told him that it was the doctor's orders, he said, "Send the doctor to me." When I came to his bedside, I said, "Young man, why do you refuse chloroform? When I found you on the battlefield you were so far gone that I thought it hardly worth while to pick you up; but when you opened those large blue eyes I thought you had a mother somewhere who might, at that moment, be thinking of her boy. I did not want you to die on the field, so ordered you to be brought here; but you have now lost so much blood that you are too weak to endure an operation without chloroform, therefore you had better let me give you some."

REMARKABLE ANSWERS TO PRAYER

He laid his hand on mine, and looking me in the face, said, "Doctor, one Sunday afternoon, in the Sabbath-school, when I was nine and a half years old, I gave my heart to Christ. I learned to trust Him then; I have been trusting Him ever since, and I can trust Him now. He is my strength and my stimulant. He will support me while you amputate my arm and leg."

I then asked him if he would allow me to give him a little brandy. Again he looked me in the face saying, "Doctor, when I was about five years old my mother knelt by my side, with her arm around my neck, and said 'Charlie, I am now praying to Jesus that you may never know the taste of strong drink; your papa died a drunkard, and went down to a drunkard's grave, and I promised God, if it were His will that you should grow up, that you should warn young men against the bitter cup.' I am now seventeen years old, but I have never tasted anything stronger than tea and coffee, and as I am, in all probability, about to go into the presence of my God, would you send me there with brandy on my stomach?"

The look that boy gave me I shall never forget. At that time I hated Jesus, but I respected that boy's loyalty to his Savior; and when I saw how he loved and trusted Him to the last, there was something that touched my heart, and I did for that boy what I had never done for any other soldier—I asked him if he wanted to see his chaplain. "Oh, yes, sir," was the answer.

When Chaplain R. came, he at once knew the boy from having often met him at the tent prayermeetings, and taking his hand said, "Well, Charlie, I am sorry to see you in this sad condition."

"Oh, I am all right, sir," he answered. "The doctor offered me chloroform, but I declined it; then he wished to give me brandy, which I also declined; and now, if my Savior calls me, I can go to Him in my right mind."

"You may not die, Charlie," said the chaplain; "but if the Lord should call you away, is there anything I can do for you after you are gone?"

"Chaplain, please put your hand under my pillow and take my little Bible; in it you will find my mother's address; please send it to her, and write a letter, and tell her that since the day I left home I have never let a day pass without reading a portion of God's word, and daily praying that God would bless my dear mother; no matter whether on the march, on the battlefields, or in the hospital."

"Is there anything else I can do for you, my lad?" asked the chaplain.

"Yes, please write a letter to the superintendent of the Sands street Sunday-school, Brooklyn, N. Y., and tell him that the kind words, many prayers, and good advice he gave me I have never forgotten; they have followed me through all the dangers of battle; and now, in my dying hour, I ask my dear Savior to bless my dear old superintendent. That is all."

Turning towards me he said, "Now, doctor, I am ready; and I promise you that I will not even groan while you take off my arm and leg, if you will not offer me chloroform." I promised, but I had not the courage to take the knife in my hand to perform the operation without first going into the next room and taking a little stimulant myself to perform my duty.

While cutting through the flesh, Charlie Coulson never groaned; but when I took the saw to separate the bone, the lad took the corner of his pillow in his mouth, and all that I could hear him utter was, "Oh Jesus, blessed Jesus! Stand by me now." He kept his promise, and never groaned.

That night I could not sleep, for whichever way I turned I saw those soft blue eyes, and when I closed mine the words, "Blessed Jesus, stand by me now," kept ringing in my ears. Between twelve and one o'clock I left my bed and visited the hospital, a thing I had never done before unless specially called, but such was my desire to see that boy. Upon my arrival there I was informed by the night steward that sixteen of the hopeless cases had died, and been carried down to the dead-house. "How is Charlie Coulson? Is he among the dead?" I asked.

"No, sir," answered the steward, "he is sleeping as sweetly as a babe." When I came up to the bed where be lay, one of the nurses informed me that, about nine o'clock, two members of the YMCA came through the hospital to read and sing a hymn. They were accompanied by Chaplain R., who knelt by Charlie Coulson's bed, and offered up a fervent and soul-stirring prayer; after which they sang, while still upon their knees, the sweetest of all hymns, *Jesus, Lover of My Soul*, in which Charlie joined. I could not understand how that boy, who had undergone such excruciating pain, could sing.

Five days after I had amputated that dear boy's arm and leg, he sent for me, and it was from him on that day I heard the first gospel sermon. "Doctor," he said, "my time has come; I do not expect to see another sunrise; but thank God, I am ready to go; and before I die I desire to thank you with all my heart for your kindness to me. Doctor, you are a Jew, you do not believe in Jesus; will you please stand here and see me die trusting my Savior to the last moment of my life?" I tried to stay, but I could not; for I had not the courage to stand by and see a Christian boy die rejoicing in the love of that Jesus whom I had been taught to hate, so I hurriedly left the room.

About twenty minutes later a steward, who found me sitting in my private office covering my face with my hand, said, "Doctor, Charlie Coulson wishes to see you."

"I have just seen him," I answered, "and I cannot see him again."

"But, doctor, he says he must see you once more before he dies." I now made up my mind to see him, say an endearing word, and let him die, but I was determined that no word of his should influence me in the least so far as his Jesus was concerned. When I entered the hospital I saw he was sinking fast, so I sat down by his bed. Asking me to take his hand, he said, "Doctor, I love you because you are a Jew; the best friend I have found in this world was a Jew." I asked him who that was.

He answered, "Jesus Christ, to whom I want to introduce you before I die and will you promise me, doctor, that what I am about to say to you, you will never forget?" I promised and he said, "Five days ago, while you amputated my arm and leg, I prayed to the Lord Jesus Christ to convert your soul."

These words went deep into my heart. I could not understand how, when I was causing him the most intense pain, he could forget all about himself and think of nothing but his Savior and my unconverted soul. All I could say to him was, "Well, my dear boy, you will soon be all right." With these words I left him, and twelve minutes later he fell asleep, "safe in the arms of Jesus."

Hundreds of soldiers died in my hospital during the war; but I only followed one to the grave, and that one was Charlie Coulson, the drummer boy; and I rode three miles to see him buried. I had him dressed in a new uniform, and placed in an officer's coffin, with a United States flag over it.

That boy's dying words made a deep impression upon me. I was rich at that time so far as money is concerned, but I would have given every penny I possessed if I could have felt towards Christ as Charlie did; but that feeling cannot be bought with money. Alas! I soon forgot all about my Christian soldier's little sermon, but I could not forget the boy himself. I now know that at that time I was under deep conviction of sin; but I fought against Christ with all the hatred of an orthodox Jew for nearly ten years, until, finally, the dear boy's prayer was answered, and God converted my soul.

About eighteen months after my conversion, I attended a prayermeeting one evening in the city of Brooklyn. It was one of those meetings when Christians testify to the loving kindness of their Savior. After several of them had spoken, an elderly lady arose and said, "Dear friends, this may be the last time that it is my privilege to testify for Christ. My family physician told me yesterday that my right lung is nearly gone, and my left lung is very much affected so at the best I have but a short time to be with you but what is left of me belongs to Jesus. Oh! It is a great joy to know that I shall meet my boy with Jesus in heaven. My son was not only a soldier for his country, but also a soldier for Christ. He was wounded at the battle of Gettysburg, and fell into the hands of a Jewish doctor, who amputated his arm and leg, but be died five days after the operation. The chaplain of the regiment wrote me a letter, and sent me my boy's Bible. In that letter I was informed that my Charlie in his dying hour sent for that Jewish doctor, and said to him, "Doctor, before I die I wish to tell you that five days ago, while you amputated my arm and leg, I prayed to the Lord Jesus Christ to convert your soul."

When I heard this lady's testimony, I could sit still no longer. I left my seat, crossed the room, and taking her hand, said, "God bless you, my dear sister; your boy's prayer has been heard and answered. I am the Jewish doctor for whom your Charlie prayed, and his Savior is now my Savior."–*Dr. M. L. R.*

God's care for the widow and orphans.

At one of our children's meetings last summer, I invited the conductor of the train running from Grand Rapids to Cincinnati, who was a Christian man, to talk to the children. After speaking of his work among the prisoner of the Cincinnati jail, he proceeded to relate an instance from his own life, proving God's willingness to supply temporal needs in answer to the prayer of faith. When he was a very young boy, his mother was left a widow, with six children dependent upon her for the supply of their temporal wants.

It was a cold winter's day when all their provisions were exhausted; and as there was no human source to which to look, they took their needs to the dear heavenly Father, who promises to hear the cry of the widow and fatherless. They had perfect confidence that He would hear and answer prayer.

After eating their last morsel, they all went to bed and slept as sweetly as though they had an abundance at hand. In the morning the mother, with great cheerfulness, went about her work, setting the table, and making arrangements for breakfast, when there came a rap. She went to the door, and found a perfect stranger, who said the Lord had sent him to supply their present wants, and he came in, bringing provisions enough to last them a long time.

The stranger said he was awakened at midnight, and something told him of the situation of this poor family. Notwithstanding he lived several miles distant, he and his good wife arose, prepared their charities, and the husband set out, finding the place in time for their breakfast. How blessed to have parents teach by precept and example such beautiful lessons of trust!–*Lily Blakeney Howe.*

A would-be murderer's arm paralyzed.

A prominent minister in Canada relates the following remarkable instance of God's miraculous care over his people: "I am frequently impressed by the Spirit to perform actions, at the time unaccountable to myself. These impressions are so vivid that I dare not disobey them.

"Some time ago, on a stormy night, I was suddenly impressed to go to the distant house of an aged couple, and here to pray. So imperative was the call that I harnessed the horse and drove to the spot, fastened the horse under the shed, and entered the house unperceived, by a door which had been left open. There, kneeling down, I poured out my petitions to God, in an audible voice, for the divine protection over the inmates; after which I departed and returned home. Months after, I was visiting one of the principal prisons in Canada, and moving amongst the prisoners, was accosted by one of them, who claimed to know me. I had no recollection of the convict, and was fairly startled when the latter said, 'Do you remember going to such a house one night, and offering prayer in the dark for the inmates.' I told him I did, and asked how he came to know anything about it. He said, 'I had gone to that house to steal a sum of money, known to be in the possession of the old man. When you drove into the yard, I thought you were he, and intended to kill you while you were hitching your horses. I saw when you spoke to the horse you were a stranger. I followed you into the house, and heard your prayer. You prayed God to protect the old people from violence of any kind, and especially from murder, and if there was any hand uplifted to strike them, that it might be paralyzed.' Then the prisoner pointed to his right arm, which hung lifeless by his side, saying; 'Do you see that arm? It was paralyzed on the spot, and I have never moved it since. Of course I left the place without doing any harm, but am here now, for other offenses.'"—*Reported by Lily Blakeney Howe.*

Dying children and youth.

The grasp of the mind of childhood upon the great truths of religion is frequently felt most perceptibly when the little sufferers are near their end. When a boy we heard the narration of a three or four-year-old daughter of good parents living in the Southern country. She sickened, and medical skill proved unavailing to restore her. The tiny creature suspected the truth herself and asked her father if the doctor had not said she must die. Being answered affirmatively, she was silent for a moment, and then said, "Papa, the grave is dark; oh, it is so dark! Won't you go down with me into it?" The stricken parent explained the impossibility, whereupon she said, "Papa, let mamma go with me, then." All who stood around the little creature were in tears, and she began in her own simple way to pray to God. Before expiring her face brightened, as she said, "Pa, the grave is not dark now. I know that you and mamma can't go with me, but Jesus will go with me into the grave."

"I went once," says Rev. C. H. Fowler, D.D., "to see a dying girl whom the world had roughly treated. She never had a father, she never knew her mother. Her home had been the poorhouse, her couch a hospital cot; and yet, as she had staggered in her weakness there, she had picked up a little of the alphabet, enough to spell out the New Testament, and she had touched the hem of the Master's garment, and had learned the new song. And I never trembled in the presence of such majesty as I did in the majesty of her presence as she came near the crossing. 'Oh, sir!' She said, 'God sends his angels. I have read in his word Are they not ministering spirits, sent forth to minister to them who shall be heirs of salvation? And when I am lying in my cot, they stand about me on this floor; and when the heavy darkness comes, and this poor side aches so severely, he comes, for he says, "Lo, I am with you," and be slips his soft hand under my aching side, and I sleep, I rest."'

The instances of heavenly ministries at the bedside of dying children are not rare. "Good-bye, papa; good-bye, mamma," said a sweet eight year old, dying in Baltimore, "the angels have come to carry me to heaven!" And, sure enough, in a few moments, the heavenly convoy were bearing his freed spirit upwards to the skies.

A contributor to the *National Era*, who was an eyewitness to the scene, narrates how a little girl—a lovely and intelligent child—who had lost her mother too early to fix the loved features in remembrance, began to fade away early. As she reclined on the lap of the friend who took a mother's care of her, she would throw her wasted arm around her neck, and say, "Now tell me about mamma." The request was never refused, and the affectionate sick child would lie for hours gazing on her mother's portrait.

But the hour came at last, and weeping neighbors assembled to see the little child die. "Do you know me, darling?" sobbed close to her ear the voice that was dearest; but it awoke no answer. All at once a brightness, as if flashed from the throne, beamed upon the colorless face. The eyelids opened, and the lips parted; the little hands were waved upwards, as, in the last impulsive effort, she looked piercingly into the far above. "Mother!" she cried, with surprise and transport in her tone—and passed with that breath to her mother's bosom. Said a distinguished divine, who witnessed the scene, "If I had never believed in the ministration of departed ones before, I could not doubt it now."

Bearing upon the same point is the story which history brings of the little son of Maria Antoinette, nine years of age, who was fastened in a cell, and his food thrust through a hole in the upper part of the door. Brought out after a year's confinement, during which period that door never once opened, he was brought out to die.

"Oh," said he, "the music, the music, how fine! I wish my sister could hear it!"

"Music? Where?" again asked his attendants.

"Up there, up there!" said the dying dauphin. "Oh, how fine! I hear my mother's voice among them." And, with these words, he went to join her, whom at that time he did *not know to be dead!*—F. H. Potts, in the *Golden Dawn*

REMARKABLE ANSWERS TO PRAYER

Does this railroad lead to Heaven?

In traveling we often meet with persons of different nationalities and languages; we also meet with incidents of various character, some sorrowful, and others joyful and instructive. One of the latter character I witnessed recently while traveling upon the cars. The train was going west, and the time was evening. At a station a little girl about eight years old came aboard, carrying a little budget under her arm. She came into the car and deliberately took a seat She then commenced an eager scrutiny of faces, but all were strange to her. She appeared weary, and placing her budget for a pillow, she prepared to try and secure a little sleep. Soon the conductor came along collecting tickets and fare. Observing him, she asked him if she might lie there. The gentlemanly conductor replied that she might, and then kindly asked for her ticket. She informed him that the had none, when the following conversation ensued. Said the conductor, "Where are you going?"

"I am going to heaven," she answered.

"Who pays your fare?" He asked again.

She then said, "Mister, does this railroad lead to heaven, and does Jesus travel on it?"

"I think not," he answered. "Why did you think so?"

"Why, sir, before my ma died she used to sing to me of a heavenly railroad, and you looked so nice and kind that I thought this was the road. My ma used to sing of Jesus on the heavenly railroad, and that He paid the fare for everybody, and that the train stopped at every station to take people on board; but my ma don't sing to me any more. Nobody sings to me now; and I thought I'd take the cars and go to ma. Mister, do you sing to your little girl about the railroad that goes to heaven? You have a little girl haven't you?"

He replied, weeping, "No, my little dear, I have no little girl now. I had one once, but she died some time ago, and went to heaven."

"Did she go over this railroad, and are you going to see her now?" She asked.

By this time every person in the coach was upon their feet, and most of them were weeping. An attempt to describe what I witnessed is almost futile. Some said, "God bless the little girl." Hearing some person say that she was an angel, the little girl earnestly replied, "Yes, my ma used to say that I would be an angel some time."

Addressing herself once more to the conductor, she asked him, "Do you love Jesus? I do; and if you love Him, He will let you ride to heaven on His railroad. I am going there, and I wish you would go with me. I know Jesus will let me into heaven when I get there, and He will let you, in too, and everybody that will ride on His railroad—yes, all these people. Wouldn't you like to see heaven, and Jesus, and your little girl?"

TOUCHING INCIDENTS AND

These words, so pathetically and innocently uttered, brought a great gush of tears from all eyes, but most profusely from those of the conductor. Some who were traveling on the heavenly railroad shouted aloud for joy.

She now asked the conductor, "Mister, may I lie here until we get to heaven?"

"Yes, dear, yes," he answered.

"Will you wake me up then, so that I may see my ma, and your little girl, and Jesus?" She asked, "for I do so much want to see them all."

The answer came in broken accents, but in words very tenderly spoken, "Yes, dear angel, yes. God bless you."

"Amen!" was sobbed by more than a score of voices.

Turning her eyes again upon the conductor, she interrogated him again, "What shall I tell your little girl when I see her? Shall I tell her that I saw her pa on Jesus' railroad? Shall I?"

This brought a fresh flood of tears from all present, and the conductor knelt by her side, and, embracing her, wept the reply he could not utter. At this juncture the brakeman called out, "H——s." The conductor arose and requested him to attend to his, the conductor's duty at the station, for he was engaged. That was a precious place. I thank God that I was a witness to this scene, but I was sorry that at this point I was obliged to leave the train.

We learn from this incident that out of the mouths of even babes God hath ordained strength, and that we ought to be willing to represent the cause of our blessed Jesus even in a railroad coach.

The sequel.

Rev. Dosh, I wish to relieve my heart by writing to you, and saying that that angel visit on the cars was a blessing to me, although I did not realize it in its fullness until some hours after. But blessed be the Redeemer, I know now that I am His, and He is mine. I no longer wonder why Christians are happy. Oh, my joy, my joy! The instrument of my salvation has gone to God. I had purposed adopting her in the place of my little daughter, who is now in heaven. With this intention I took her to G——b, and on my return trip I took her back to S——n, where she left the cars. In consultation with my wife in regard to adopting her, she replied, "Yes, certainly, and immediately too, for there is a Divine providence in this. Oh," said she, "I never could refuse to take under my charge the instrument of my husband's salvation."

I made inquiry for the child at S——n, and learned that in three days after her return she died suddenly, without any apparent disease, and her happy soul had gone to dwell with her ma, my little girl, and the angels in heaven. I was sorry to hear of her death, but my sorrow is turned to joy when I think my angel daughter received intelligence from earth concerning her pa, and that he is on the heavenly railway. Oh! Sir, methinks I see her near the Redeemer. I think I hear her sing, "I'm safe at home, and pa and ma are coming;" and I find myself sending back the reply, "Yes, my darling, we are coming, and will soon be there." Oh, my dear sir, I am glad that I ever formed your acquaintance. May the blessing of the great God rest upon you. Please write to me, and be assured, I would most happy to meet you again.—*Rev. F. M. Dosh, in* Christian Expositor

3

For His sake

YOU ASK ME, "HOW did you come into these new notions of giving?"

Well, it was this way: A year ago this winter our house took fire. It was in the middle of the night, and we were all asleep. The flames were first discovered by a poor neighbor, who at once gave the alarm, and then burst in the door. The house was full of smoke, and the fire had already attacked the staircase which led to the rooms in which we were still sleeping. It seems almost a miracle that we were got out alive. We were dazed and suffocated, and it was only the heroic courage and strength of our neighbor that brought us down the blazing stairway into the open air.

But it nearly cost him his life. Indeed, we thought the poor man, gasping for breath, would die on the spot. Intent on protecting us, he had exposed himself so that he was terribly burned about the arms and chest. He had, too, drawn into his lungs the almost furnace-like air. As he stumbled out of the door with the last child in his arms, he fell down, utterly spent. I shall never forget the anguish of that hour. He had saved us, but himself seemed dying—dying for our sakes. All thought or our misfortune at once left us. The best physicians were summoned, and we bore him tenderly to his own house. When the immediate danger had been averted, it became plain that it would take careful nursing of many months to bring him back to his ordinary health, if, indeed, he had not become disabled for life.

And now it was our turn. He was a laborer, and his family was wholly dependent on his daily earnings. It did not take us long to decide upon our course. In fact, there was no debate or counseling about it. The immediate and common thought of each of us, down to the youngest child was, that we should at once take the whole care of his family upon ourselves. They were now allied to us by a tie stronger than any body of kindred, and we did not for a moment hesitate what to do.

REMARKABLE ANSWERS TO PRAYER

I had a business that gave us comfortable support, though we had followed the custom of our acquaintances generally, of living in a liberal way, quite up to the extent of our means. But we did not stay to ask whether we could afford it or not. We just settled it at once that this should be done first, and then we would somehow contrive to live on what remained.

We arranged that the women of our family should relieve the heartbroken wife of the poor man from all household cares, that she might devote herself wholly to him. They were very tenderly attached, and no one could care for him as she could

"It was just like Joe," she said, as she patiently sat by his bedside; "he never thinks of himself." But a happy smile flitted across her wan face, as she added, "I wouldn't have him different."

My oldest daughter soon secured a class in music, and the next one found a place in kindergarten. It was a great delight to me, and a stimulus to my own efforts, to see how intent the younger children were, each one of the, to earn or save something for the great purpose which had now come into our hearts. It sometimes brought the tears to see especially how Charlie, the last one saved, took wholly upon himself to look after one of the children of our brave friend, a boy about a year younger than himself. He could enjoy nothing, neither garment, schoolbook nor plaything, until he had seen to it that his little mate was fitted out as he himself was. And often this was done at a real sacrifice by the little fellow.

Indeed, this was the way with us all. It did not occur to us to ask whether we could do what we had undertaken without feeling it. *We wanted to feel it.* We could not take upon ourselves any of the bodily anguish of this poor suffering man; suffering for our sakes. But it was a genuine satisfaction to be doing something for him, at some cost to ourselves, some real self-denial, that should be as constant as was the pain he was enduring. We somehow felt that it was the only way we could emphasize to our own hearts our great obligation, and show to him our gratitude; the only way in which we could in some small measure—it seemed very small to us sometimes—suffer with him in his great suffering for us.

I do not say that there was no conflict in doing this. After the excitement of the first few days was passed, it was often necessary to reinforce our variable impulses by calling up to our minds a sense of duty. The close quarters into which we had moved were inconvenient. Our former tastes and luxurious indulgences now and then stoutly asserted themselves. They had grown into headstrong habits, and it sometimes cost a real conflict to put them down.

There was one untidy and expensive habit, which, it seems to me, I never could have broken off, had it not been for this new power that had come into my life. Upon a little calculation I found that it cost me more than a hundred dollars a year. This might be saved. It was a defiling and unwholesome thing, and I could not but feel a loss of self-respect every time I gave way to its use. But I had no idea it had gained such a mastery over me; and when the intense craving for my daily indulgence came on, the battle would certainly have gone against me had I not been wont to say over to myself; "it is for his sake—for his sake!" That one word gave me the victory, and it was a real deliverance.

There was another stout fight I had to make.

One day a business friend of mine drove up with his well matched span, and took me to see the new house he was building. I was glad to look it over, for I had planned that, some day, I would build such a house for myself. The rooms were spacious and many. The outlook from the bay windows was delightful. No modern convenience or appliance for comfort had been omitted. It was not strange that for a time my former desire for such a mansion-like residence came upon me with almost overpowering strength. It was a moment of weakness. The spirit of self-indulgence came back to its old home, and before I was aware, the chafing and impatience of my heart at the new expenses laid on me grew into a tumult; but it was only for a moment. As I walked away, and began to come to myself, and to see what I was really thinking about, what do you suppose I did?

I just stood still and hated myself for about half an hour!

Oh, what indignation! What clearing of myself! Yea, what revenge! To make sure that I had utterly rid myself of the meanness of this contemptible thought, I immediately went with my wife and bargained for a neat cottage in the next block, arranging easy terms which I could meet in the year to come; and then directed that the deed should be given to my brave, suffering deliverer, the first day he should be able to walk out. I felt as if I had grievously wronged him, and that nothing short of this would satisfy the demands of the case.

As our friend began to be able to walk, we found that there was something weighing upon his mind. It soon came out that he was the superintendent of a little Mission School which he had gathered in a neglected part of the town. Somehow it had come to him that in his absence it had sadly run down. You may be sure the whole teaching force of our family was turned into that school the very next Sunday. I am ashamed to say that it was new business to us; but for his sake we were there, and we threw our whole souls into it. And it was a great satisfaction to see how like medicine it was to the poor man, to hear our weekly report of the growing interest and numbers. And when in the winter there came a blessed revival, his joy knew no bounds. It was noticeable that from that time on, he showed a marked improvement.

REMARKABLE ANSWERS TO PRAYER

There was a natural, unlooked-for result from the self-denials and solicitudes of this year. We were drawn, not only to this man, who was making a brave fight for life in at the next door—for we were continually running in and out—but we were also drawn to each other as we had never been before. A new tenderness and patience came into our lives. Somehow the common service and sacrifice upon which all our hearts were set, softened us and brought us together in a sympathy and oneness of feeling which was altogether new; and thus it proved to be the happiest period of our domestic life.

It is a year now since that terrible night. Our neighbor, to our great joy, has so far recovered that he has moved to the new house, and will soon be back again to his accustomed work.

Yesterday, as I looked over the footings of my inventory, I found, to my surprise, that after all, it had been one of my most successful years. Indeed, I had scarcely ever had so large a balance in hand. This was altogether unexpected. There had been no marked successes, or special interposition's. But I could see, on looking back, that my own business habits had been toned up by the necessities which faced us; that needless expenses had been cut off. That my business men had steadily improved, and that I had been somehow kept from mistakes, and had adventures, and misplaced credits. Indeed, we have a settled and sweet consciousness that the hand of good Providence had been constantly with us.

Last evening, as it was the anniversary of the fire, we gave up the accustomed hour of family worship to a review of the experiences. It was a delightful and precious season. We felt with humble gratitude, that we had come up to a higher plane of life, and no one of us desires to go back to the old way of self-indulgence. There had been quietly growing in our hearts for some months, the thought, If for this man's sake, why not even more for Christ's sake?

When we had read at our morning worship such passages as the 53rd chapter of Isaiah, or the closing scenes of our Lord's life in the Gospels, and many expressions in the Epistles. The sufferings, sometimes the intense anguish at the next door—of which we were often the witness, and which were almost never out of our thoughts—seemed to make very real to us our Lord's sacrifice and sufferings for us. We were also much moved by the beautiful patience of our neighbor, and by his joy in what he had done. He seemed to feel, with all his lowliness, a sense of having somehow gained an ownership in us, and in a quiet way, he rejoiced over us as if we were the trophies of a great victory. We were, indeed, as "brands plucked from the burning;" and often led us to turn to the Lord Jesus, with much yearning and tenderness of soul. And there would sometimes appear to us, with the vividness of a new revelation, the words, "Ye are bought with a great price... Ye are not your own." And so, at the close of our review, there came out, in a formal covenant, the purpose which had thus been quietly growing in all our hearts, that we would never, any more, live unto ourselves; that we would keep right on doing for our Lord, just what we had been doing for this man. It seemed easy and natural, and the most reasonable thing in the world, that for the next year, and for all the years, we would make Christ's business our business; that we would take to our hearts the things that were nearest to His heart. That henceforth His Church, His poor, His little ones, and the salvation of the world, for which His soul is still in travail, should be the chief care of our lives.

Our daughters have wrought and hung on the walls of our rooms a motto. It is only a faint reflection of that which is deeply, and we believe, permanently graven in our hearts: *For His sake, for His sake!*

And so I have answered your question, *How did you come into these new notions of giving?*—S. J. Humphrey

Experience of a minister's wife on the frontier

I remember a day during one winter that stands out like a boulder in my life. The weather was unusually cold, our salary had not been regularly paid, and it did not meet our needs when it was. My husband was away traveling from one district to another much of the time. Our boys were well, but my little Ruth was ailing, and at best none of us were decently clothed. I patched, and re-patched, with spirits sinking to their lowest ebb. The water gave out in the well, and the wind blew through the cracks in the floor.

The people in the parish were kind, and generous, too; but the settlement was new, and each family was struggling for itself. Little by little, at the time I needed it most, my faith began to waver. Early in life I was taught to take God at His word, and I thought my lesson was well learned. I had lived upon the promises in dark times, until I knew as David did, "who was my fortress and deliverer." Now a daily prayer for forgiveness was all that I could offer. My husband's overcoat was hardly thick enough for October, and he was often obliged to ride miles to attend some meeting or funeral. Many times our breakfast was Indian cake, and a cup of tea without sugar. Christmas was coming; the children always expected their presents. I remember the ice was thick and smooth, and the boys were each craving a pair of skates. Ruth, in some unaccountable way, had taken a fancy that the dolls I had made were no longer suitable; she wanted a nice, large one, and insisted in praying for It. I knew it was impossible; but, oh! how I wanted to give each child its present. It seemed as if God had deserted us, but I did not tell my husband all this. He worked so earnestly and heartily, I supposed him to be as hopeful as ever. I kept the sitting-room cheerful with an open fire, and tried to serve our scanty meals as invitingly as I could.

REMARKABLE ANSWERS TO PRAYER

The morning before Christmas, James was called to see a sick man. I put up a piece of bread for his lunch—it was the best I could do—wrapped my plaid shawl around his neck, and then tried to whisper a promise, as I often had, but the words died away upon my lips. I let him go without it. That was a dark, hopeless day. I coaxed the children to bed early, for I could not bear their talk. When Ruth went, I listened to her prayer; she asked for the last time most explicitly for her doll, and for skates for her brothers. Her bright face looked so lovely when she whispered to me, "You know I think they'll be here early tomorrow morning, mamma," that I thought I could move heaven and earth to save her from disappointment. I sat down alone, and gave way to the most bitter tears.

Before long James returned, chilled and exhausted. He drew off his boots; the thin stockings slipped off with them, and his feet were red with cold. "I wouldn't treat a dog that way; let alone a faithful servant," I said. Then, as I glanced up and saw the hard lines in his face and the look of despair, it flashed across me, James had let go, too. I brought him a cup of tea, feeling sick and dizzy at the very thought. He took my hand, and we sat for an hour without word. I wanted to die and meet God, and tell Him his promise wasn't true; my soul was so full of rebellious despair.

There came a sound of bells, a quick stomp, and a loud knock at the door. James sprang up to open it. There stood Deacon White. "A box came for you by express just before dark. I brought it around as soon as I could get away. Reckoned it might be for Christmas; at any rate, they shall have it tonight. Here is a turkey my wife asked me to fetch along, and these other things I believe belong to you." There was a basket of potatoes and a bag of flour. Talking all the time, he hurried in the box, and then with a hearty goodnight rode away. Still, without speaking, James found a chisel and opened the box. He drew out first a thick red blanket, and we saw that beneath was full of clothing. It seemed at that moment as if Christ fastened upon me a look of reproach. James sat down and covered his face with his hands.

"I can't touch them," he exclaimed; "I haven't been true, just when God was trying me to see if I could hold out. Do you think I could not see how you were suffering and I had no word of comfort to offer? I know now how to preach the awfulness of turning away from God."

"James," I said, clinging to him, "don't take it to heart like this; I am to blame, I ought to have helped you. We will ask Him together to forgive us."

"Wait a moment, dear, I cannot talk now;" then he went into another room. I knelt down, and my heart broke; in an instant all the darkness, all the stubbornness rolled away. Jesus came again and stood before me, but now with the loving word, "Daughter!" Sweet promises of tenderness and joy flooded my soul, I was so lost in praise and gratitude that I forgot everything else. I don't know how long it was before James came back, but I knew he too had found peace.

"Now, my dear wife," said he, "let us thank God together;" and then he poured out words of praise; Bible words, for nothing else could express our thanksgiving. It was eleven o'clock, the fire was low, and there was the great box, and nothing touched but the warm blanket we needed. We piled on some fresh logs, lighted two candles, and began to examine our treasures. We drew out an overcoat; I made James try it on; just the right size, and I danced around him; for all my lightheartedness had returned. Then there was a cloak, and he insisted on seeing me in it. My spirits always infected him, and we both laughed like foolish children. There was a warm suit of clothes also, and three pair of woolen hose. There was a dress for me, and yards of flannel, a pair of arctic overshoes for each of us, and in mine was a slip of paper. I have it now, and mean to hand it down to my children.

It was Jacob's blessing to Asher: "Thy shoes shall be iron and brass, and as thy days so shall thy strength be." In the gloves, evidently for James, the same dear hand had written, "I, the Lord thy God, will hold thy right hand, saying unto thee: Fear not, I will help thee." It was a wonderful box, and packed with thoughtful care. There was a suit of clothes for each of the boys, and a little red gown for Ruth. There were mittens, scarves, and hoods; down in the center, a box; we opened it, and there was a great wax doll. I burst into tears again; James wept with me for joy. It was too much; and then we both exclaimed again, for close behind it came two pair of skates. There were books for us to read; some of them I had wished to see; stories for the children to read, aprons and underclothing, knots of ribbon, a gay little tidy. A lovely photograph, needles, buttons and thread; actually a muff, and an envelope containing a ten dollar gold piece.

At last we cried over everything we took up. It was past midnight, and we were faint and exhausted even with happiness. I made a cup of tea, cut a fresh loaf of bread and James boiled some eggs. We drew up the table before the fire; how we enjoyed our supper! And then we sat talking over our life, and how sure a help God always proved.

You should have seen the children the next morning; the boys raised a shout at the sight of their skates. Ruth caught up her doll, and hugged it tightly without a word; then she went into her room and knelt by her bed. When she came back she whispered to me, "I knew it would be here, mamma, but I wanted to thank God just the same, you know."

"Look here, wife, see the difference." We went to the window and there were the boys out of the house already, and skating on the crust with all their might. My husband

and I both tried to return thanks to the church in the East that sent us the box, and have tried to return thanks unto God every day since.

Hard times have come again and again, but we have trusted in Him; dreading nothing so much as a doubt of His protecting care. Over and over again we have proved that, "they that seek the Lord shall not want for any good thing." —*Christian Witness*

Superhuman control of the locomotive, in answer to prayer

The following instance is given in the experience of a correspondent of *The Christian*, which occurred in the latter part of November, 1864, while traveling with her aged father and two small girls.

"We started from New Hampshire on Thursday morning expecting to get through to Indiana before Saturday night; but, after we crossed the St. Lawrence River, the next day, I think, there was a smashup on a freight train which hindered our train about two hours. I began to feel anxious, as I knew our limited means would not permit us to stop long on the way. After the cars had started again I inquired of the conductor what time we should get to Toledo, fearing we should not reach there in time for the down train. He said it would be impossible to gain the time. Soon they changed conductors, and I made a similar inquiry, getting about the same answer. Still I hoped, till we reached the Detroit River. Here I found that, though they had put on all steam they dared to, they were almost an hour behind time, so I should have to stay over till Sunday night.

"After getting seated in the cars on the other side, I ventured to ask the conductor if we should get to Toledo in time for the down train. He readily said, 'No madam; impossible! If we put on all the steam we dare to we shall be more than half an hour behind time. If we were on some trains, we might hope they would wait; but on this, never! He is the most exact conductor you ever saw. He was never known to wait a second, say nothing about a minute, beyond the time.' I then inquired if we could not stay at the depot. He said 'No, you would all freeze to death, for the fire is out till Sunday evening.'

"A gentleman sitting in front of us said he would show us a good hotel near by, as he was acquainted there. I thanked him, but sunk back on my seat. Covering my eyes with my hand, and raising my heart to God, I said, 'Oh God, if thou art my Father, and I am thy child, put it into the heart of that conductor to wait till we get there.'

"Soon I became calm, and fell asleep, not realizing that God would answer my poor prayer; but, when we reached Toledo, to the astonishment of us all, there stood the conductor, wanting to know the reason why he had to wait; when our conductor told him there was a lady with her crippled father and two little daughters, who were going down on that train.

"Soon as all were out of the car, both conductors came with their lanterns, and gave their aid in helping my father to the other train, where they had reserved seats by keeping the door locked. All was hurry and confusion to me, as I had my eye on father, fearing he might fall, it being very slippery, when the baggage master said, "Your checks, madam!' I handed them to him, and rushed into the car; but, before I got seated, the car started, and I had no checks for my baggage. Again my heart cried out, 'Oh Thou that hearest prayer, take care of my baggage!' Believing He could do that as well as make the conductor wait.

"In a few moments the conductor came to me with a face radiant with smiles, saying, 'Madam, I waited a whole half hour for you; a thing I never did before since I was a conductor, so much as to wait one minute after my time.' He said, 'I know it was your father that I was waiting for, because there was nothing else on the train for which I could have waited.'

"I exclaimed, in a half-suppressed tone. 'Praise the Lord!' I could not help it; it gushed out.

"Then he said, 'At the very moment all were on board, and I was ready to start, such a feeling came over me as I have never had in my life before. I could not start. Something kept saying to me, you must wait, for there is something pending on that train you must wait for. I waited, and here you are all safe.'

"Again my heart said, 'Praise the Lord!' And he started to leave me, when I said, 'But there is one thing.'

" 'What is it?' was his quick reply. 'I gave the baggage-master my checks, and have none in return.'

" 'What were the numbers?' I told him.

" 'I have them,' he said, handing them to me; 'but your baggage will not be there till Monday morning. We had no time to put it on, we had waited so long.'"—*Selected*.

Married to a drunkard

She arose suddenly in the meeting, and spoke as follows: "Married to a drunkard! Yes, I was married to a drunkard. Look at me! I am talking to the girls."

We all turned and looked at her. She was a wan woman, with dark, sad eyes, and white hair, placed smoothly over a brow that denoted intellect.

"When I married a drunkard, I reached the acme of misery," she continued. "I was young, and oh, so happy! I married the man I loved, and who professed to love me. He was a drunkard, and I knew it—knew it, but did not understand it. There is not a young girl in this building that does understand it, unless she has

REMARKABLE ANSWERS TO PRAYER

a drunkard in her family; then, perhaps, she knows how deeply the iron enters the soul of a woman, when she loves, and is allied to a drunkard; whether father, husband, brother or son. Girls, believe me when I tell you, that to marry a drunkard, to love a drunkard, is the crown of all misery. I have gone through deep waters, and know. I have gained that fearful knowledge at the expense of happiness, sanity, almost life itself. Do you wonder my hair is white? It turned white in a night, 'bleached by sorrow,' as Marie Antoinette said of her hair. I am not forty years old, yet the snows of seventy rest upon my head; and upon my heart. Ah! I cannot begin to count the winters resting there," she said, with unutterable pathos in her voice.

"My husband was a professional man. His calling took him from home frequently at night, and when he returned, he returned drunk. Gradually he gave way to temptation in the day, until he was rarely sober. I had two lovely little girls and a boy." Here her voice faltered, and we sat in deep silence listening to her story. "My husband had been drinking deeply. I had not seen him for two days. He had kept away from his home.

"One night I was seated beside my sick boy; the two little girls were in bed in the next room, while beyond was another room, into which I heard my husband go, as he entered the house. The room communicated with the one in which my little girls were sleeping. I do not know why, but a feeling of terror took possession of me, and I felt that my little girls were in danger. I arose and went to the room. The door was locked. I knocked on it frantically, but no answer came. I seemed to be endowed with superhuman strength, and throwing myself with all my force against the door, the lock gave way and the door flew open. Oh, the sight! The terrible sight!" She wailed out in a voice that haunts me now; and she covered her face with her hands, and when she removed them it was whiter and sadder than ever.

"Delirium tremens! You have never seen it, girls; God grant that you never may. My husband stood beside the bed, his eyes glaring with insanity, and in his hand a large knife. 'Take them away!' he screamed. 'The horrible things, they are crawling all over me. Take them away, I say!' And he flourished the knife in the air. Regardless of danger, I rushed up to the bed, and my heart seemed suddenly to cease beating. There lay my children, covered with their lifeblood, slain by their own father! For a moment I could not utter a sound. I was literally dumb in the presence of this terrible sorrow, I scarcely heeded the maniac at my side—the man who had wrought me all this woe. Then I uttered a loud scream, and my wailings filled the air. The servants heard me and hastened to the room, and when my husband saw them, he suddenly drew the knife across his own throat. I knew nothing more. I was borne senseless from the room that contained the bodies of my slaughtered children, and the body of my husband. The next day my hair was white, and my mind so shattered that I knew no one."

She ceased! Our eyes were riveted upon her wan face. Some of the women present sobbed aloud, while there was scarcely a dry eye in the temperance meeting. We saw that she had not done speaking, and was only waiting to subdue her emotion to resume her story.

"Two years," she continued, "I was a mental wreck; then I recovered from the shock, and absorbed myself in the care of my boy. But the sin of the father was visited upon the child, and six month ago my boy of eighteen was placed in a drunkard's grave; and as I, his loving mother, stood and saw the sod heaped over him, I said, "Thank God! I'd rather see him there than have him live a drunkard;' and I turned unto my desolate home a childless woman—one on whom the hand of God had rested heavily.

"Girls, it is you I wish to rescue from the fate that overtook me. Do not blast your life as I blasted mine; do not be drawn into the madness of marrying a drunkard. You love him! So much the worse for you; for married to him, the greater will be your misery because of your love. You will marry and then reform him, so you say. Ah! A woman sadly overrates her strength when she undertakes to do this. You are no match for the giant demon Drink when he possesses a man's body and soul. You are no match for him, I say. What is your puny strength beside his gigantic force? He will crush you, too. It is to save you, girls, from the sorrows what wrecked my happiness, that I have unfolded my history to you. I am a stranger in this great city. I am merely passing through it; and I have a message to bear to every girl in America—never marry a drunkard!"

I can see her now, as she stood there amid the hushed audience, her dark eyes glowing, and her frame quivering with emotion, as she uttered her impassioned appeal. Then she hurried out, and we never saw her again. Her words, "fitly spoken," were not without effect, however, and because of them there is one girl single now.—*Selected.*

<u>Kicked for Christ's sake</u>

An evangelist said, "A little girl of eight years was sent on an errand by her parents. While on her way, she was attracted by the singing of a gospel meeting in the open air, and drew near. The conductor of the meeting was so struck with the child's earnestness that he spoke to her, and told her about Jesus. She being the child of Roman Catholics, did not know much about Him, but the gentleman told her of His love to her. On returning home her father asked her what had detained her. She told him, and he cruelly beat her, forbidding her to go to any such meeting again.

REMARKABLE ANSWERS TO PRAYER

About a fortnight afterwards, she was so taken up with what she had previously heard of Jesus, that she forgot all about her message. She saw the same gentleman, who again told her more about the Savior. On her return home, she again told her father, as before, where she had been, and that she had not brought what she had been sent for, but that she had brought Jesus. Her father was enraged, and kicked the poor little creature until the blood came. She never recovered from this brutal treatment. Just before she breathed her last, she called her mother and said, "Mother, I have been praying to Jesus to save you and father." Then pointing to her little dress, she said, "Mother, cut me a bit out of the bloodstained piece of my dress." The mother, wondering, did so.

"Now," said the dying child, "Christ shed His blood for my sake, and I am going to take this to Jesus to show Him that I shed my blood for His sake." Thus she died, holding firmly the piece of her dress, stained with her own blood. The testimony of that dear child was the means of leading both father and mother to Christ.—*Selected*

An effectual prayer

"No," said the lawyer, "I shan't press your claim against that man; you can get someone else to take your case, or you can withdraw it, just as you please."

"Think there isn't any money in it!"

"There would probably be some money in it, but it would, as you know, come from the sale of the little house the man occupies and calls home; but I don't want to meddle with the matter, anyhow."

"Got frightened out of it, eh?"

"No, I wasn't frightened out of it."

"I suppose likely the old fellow begged hard to be let off?"

"Well, yes he did."

"And you caved, likely?"

"No, I didn't speak a word to him."

"Oh, he did all the talking, did he?"

"Yes."

"And you never said a word?"

"Not a word."

"What in creation did you do?"

"I believe I shed a few tears."

"And the old fellow begged you hard, you say?"

"No, I didn't say so; he didn't speak a word to me."

"Well, may I respectfully inquire whom he did address in your hearing?"

"God Almighty."

"Ah, he took to praying, did he?"

"Not for my benefit, in the least. You see"—and the lawyer crossed his right foot over his left knee, and began stroking his lower leg up and down, as if to state his case concisely. "You see, I found the little house easily enough, and knocked at the outer door, which stood ajar. But nobody heard me, so I slipped into the hall, and saw, through the crack of another door, just as cozy a sitting room as there ever was. There on a bed, with her silver head way up high on the pillows, was an old lady, who looked for all the world just my mother did the last time I ever saw her on earth.

"Well, I was right on the point of knocking, when she said as clearly as could be, 'Come, father, begin; I'm ready.' And down on his knees by her side went an old, white-haired man, still older than his wife, I should judge; and I could not have knocked then for the life of me. Well, he began; first he reminded God they were still His submissive children, mother and he; and no matter what He saw fit to bring upon them they shouldn't rebel at his will! Of course, 'twas going to be terrible hard for them to go out homeless in their old age, especially with poor mother so sick and helpless; but still they'd seen sadder things than ever that would be.

"He reminded God, in the next place, how different all might have been if only one of their boys might have been spared them; then his voice kind of broke, and a thin, white hand stole from under the coverlet, and moved softly over his snowy hair; then he went on to repeat, that nothing could be so sharp as the parting of those three sons—unless mother and he should be separated. But at last he fell to comforting himself with the fact that the dear Lord knew it was through no fault of his own, that mother and he were threatened with the loss of their dear little home, which meant beggary and the almshouse; a place they prayed to be delivered from entering, if it could be consistent with God's will. And then he fell to quoting a multitude of promises concerning the safety of those who put their trust in the Lord; yes, I should say he begged hard; in fact it was the most thrilling plea to which I ever listened. And at last he prayed for God's blessing on those who were about to demand justice." The lawyer stroked his lower limb in silence for a moment or two, then continued more slowly that before, "And, I believe, I'd rather go to the poorhouse myself, tonight, than to stain my heart and hands with the blood of such a prosecution as that."

"Little afraid to defeat the old man's prayer, eh?" queried the client.

"Bless your soul, man, you could not defeat it!" roared the lawyer. "It doesn't admit of defeat! I tell you, he left it all subject to the will of God; but he left no doubt as to his wishes in the matter; claimed that we were told to make known our desires unto God; but of all the pleading I ever heard that beat all. You see, I was taught that kind of thing myself in my childhood; and why I was sent to hear that prayer I'm sure I don't know, but I hand the case over."

"I wish," said the client, twisting uneasily, "you hadn't told me about the old fellow's prayer."

"Why so?"

"Well, I greatly want the money the place would bring, but was taught the Bible all straight when I was a youngster; and I'd hate to run counter to such a harangue as that you tell about. I wish you hadn't heard a word of it; and another time I wouldn't listen to petitions not intended for your ears."

The lawyer smiled.

"My dear fellow," he said, "you're wrong again; it was intended for my ears, and yours, too, and God Almighty intended it. My old mother used to sing about God's moving in a mysterious way, I remember."

"Well, my mother used to sing it, too," said the claimant, as he twisted his claim-papers in his fingers. "You can call him in the morning, if you like, and tell mother and him the claim has been met."

"In a mysterious way," added the lawyer, smiling.—Selected by Mrs. E. C. Best.

Bishop Simpson's recovery

Bishop Bowman, of the M. E. Church, gives the following instance from his own experience:

"In the fall of 1858, whilst visiting Indiana, I was at an annual conference where Bishop Janes presided. We received a telegram that Bishop Simpson was dying.

"Said Bishop Janes, 'Let us spend a few moments in earnest prayer for the recovery of Bishop Simpson.' We kneeled to pray. William Taylor, the great California Street-preacher was called to pray; and such a prayer I never heard since. The impression seized upon me irresistibly, *Bishop Simpson will not die.* I rose from my knees perfectly quiet. Said I, 'Bishop Simpson will not die.'

'Why do you think so?'

'Because I have had an irresistible impression made upon my mind during prayer.'

"Another said, 'I have the same impression.' We passed it along from bench to bench, until we found that a very large proportion of the conference had the same impression.

"I made a minute of the time of day, and when I next saw Simpson, he was attending his daily labor. I inquired of the bishop, 'How did you recover from your sickness?'

"He replied, 'I cannot tell.'

" 'What did your physician say?'

" 'He said it was a miracle.'

"I then said to the bishop, 'Give me the time and circumstances under which the change occurred.' He fixed upon the day, and the very hour, making allowance for the distance—a thousand miles away—that the preachers were engaged in prayer at this conference. The physician left his room and said to his wife, 'It is useless to do anything further; the bishop must die.'

"In about an hour he returned, and started back, inquiring, 'What have you done?'

" 'Nothing,' was the reply.

" 'He is recovering rapidly,' said the physician; 'a change has occurred in the disease within the last hour beyond anything I have ever seen; the crisis is past, and the bishop will recover.' And he did."

The doctor was puzzled; it was beyond all the course and probabilities of nature, and the laws of science. What was it that made those ministers so sure—what was it that made the patient recover, at the exact hour that they prayed? There is only one answer: "The ever-living power of a Superior Spirit which rules the world."—*Wonders of Prayer*

<u>Healed of diphtheria</u>

In the fall of 1885 our oldest boy, then two and one half years old, was taken very ill. Diphtheria had for some time been raging to a considerable extent in the city of Grand Rapids, where we then resided. But a short time before, friends who had just buried a little daughter, who had died of that disease, had visited at our home. Our little Rolin's throat was badly cankered, he could no longer lie down without strangling; and we felt that by naught but the power and mercy of God, could he be spared to us. With a sad, aching heart, I laid away his little playthings, thinking I might never see him use them again; and as I looked over the cemetery on the hill beyond us, a great yearning cry of anguish went up from my soul, as I thought that, in all human probability, I might be called within a few days, to there lay away the form of my little darling.

More from a sense of regard for the feelings and convictions of others, than because of any confidence in the power of human remedies to meet the demands of the case, husband sent for a physician. As the one sent for was not in his office, the friend who went for him brought another, prominent for skill and experience. After careful examination, he pronounced the child dangerously ill of diphtheria, and said to the friend who brought him, "They do not realize how sick that child is; whatever is done for him must be done quickly." He would leave no medicine, unless we gave him entire charge of the case, and this we did not feel ready to do. After his departure, husband said to me, "If you wish me to send for the other physician, I will do so; but for myself, I can as easily exercise faith in God to heal Rolin as to trust Him for means to pay a doctor."

Then while I sat with Rolin in my arms, he knelt and prayed. As he pled with God that, if it were according to His will and for His glory, He would spare and heal the child he had given us, I knew he was wonderfully helped of the Spirit.

When he arose he told me that he had the positive assurance that his prayer was heard, and that Rolin would recover.

For hours previous, the sick one had been suffering greatly; but *he immediately appeared very much better*, and soon after returned, and *that night we all slept well.* The next morning, Rolin was up, dressed, and playing as usual about the house, and there was no more sign of diphtheria in his case.

In a short time a sister in the Lord, who had been with us the previous afternoon, but who left at about the time we sent for the physician, and who knew nothing of what had transpired in her absence, came to the door. As I met her she said, "I have good news for you. Rolin is going to get well." And upon careful inquiry we found that at very nearly, if not exactly, the same time that husband said to me that God has assured him that Rolin would recover, this sister, then a mile and a half away, had testified the very same thing to those that were with her.

A few weeks later, husband was just as miraculously healed of the same disease, and the very next day rode over twenty miles in a cutter; and though it was a very cold, raw, windy November day, his throat did not trouble him in the least.

Yours in the love of Jesus,
Mrs. S. B. Shaw.

A widow's wonderful deliverance

In the winter of 1855, in the state of Iowa, the snow fell early in November to the depth of two feet. The storm was such that man nor beast could move against it.

In a log cabin, six miles from her nearest relative, lived a woman with five children, ranging from one to eleven years. The supply of food and fuel was but scant when the snow began falling; and day after day the small store melted away, until the fourth evening, when the last provisions were cooked for supper, and barely enough fuel remained to last one day more. That night, as was her custom, the little ones were called around her knee to hear the scripture lesson read, before commending them to the Heavenly Father's care. Then, bowing in prayer, she pleaded as only those in like condition can plead, that help from God might be sent.

While wrestling with God in prayer, the Spirit took the words of the Psalmist and impressed them on her heart, "I have been young, and now am old, yet have I not seen the righteous forsaken, nor his seed begging bread." And again, these words came as if spoken audibly, "The young lions do lack and suffer hunger, but they that wait on the Lord shall want no good thing." Faith took God at His word; and with an assurance that help would come, she prayed God who heareth prayer, and retired to rest without a care or fear for the morrow. When again the morning broke, that mother arose, kindled her fire, and put on the kettle as she had done on other days before the food was all gone. Just as the sun arose, a man in a sleigh drove up to the house, and hastening in inquired how they were getting along. Her heart at first was too full for utterance; but in a short time he was told something of their destitution, and of her cry to God for help.

He replied, "Last night about nine o'clock, wife and I were both impressed that you were in need. Spending almost a sleepless night, I hastened at early dawn to come and inquire about the case."

Then returning to his sleigh he took into the house breadstuff, meat and groceries, so that mother had abundance to prepare breakfast for the little ones, who had eaten the last bread the night before. And as if to make the case above mentioned a special providence, without a doubt remaining, the individual who was thus impressed—and that at the very hour that mother was crying to God—was a stranger to the circumstances and surroundings of this family. Indeed, he had never been in that house before, nor had ever showed any interest in the person referred to, but he ever afterwards proved a friend indeed.

Now, after years have rolled around, and these children are all married and settled in homes of their own, that mother's heart is still strengthened to bear hardships and trust in God, by the recollections of that hour, when faith in God was so tested, and yet was so triumphant.

Let skeptics ridicule the idea of a special Providence, or lightly speak of prayer. One heart will ever believe God's ear in mercy is open to the cry of the feeblest of His children, when in distress their cry goes up for help to Him.— E. M. *Dodson, of Orworth, Kansas, in* Michigan Holiness Record

The conversion of Hudson Taylor

Hudson Taylor, founder of China Inland Mission, says that about 1830 his father became so interested in the spiritual condition of China, that he was led to pray that if God ever gave him a son, he might be privileged to labor as a missionary there; a prayer unknown to the son until after seven years of service in that mission field. Though carefully trained to the study of God's word and a life of devotion, yet at the age of fifteen the lad was a skeptic.

Of his conversion he says, "One day, which I shall never forget, when I was about fifteen years old, my dear mother being absent from home some eighty miles away, I had a holiday. I searched through the library for a book to while away time. I selected a gospel tract which looked unattractive, saying, there will be an interesting story at the commencement, and a sermon or moral at the end; I will take the former, and leave the latter for those who like it. I little knew what was going on in the heart of my dear mother. She arose from the dinner table with an intense yearning for the conversion of her boy, and feeling that, being from home, and having more leisure than she otherwise would, there was a special opportunity afforded her of pleading with God for me. She went to their bedroom, and turned the key in the door, and resolved not to leave the room until her prayers were answered.

Hour after hour did that dear mother plead for me, until she could only praise God for the conversion of her son. In the meantime, as I was reading the tract, *The Finished Work of Christ*, a light was flashed into my soul by the Holy Spirit, that there was nothing to be done, but to fall on my knees and accept this Savior and his salvation, and praise God forevermore. While my mother was praising God in her closet, I was praising Him in the old warehouse where I had retired to read my book. When I met mother at the door on her return with the glad news, she said, "I know, my boy; I have been rejoicing for a fortnight in the glad tidings you have to tell me!"

Many souls are lost for want of persistent pleading with God in their behalf. Time that might be used in prayer is consumed in other ways, and souls and opportunities pass forever from our reach. For those hours of pleading with God, this faithful mother received not only her son for God, but the great work God put into his hands—China Inland Mission. Hudson Taylor has led out into the heart of China more than one hundred and seventy apostolic missionaries, none of whom receive support except through faith in God.—Anna Abrams, in *Vanguard*.

Awful providences

The following are selected from a list of incidents recorded by Thomas Graham, the noted revivalist preacher, of the Erie Conference of the M. E. Church. After his death they were found entered, under the above heading, in a small passbook, as facts worth of preservation, from the experience of almost fifty years in the ministry.

When the Rev. Mr. Knapp, a Regular Baptist minister, was holding a protracted meeting in Erie, he was interrupted by one Gifford, a Universalist preacher. Mr. Knapp felt his patience tried. At the conclusion of his sermon he prayed publicly that if said Gifford was within reach of salvation that God would have mercy upon him; but if not that God would take away his speech, so that he might deceive the people no longer. And Mr. Gifford went out of the house that night a perfect mute, nor did he speak another word for more than four years. He said himself he believed he could speak if he would will to do it. He carried a slate about with him all the time, on which he wrote what he wished to say. All physicians who examined him said there was no disease of the organs of speech. It was a direct visitation in answer to prayer. He went to New York, Boston, and other places, to consult the best physicians; but it was of no use.

Soon after the publication of this item in the *Michigan Holiness Record*, August, 1887, the editor received the following testimony from Mrs. Clarissa Olds Keeler, who, with her husband, edited the *Banner of Love*, in Washington, D. C.: "I have just been looking over the last *Record*, and I see the account of Elder Knapp's prayer in Erie. I was a little girl when that incident occurred, but I remember it. Elder Knapp was preaching in our church (or rather the church my parents belonged to, the one we all of us children attended), and his prayer was answered as related, 'God is not mocked.'"

When Rev. George Howe was holding a protracted meeting, at which many were converted, the family of a noted infidel experienced religion, which affected him much. Returning home one evening from meeting, he seemed more than usually melancholy; and after going to bed, he began to abuse his wife for letting the children have a certain rope to play with that day, for they had now lost it. She remarked to him that it was not lost, that she knew it was in a certain place which she designated. Apparently he became satisfied, and fell asleep. That night one of the members of the Methodist society in the neighborhood came to two others of the brethren, stating to them that he was impressed with the idea of going to this infidel's house, and wanted them to go along with him. They all started off immediately. They came to the infidel's door and rapped, but received no answer. After waiting some time, they opened the door, and coming in, found the man of the house with the rope around his neck, and in the act of putting it over a beam to hang himself. Immediately he dropped on his knees, and cried for mercy, and before they left him he was happily converted to God. His name was John James. Ten minutes more and he would have been in eternity.

When Rev. William Swazy and Rev. John Chandler were holding a quarterly meeting in Greenville, Pennsylvania, they gave an opportunity for seekers of religion to come to the altar on Saturday evening. Many came. One young man, who was almost induced to go, held back. The thought, however, that it "was now or never" haunted him, so that at last he arose and went part way down the aisle with the intention of going forward; he stopped, however, and going back resumed his seat. Still this idea troubled him. He arose and went part way a second time. A third time he arose and went down, but instead of kneeling down at the altar, he went out of the house intending to go home; but being impressed with the idea that it was "now or never," he turned about and came back, and stood at the altar, and looked on the scene for a short time; then clenching his fist, and shaking it in the air, he shouted, "God Almighty, I will not!" and left the house. From that moment he said his feelings left him.

He walked on home; but as he stepped on his own doorstep and put his hand to the door to open it, he said a light shone around him, and a voice distinctly said, "He is joined to his idols, let him alone;" and, shrieking aloud, he fell on the pavement. His neighbors came and carried him in. They sent for Swazy and Chandler, who came and offered him the consolation of the gospel, but without avail. His reply was, "It is too late! Too late! Too late!" And continued thus to exclaim until about sunrise the next morning, when his spirit took its flight to God, whom he had refused and insulted.

4

John Byers' prevailing prayer

MAGGIE, AN IRISH GIRL of about twenty years, burned herself by lighting the morning fire with kerosene. Dr. Benjamin, the leader of the infidel club here, was called, who bound her up in cotton and oil.

A neighbor sent for John Byers, an old Scotch shoemaker, to pray with her. As he came into the house, the doctor was coming out, and ordered him away, saying, he didn't want any praying done about any of his patients. But Brother Byers paid him no heed, and taking the girl's hand, asked her, "Maggie, are you in great pain?"

"Oh! Awful, sir," was her answer.

"Well, we will ask God to take it away." He said; and falling upon his knees at her bedside, paying no more attention to the room full of women that stood about, than if they had been so many flies, he asked the Lord to take all the pain away, so that he could talk to her about her soul; and very soon he got the perfect assurance that his prayer was heard. So he arose and said, "Do you feel any pain now, Maggie?"

"No, sir, it has all gone away." Then he presented a Savior to her mind, as dying for dying Maggie, so that she, by believing on Him, might live forever; and soon she accepted Him as her Redeemer.

After a little while she opened her eyes, and looking around, said to the women, "Don't you hear it?"

"No, we don't hear anything, Maggie," they replied.

"Oh, I never heard such singing before! And the music! I can't tell you how fine it is." And then she lay, listening—till starting up, she sat up in bed, and pointing upward, said, "Don't you see them? Oh, how beautiful they are! What are they?"

"They are angels, coming to take you home, Maggie," said Brother Byers. Then she laid back again on her pillow perfectly quiet, as if fearing to lose sight of the beautiful vision.

Brother Byers turned to go home, but had not got a hundred steps from the house, when one of the women called out to him, "She's gone, sir."

But the case of the doctor lay heavily on John Byers' mind; and that night, he did not go to bed until he had made the case a subject of earnest prayer, and had received the assurance that he should be converted. Seeing the doctor a few days after that, he told him of his answer to prayer for him. But the doctor laughed at the idea of such a fool getting any such a promise for the Maker of the universe.

But the next fall the doctor went to Florida for his health, and within two months, the news came back that Benjamin had knelt at a Methodist mourner's bench, and was converted.

The next spring he died, rejoicing in the faith.—*Dr. H. Durham.*

<u>A vision of heaven</u>

That heaven is real there can be no doubt. That others beside St. Paul have been allowed a view of Paradise, is evident from the testimony of the most reliable witnesses, such as Dr. Tennent, of New Jersey, Dr. Coke, and many others. One of the most interesting and touching incidents of this character is related by Rev. James B. Finley, in his *Autobiography*. It occurred in 1842, when he was presiding elder of the Lebanon District, Ohio Conference.

He tells us that he was "winding up the labors of a very toilsome year. I had scarcely finished my work till I was most violently attacked with bilious fever, and it was with great difficulty I reached my home." He sank rapidly. The best medical skill failed to arrest the disease, and life was utterly despaired of.

"On the seventh night," he says, "in a state of entire insensibility to all around me, when the last ray of hope had departed, and my weeping family and friends were standing around my couch, waiting to see me breathe my last, it seemed to me that a heavenly visitant entered my room. It came to my side, and in the softest and most silvery tones, which fell like rich music on my ear, it said, 'I have come to conduct you to another state and place of existence.' In an instant I seemed to rise, and gently borne by my angel guide, I floated out upon the ambient air. The earth was lost in the distance, and around us on every side were worlds of light and glory. On, on, away, away, from world to luminous worlds afar, we sped with the velocity of thought. At length we reached the gates of Paradise; and oh, the transporting scenes that fell upon my vision, as the emerald portals, wide and high, rolled back upon their golden hinges! Then in its fullest extent, I did realize the invocation of the poet:

> Burst, ye emerald gates, and bring
> To my raptured vision,
> All the ecstatic joys that spring
> Round the bright Elysian.

"Language, however, is inadequate to describe what then, with unveiled eyes I saw. The vision is indelibly pictured on my heart. Before me, spread out in beauty, was a broad sheet of water, clear as crystal, not a single ripple on its surface, and its purity and clearness indescribable.

"While I stood gazing with joy and rapture at the scene, a convoy of angels was seen floating in the pure ether of that world. They all had long wings, and although they went with the greatest rapidity, yet their wings were folded close to their sides. While gazing, I asked my guide who these were, and what their mission. To this he responded, 'They are angels, dispatched to the world from whence you came, on an errand of mercy.' I could hear strains of the most entrancing melodies all around me, but no one was discoverable but my guide.

"At length I said, 'Will it be possible for me to have a sight of some of the just made perfect in glory?' Just then there came before us three persons; one had the appearance of a male, the other a female, and the third was an infant. The appearance of the first two was somewhat similar to the angels I saw, with the exception that they had crowns upon their heads of the purest yellow, and harps in their hands. Their robes, which were full and flowing, were of the purest white. Their countenances were lighted up with heavenly radiance, and they smiled upon me with ineffable sweetness.

"There was nothing with which the blessed babe or child could be compared. Its wings, which were most beautiful, were tinged with all the colors of the rainbow. Its dress seemed to be of the whitest silk, covered with the softest white down. The driven snow could not exceed it for whiteness of purity. Its face was all radiant with glory; its very smile now plays around my heart. I gazed and gazed with wonder upon this heavenly child.

"At length I said, 'If I have to return to earth, from whence I came, I should love to take this child with me, and show it to the weeping mothers of earth. Methinks when they see it, they will never shed another tear over their children when they die.' So anxious was I to carry out the desire of my heart, that I made a grasp at the bright and beautiful one, desiring to clasp it in my arms; but it eluded my grasp and plunged into the river of life. Soon it rose up from the water; and, as the drops fell from its expanding wings, they seemed like diamonds, so brightly did they sparkle. Directing its course to the other shore, it flew up to one of the topmost branches of one of life's fair trees. With a look of most seraphic sweetness it gazed upon me, and then commenced singing in heaven's own strain, 'To Him that hath loved me, and washed me from sins in His own blood, to Him be glory, both now and forever. Amen.'

"At that moment, the power of the eternal God came upon me, and I began to shout; and clapping my hands, I sprang from my bed, and was healed as instantly as the lame man in the beautiful porch of the temple, who 'went walking, and leaping, and praising God.' Overwhelmed with the glory I saw and felt, I could not cease praising God.

"The next Sabbath, I went to campmeeting, filled with the love and power of God. There I told the listening thousands what I saw and felt, and what God had done for me; and loud were the shouts of glory that reverberated through the forest."

This is a most remarkable case. Gather Adams, a member of the Ohio Conference, now residing at Orange, South Carolina, told us that he was present at the campmeeting and heard Mr. Finley relate the circumstances, when such power fell on the people that not less than five hundred sinners were crying to God for mercy, while the saints of God shouted for joy.

The healing was divine—done by the power of God. The man was made whole in a moment, after all hope of life had fled.—*Christian Witness.*

Miracle of healing.

From *Remarkable Answers to Prayer*, by Patton, the following extract is made:

The author has received a letter from James H. Blackman of Sharon, Mass., (P.O. address at Canton, Mass.,) which is of extraordinary interest. Some of the facts have been given before, but never so fully as now. Slightly abridged, it is as follows, under the date of Octaober 23, 1875:

"In the spring of 1870, my wife was taken sick with kidney complaint. She continued to grow worse during the summer. I took a bottle of urine to Dr. Erasmus D. Miller, a celebrated physician of Boston, to be tested. He sent me a note saying, 'Her disease is Bright's disease of the kidneys, in a far advanced stage, and incurable.' The water was afterward tested by several physicians, who agreed with Dr. Miller. An increase of albumen was apparent at every test, and the last, a 2 oz. bottle, tested by Dr. A. A. Holmes, of Canton, contained nothing but albumen. The water finally decreased in quantity, and finally stopped altogether, and for two years nothing passed. It is well known that physicians do not profess to cure this disease. During my wife's illness her left limb became completely paralyzed, and withered away to the size of a man's wrist in the largest place, without any feeling even to pins and boiling water. She tipped a milk pan of boiling water upon her feet, but did not know that this limb was scalded till she began to dress the well foot. For three years and two months she did not walk; for two years she crept upon her knees, drawing the lame leg after her; and for the last year she moved herself around in a wheeled invalid chair. During these three years she was taken out of her bed in the morning and put into it again at night. For the two years and four months no physician had been in the house, and she had taken no medicine, resorted to no bathing or rubber. She ate but once a day, and immediately vomited.

"During her sickness, God gave me a new heart, and I prayed for her conversion, which occurred in January, 1874, and then for that of our daughter, which took place in February. Previously I was a Unitarian, unacquainted with evangelical doctrines. Not knowing that the Christian world had decided that the day of miracles had passed, in my ignorance and simplicity, I went to praying with faith in Christ's promise, that my wife might be healed—my wife and daughter joining after their conversion. God gave me the assurance that our prayers were accepted, and I became bold to say to others that she would soon walk. I made this declaration to James Jennison, Congregational minister at Canton, and he replied, 'Why, you can't expect God to do a miracle!'

"My assurance grew stronger and stronger, and filled me with joy and gratitude. Just then the water came back in large quantity, and on being tested by Dr. Holmes, proved free of albumen. On the morning of February 25, 1873, I prayed earnestly in secret, and then placed my wife on her knees at the family altar, and again prayed earnestly that she might walk. At the close of the prayer she was unconscious, and apparently dead. She remained thus about three minutes, when she exclaimed, 'I can walk! I know I can walk! Praise God, I can walk!' She got up off her knees, and walked twice around the room, exclaiming, 'Praise God, I can walk! Why don't you praise God that I can walk?'

"Then we commenced shouting, 'Glory to God!' Oh, the rapture of that moment! We bowed before God and thanked Him for the great miracle He had performed.

"I opened the door, and she walked out upon the plaza; and about an hour afterward she walked out and shook hands with a neighbor, who was so surprised that he lost all power of speech. The paralyzed limb became immediately enlarged, and in a few days was plump and round, and stronger than the other. The appetite came back, the vomiting ceased, and Bright's disease, with all its attendant pains, passed away. She is in better health than ever before, and, like the impotent man at the Beautiful Gate, goes about leaping and praising God, after walking eight and ten miles a day without limping or fatigue.

"We got our faith by prayer and reading the promises. How could we, after having been born again, refuse to accept those promises as true? Our hearts had been given to Him, and we prayed for her recovery, that each might be enabled to go out into the world and make known the wonderful things God had done for us, in giving us clean hearts; and by the grace of God, so we will ever do."

Remarkable healing of Mrs. Susan E. Miller

When I was twelve years of age I felt the need of a new heart. I asked God for it, and He gave it to me. I am now forty-six years old, and oh, how wonderfully the Lord has led me! I must say, there is nothing so grand and glorious as to know that we are of God's chosen ones.

When I came to Grand Rapids five years ago I became acquainted with S. B. Shaw, President of the Michigan Holiness Association, and his very worthy wife. I saw them live by faith alone for all things, both spiritual and temporal; and of them I learned how to consecrate myself wholly unto the Lord.

I had been afflicted with rheumatism from a child; and had spent large sums of money for my recovery, but could only find relief for a few weeks at a time. I was sick and helpless in bed with inflammatory rheumatism, when I heard through Mrs. Shaw of Mrs. Dora Griffin. I sent for her to anoint me. After she had done so, and while she was praying for a recovery, the Lord touched my body, and I was healed that very same hour, and have never been troubled with rheumatism since; praise God!

One year after this, the piles came upon me, and I suffered greatly. After trying many remedies and doctors without relief, I said, "The Lord has healed me and will heal me again;" so I went to the *Beulah Rest*, and after prayer and anointing, I was healed, and went home happy, healed and saved in both soul and body; praise His name forever!

Dear friends, you who are sick of sin and sick in body, come to Jesus, and be healed, soul and body.–Mrs. Susan E. Miller

Instantly healed of rupture

During the fall of 1888 we witnessed the remarkable healing of Brother J. S. Whiting, then a pastor at Hilliards, Michigan. The night of his cure we were wonderfully led out in prayer. We give the circumstances in his own words, as published in the *Holiness Record* a short time afterwards.

He says, "About three weeks after my conversion the Lord told me to go preach His gospel. I obeyed the call the best I could, but have been trying to believe that I could work in the mill through the week and just preach on Sunday; but found that the Lord wanted me to give up all and work for Him. Still I hesitated. About one year ago while about my work, I fell, and ruptured myself very badly—was so that I could not stand on my feet without a truss, and sometimes even that was not sufficient, and I had to lie on my back.

"Last Thursday night, while I was preaching, my rupture began to pain me so badly that I had to stop and let Brother Shaw finish. That night we went to stay with one of the members. I suffered a great deal of pain all the next day. When night came, it rained so hard we could not have any meeting, so remained where we were. During the evening I lay on the couch, as I was unable to be on my feet, or even sit up with any comfort.

"Finally Brother Shaw said, 'Let us pray.' At first I thought I could not get on my knees, but with the Lord's help I got down, and began to pray for God to heal my body.

"Then I thought something said, 'Get up, and take off your truss.' So I got up, and took it off, and went to the stove, opened the door, and threw it into the fire, as I felt clearly directed to do. Then God came and made a sound man of me. I can jump and praise Him now, and all is right."

From what he told us, we think the Lord has done more for him than would be inferred from his words. We were with him one week before his healing, and a few days after, and certainly God wrought a most wonderful cure in his case. When we met him months afterward, we found him still well and sound. May God use this and other similar cases to inspire faith in others.

The young martyr

On the afternoon of August 9, 1853, a little Norwegian boy, named Kund Iverson, who lived in the city of Chicago, Illinois, was going to the pastures for his cow, as lighthearted, I suppose, as boys usually are when going to the pasture on a summer afternoon. He came at length to a stream of water, where there was a gang of idle, ill-looking, big boys, who, when they saw Kund, came up to him, and said they wanted him to go into Mr. Elston's garden and steal some apples.

"No," said Kund promptly; "I cannot steal, I am sure."

"Well, but you've got to," they cried.

They threatened to duck him, for these wicked big boys had often frightened little boys into robbing gardens for them. Little boys, they thought, were less likely to get found out.

REMARKABLE ANSWERS TO PRAYER

The threat did not frighten Kund, so, to make their words good, they seized him and dragged him into the river, and, in spite of his cries and struggles, plunged him in. But the heroic boy, even with the water gurgling and choking in his throat, never flinched, for he knew that God had said, "Thou shalt not steal," and God's law he had made his law; and no cursing, or threats, or cruelty of the big boys would make him give up. Provoked by his firmness, I suppose, they determined to see if they could not conquer.

So they ducked him again, but still it was "No, no;" and they kept him under the water. Was there no one near to hear his distressing cries, and to rescue the poor child from their cruel grip? No, there was none to rescue him; and gradually the cries of the drowning child grew fainter and fainter, and his struggles less and less, and the boy was drowned. He could die, but would not steal.

A German boy who had stood near, much frightened by what he saw, ran home to tell the news. The agonized parents hastened to the spot, and all night they searched for the lifeless body of their lost darling. It was found the next morning; and who shall describe their feelings as they clasped the little form to their bosoms? Early piety had blossomed in his little life. He loved his Bible and his Savior. His seat was never vacant at Sunday school, and so intelligent, conscientious and steadfast had he been, that it was expected that he would soon be received in the church of his parents.

Perhaps the little boy used often to think how, when he grew up, he would like to be a preacher or a missionary, and do something for his Lord and Master. He did not know what post he might be called to occupy, even as a little child; and, as he left home that afternoon and looked his last look in his mother's face, he thought he was only going after his cow; and other boys, and the neighbors, if they saw him, thought so too. They did not then know that instead of going to the pasture, he was going to preach one of the most powerful sermons of Bible law and Bible principles the country ever heard. They did not know that he was going to give an example of steadfastness of purpose and of unflinching integrity, such as should thrill the heart of this nation with wonder and admiration. He was then only a Norwegian boy, Kund Iverson, only thirteen years old, but his name was soon to be reckoned with martyrs and heroes.

As the story of this moral heroism winged its way from state to state and city to city, and village to village, how many mothers cried, with full hearts, "May his spirit rest upon my boy!" And strong men have wept over it and exclaimed, "God be praised for the lad!" And rich men put their hands in their pockets, and said, "Let us build him a monument; let his name be perpetuated, for his memory is blessed."

May there be a generation of Kund Iverson's, strong in their integrity, true to their Bibles, ready to die rather than do wrong.—*The Cynosure.*

Revivals vs. fairs—wonders of prayer

The Methodist Preachers' Meeting of Boston was well attended last Monday, and Rev. W. N. Brodbeck, D.D., the pastor of the Tremont Street Church of this city, thrilled the brethren with an address on *The Relation of the Ministers to Revivals,* during which he pointedly referred to church fairs and festivals as barriers to revivals.

He declared that some ministers and churches would never have a revival, because they would not do the hard work, and make to sacrifice essential to secure said results. At Urbana, Ohio, he began revival services, but at first only doubtful characters came to the altar, in whom the public had no confidence. Many were offended, and some said, "Do you know these people that are coming to the altar?"

He replied, "Yes, I know them; they are immortal souls for whom Christ died." When the meetings had run three weeks, one of his leading members came to him and said, "I think it is time these meetings were stopped; we have held them for three weeks, and we want to hold a fair, and have some entertainments."

The pastor firmly and promptly replied, "You may do as you please, but these meetings will not stop."

His heart was broken, and so was the heart of one of the devout women members. They expressed their feelings to each other and parted. They both spent the night in prayer, and at ten o'clock the next morning, the pastor gained the evidence that his prayers were answered. After dinner he went out, and met the devout lady on the street, her face shining with the glory of God. She said, "The victory is coming."

"How do you know?"

"I got the evidence at ten o'clock this morning, after spending a whole night in prayer."

This was the very time that the pastor gained the evidence. That very night, while the pastor was preaching, a young man arose and came to the altar; others followed, so that the pastor had to stop preaching. God was among the people in power; the church was quickened, backsliders were reclaimed, hundreds of sinners were converted. Places of amusement and saloons were closed. The face of the community was changed, and 275 converts joined that one church, and the fair was not held, all because they refused to have the fair. Oh, for more nights of prayer! Oh, for more agony of soul for perishing sinners! Oh! For more of the mind of Christ! Then would revivals prevail, and thousands would be converted to God.—*Christian Witness.*

REMARKABLE ANSWERS TO PRAYER

An army miraculously delivered

We clip the following from an epistle of the Roman Emperor, Marcus Aurelius, who was born in the year 121, and died in the year 180, as found in Volume 2 of the *Anti-Nicene Christian Library*. —Editor

The Emperor Caesar Marcus Aurelius Antonius, to the people of Rome, and to the sacred senate: Greeting.

I explained to you my grand design, and what advantages I gained on the confines of Germany, with much labor and suffering, in consequence of the circumstance that I was surrounded by the enemy; I myself being shut up in Carauntum by seventy-four cohorts, nine miles off. And the enemy being at hand, the scouts pointed out to us, and our general Pompeianus showed us, that there was close on us a mass of a mixed multitude of 977,000 men, which, indeed, we saw; and I was shut up by this vast host, having with me only a battalion composed of the first, tenth, double and marine legions. Having then examined my own position, and my host, with respect to the vast mass of barbarians and of the enemy; But being disregarded by them, I summoned those who among us go by the name of Christians. And having made inquiry, I discovered a great number and vast host of them, and raged against them, which was by no means becoming; for afterwards I learned their power. Wherefore they began the battle, not by preparing weapons, nor arms, nor bugles; for such preparation is hateful to them, on account of the God they bear about in their conscience. Therefore it is probable that those whom we suppose to be atheists have God as their ruling power entrenched in their conscience. For having cast themselves on the ground, they prayed not only for me, but also for the whole army as it stood, that they might be delivered from the present thirst and famine. For during five days we had got no water, because there was none; for we were in the heart of Germany, and in the enemy's territory. And simultaneously with their casting themselves on the ground, and praying to God, a God of whom I am ignorant, water poured from heaven upon us, most refreshingly cool, but upon the enemies of Rome a withering hail. And immediately we recognized the presence of God following on the prayer—a God unconquerable and indestructible. Founding upon this, then, let us pardon such as are Christians, lest they pray for and obtain such a weapon against ourselves. And I counsel that no such person be accused on the ground of his being a Christian. But if anyone be found laying to the charge of Christian that he is a Christian, I desire that it be made manifest that he who is accused as a Christian, and acknowledges that he is one, is accused of nothing else than only this, that he is a Christian; but that he who arraigns him be burned alive. And I further desire, that he who is entrusted with the government of the province shall not compel the Christian, who confesses and certifies such a matter, to retract; neither shall he commit him. And I desire that these things be confirmed by a decree of the Senate. And I command this my edict to be published in the Forum of Trajan, in order that it may be read. The prefect Vitrasius Pollio will see that it be transmitted to all the provinces round about, and that no one who wishes to make use of or to possess it be hindered from obtaining a copy from the document I now publish.

Little mother

She was a clear-eyed, fresh-cheeked little maiden, living on the banks of the great Mississippi, the oldest of four children, and mother's "little woman" always. They called her so because of her quiet, matronly care of the younger Mayfields—that was the father's name. Her own name was the beautiful one of Elizabeth, but they shortened it to Bess.

She was thirteen when one day Mr. Mayfield and his wife called to the nearest town, six miles away. "Be mother's little woman, dear," said Mrs. Mayfield, as she kissed the rosy face. Her husband added, "I leave the children in your care, Bess; be a little mother to them."

Bess waved her old sunbonnet vigorously, and held up the baby Rose, that she might watch them to the last. Old Daddy Jim and Mammy had been detailed by Mr. Mayfield to keep an unsuspected watch on the little nestlings, and were to sleep at the house. Thus two days went by, when Daddy Jim and Mammy begged to be allowed to go to their home to see if their own daughter was all right. "Jennie, who was bad with a toothache." They declared they would be back by evening, so Bess was willing. She put the little girls to bed, and persuaded Rob to go; then seated herself by the table with her mother's work basket, in quaint imitation of Mrs. Mayfield's industry in the evening time.

But what was this? Her feet touched something cold! She bent down and felt around with her hand. A pool of water was spreading over the floor. She knew what it was; the Mississippi had broken through the levee. What should she do? Mammy's stories of how houses had been washed away and broken in pieces, were in her mind. "Oh, if I had a boat!" she exclaimed, "but there isn't anything of the sort on the place." She ran wildly out to look for Mammy; and stumbled over something sitting near the edge of the porch. A sudden inspiration took her. Here was her boat! A very large, old fashioned, oblong tub. The water was now several inches deep on the porch, and she contrived to half float, half roll the tub into the room.

Without frightening the children she got them dressed in the warmest clothes they had. She lined the oblong tub with a blanket, and made ready bread and cold meat left from supper. With Rob's assistance she dragged the tub upstairs. There was a single

REMARKABLE ANSWERS TO PRAYER

large window in the room, and they set the tub directly by it, so that when the water rose the tub would float out. There was no way for the children to reach the roof, which was a very steep, inclined one. It did not seem long before the water had very nearly risen to the top of the stairs leading from below.

Bess flung the window open, and made Rob get into their novel boat; then she lifted in Kate, and finally baby Rose, who began to cry, was given into Rob's arms, and now the little mother, taking the basket of food, made ready to enter too, but Lo! There was no room for her with safety to the rest. Bess paused a moment, drew a long breath, and kissed the children quietly. She explained to Rob that he must guard the basket, and that they must set still.

"Good-bye, dears. Say a prayer for sister, Rob. If you ever see father and mother, tell them I took care of you." Then the water seized the insecure vessel, and out into the dark night it floated.

The next day Mr. Mayfield, who, with his neighbors, scoured the broad lake of eddying water that represented the Mississippi, discovered the tub lodged in the branches of a sycamore with the children weeping and chilled, but safe.

And Bess? Ah, where was Bess, the "little mother," who in that brief moment resigned herself to death? They found her later, floating on the water with her brave childish face turned to the sky; and as strong arms lifted her into the boat, the tears from every eye paid worthy tribute to the "little mother."—*Detroit Free Press*.

The Quaker who refused to fight

We clip the following from *Lossing's Pictorial Field Book of the Civil War*, Volume 3, page 79. It is certainly a remarkable evidence of God's power to deliver them that put their trust in Him.—*Editor*.

There were some Friends or Quakers from South Carolina in the battle of Gettysburg, who were forced into the ranks, but who, from the beginning to the end, refused to fight. They were from Guilford county, which was mostly settled by their sect, and as the writer can testify by personal observation, presented the only region in that state where the evidences of thrift, which free labor gave in a land cursed by slavery, might be seen. These excellent people were robbed and plundered by the Confederates without mercy. About a dozen of them were in Lee's army at Gettysburg and were among the prisoners captured there. They had steadily borne practical testimony to the strength of their principles in opposing war. They were subjected to great cruelties. One of them who refused to fight was ordered by his colonel to be shot. A squad of twelve men were drawn up to shoot him. They loved him as a brother because of his goodness, and when ordered to

TOUCHING INCIDENTS AND

fire every man refused. The remainder of the company was called up and ordered to shoot the first twelve if they did not execute the order. The intended victim folded his hands, and raised his eyes, and said, "Father, forgive them, for they know not what they do."

The entire company threw down their muskets and refused to obey the order. Their exasperated captain, with a horrid oath, tried to shoot him with his pistol The cap would not explode. Then he dashed upon him with his horse, but the meek conscript was unharmed. Just then a charge of some of Mead's troops drove the Confederates from their position, and the Quaker became a prisoner. He and his co-religionists were sent to Fort Delaware. When the fact was made known to some of their sect in Philadelphia, it was laid before the President, and he ordered their release.

A child's prayer answered

The following touching incident, which drew tears from my eyes, was related to me a short time since, by a dear friend who had it from an eyewitness of the same. It occurred in the great city of New York, on one of the cold days in February:

A little boy about ten years old was standing before a shoestore in Broadway, barefooted, peering through the window, and shivering with cold.

A lady riding up the street in a beautiful carriage, drawn by horses finely caparisoned, observed the little fellow in his forlorn condition, and immediately ordered the driver to draw up and stop in front of the store. The lady, richly dressed in silk, alighted from her carriage, went quickly to the boy, and said, "My little fellow, why are you looking so earnestly in that window?"

"I was asking God to give me a pair of shoes," was the reply. The lady took him by the hand and went into the store, and asked the proprietor if he would allow one of his clerks to go and buy half a dozen pair of stockings for the boy. He readily assented. She then asked him if he could give her a basin of water and a towel, and he replied, "Certainly," and quickly brought them to her.

She took the little fellow to the back part of the store, and, removing her gloves, knelt down, washed those little feet and dried them with the towel.

By this time the young man had returned with the stockings. Placing a pair upon his feet, she purchased and gave him a pair of shoes, and tying up the remaining pairs of stockings, gave them to him, and patting him on the head said, "I hope, my little fellow, that you now feel more comfortable."

As she turned to go, the astonished lad caught her hand, and looking up in her face, with tears in his eyes, answered her question with these words, "Are you God's wife?"—*Parish Register.*

Send food to John.

On the summit of Washington mountain, overlooking the Housatonic valley, stood a hut, the home of John Barry, a poor charcoal-burner, whose family consisted of his wife and himself. His occupation brought him in but a few dollars, and when cold weather came he had managed to get together only a small provision for winter. The fall of 1874, after a summer of hard work, he fell sick and was unable to keep his fires going. So, when the snow of December, 1874 fell, and the drifts had shut off communication with the village at the foot of the mountain, John and his wife were in great straits.

Their entire stock of food consisted of only a few pounds of salt pork and a bushel of potatoes; sugar, flour, coffee and tea had, early in December, given out; and the chances for replenishing the larder were slim indeed. The snow storms came again, and the drifts deepened. All the roads, even in the valley, were impassable, and no one thought of try to open the mountain highways, which, even in summer, were only occasionally traveled; and none gave the old man and his wife a thought.

December 15th came, and with it the heaviest fall of snow experienced in Berkshire county in many years. The food of the old couple was now reduced to a day's supply, but John did not yet despair. He was a Christian and a God-fearing man, and His promises were remembered; and so, when evening came, and the northeast gale was blowing, and the fierce snow storm was raging, John and his wife were praying and asking for help.

In Sheffield village, ten miles away, lived Deacon Brown, a well-to-do farmer fifty years old, who was know for his piety and consistent deportment; both as a man and a Christian. The deacon and his wife had gone to bed early, and, in spite of the storm without, they were sleeping soundly, when with a start the deacon awoke, and said to his wife, "Who spoke? Who's there?"

"Why," said his wife, "no one is here but you and me; what is the matter with you?"

"I heard a voice," said the deacon, "saying, 'send food to John.'"

"Nonsense," replied Mrs. Brown; "go to sleep. You have been dreaming." The deacon laid his head on his pillow, and was asleep in a minute.

Soon he started up again, and waking his wife, said, "There, I heard that voice again, 'Send food to John.'"

"Well, well!" Said Mrs. Brown. "Deacon, you are not well; your supper has not agreed with you. Lie down and try to sleep."

Again the deacon closed his eyes, and again the voice was heard, "Send food to John."

This time the deacon was thoroughly awake. "Wife," said he, "whom do we know named John who needs food?"

"No one I remember," replied Mrs. Brown, "unless it be John Barry, the old charcoal-burner on the mountain."

"That's it," exclaimed the deacon, "Now I remember, when I was at the store in Sheffield the other day, Clark, the merchant, speaking of John Barry, said, 'I wonder if the old man is alive, for it is six weeks since I saw him, and he has not yet laid in his winter stock of groceries.' It must be old John is sick and wanting food."

So saying, the good deacon arose and proceeded to dress himself. "Come, wife," said he, "waken our boy Willie and tell him to feed the horses, and get ready to go with me; and do you pack up in the two largest baskets you have a good supply of food, and get us an early breakfast; for I am going up the mountain to carry the food I know John Barry needs."

Mrs. Brown, accustomed to the sudden impulses of her good husband, and believing him to be always in the right, cheerfully complied; and after a hot breakfast, Deacon Brown and his son Willie, a boy of nineteen, hitched up the horses to the double sleigh, and the, with a month's supply of food, and a "Good-bye, mother," started at five o'clock on that cold December morning for a journey that almost any other than Deacon Brown and his son Willie would not have dared to undertake.

The northeast storm was still raging, and the snow falling and drifting fast; but on, on went the stout, well-fed team on its errand of mercy, while the occupants of the sleigh, wrapped up in blankets and extra buffalo robes, urged the horses through the drifts and in the face of the storm. That ten mile ride, which required in the summer hardly an hour or two, was not finished until the deacon's watch showed that five hours had passed.

At last they drew up in front of the hut where the poor, trusting Christian man and woman were on their knees praying for help to Him who is the "hearer and answerer of prayer;" and as the deacon reached the door, he heard the voice of

REMARKABLE ANSWERS TO PRAYER

supplication, and then he knew that the message which awakened him from sleep was sent from heaven. He knocked at the door, it was opened, and we can imagine the joy of the old couple, when the generous supply of food was carried in, and the thanksgivings that were uttered by the starving tenants of that mountain hut.—*Albany Journal.*

Kiss me, mama

The child was so sensitive, so like that little shrinking plant that curls at the breath, and shuts its heart from the light. The only beauties she possessed were and exceedingly transparent skin, and the most mournful, large blue eyes.

I had been trained by a very stern, strict, conscientious mother, but I was a hardy plant, rebounding after every shock; misfortune could not daunt, though discipline tamed me. I fancied, alas! that I must go through the same routine with this delicate creature; so one day, when she had displeased me exceedingly by repeating an offense, I was determined to punish her severely. I was very serious all day, and upon sending her to her little couch I said, "Now, my daughter, to punish you, and show you how very, very naughty you have been, I shall not kiss you tonight."

She stood looking at me, astonishment personified, with her great mournful eyes wide open. I suppose she had forgotten her misconduct till then; and I left her with big tears dropping down her cheeks, and her little red lips quivering.

Presently I was sent for. "Oh, mamma! You will kiss me, I can't go to sleep if you don't!" She sobbed, every tone of her voice trembling, and she held out her little hands.

Now came a struggle between love and what I falsely termed duty. My heart said give her a kiss of peace; my stern nature urged me to persist in my correction, that I might impress the fault upon her mind. This was the way I had been trained, till I was a most submissive child; and I remembered how I had often thanked my mother since for her straightforward course.

I knelt by the bedside. "Mother can't kiss you, Ellen," I whispered, though every word choked me. Her hand touched mine; it was very hot, but I attributed it to her excitement. She turned her little grieving face to the wall; I blamed myself as the fragile form shook with self-suppressed sobs, and saying, "Mother hopes little Ellen will learn to mind after this," left the room for the night. Alas! In my desire to be severe I forgot to be forgiving.

It must have been twelve o'clock when I was awakened by my nurse. Apprehensive, I ran eagerly to the child's chamber; I had had a fearful dream.

Ellen did not know me. She was sitting up, crimsoned from the forehead to the throat, her eyes so bright that I almost drew back aghast at their glances.

From that night a raging fever drank up her life; and what think you was the incessant plaint that poured into my anguished heart? "Oh! Kiss me, mamma, do kiss me; I can't go to sleep. I won't be naughty if you'll only kiss me! Oh! Kiss me, dear mamma; I can't go to sleep."

Little angel! She did go to sleep one gray morning, and she never woke again, never! Her hand was locked in mine, and all my veins grew icy with its gradual chill. Faintly the light faded out of the beautiful eyes; whiter and whiter grew the tremulous lips. She never knew me; but with her last breath she whispered, "I will be good, mamma, if you'll only kiss me."

Kiss her! God knows how passionate but unavailing were my kisses upon her cheek and lips after that fatal night. God knows how wild were my prayers that she might know, if but only once, that I kissed her. God knows how I would have yielded up my very life, could I have asked forgiveness of that sweet child.

Grief is unavailing now! She lies in her little tomb. There is a marble urn at the head, and a rose bush at her feet; there grow sweet summer flowers; there waves the grass; there birds sing their matins and their vespers; there the blue sky smiles down today, and there lies buried the freshness of my heart.—*Ladies' Home Journal.*

REMARKABLE ANSWERS TO PRAYER

5

The converted infidel

SOME TWO MILES FROM the village of C., on a road that wound in among the hills, stood a great white house. It was beautifully situated upon a gentle slope facing the south, and overlooking a most charming landscape. Away in the distance a mountain lifted itself against the clear blue sky. At its base rolled a broad, deep river. Nestling down in the beautiful valley that intervened, reposed the charming little village, with its neat cottages, white church, little red Schoolhouse, and one or two mansions that told of wealth. Here and there in the distance a pond was visible, while farmhouses and humbler dwellings dotted the picture in every direction.

Such was the home of three promising children, who for the last three months, had been constant members of the village Sabbath school. The eldest was a girl of some fourteen years. John, the second, was a bright, amiable lad of eleven. The other, the little rosy-cheeked, laughing Ella, with her golden curls and sunny smile, had just gathered the roses of her ninth summer.

The father of these interesting children was the rich Captain Lowe. He was a man of mark, such, in many respects, as are often found in rural districts. Strictly moral, intelligent and well read, kindhearted and naturally benevolent, he attracted all classes of community to himself, and wielded great influence in his town.

But, notwithstanding all these excellences, Mr. Lowe was an **infidel**. He ridiculed, in his good-natured way, the idea of prayer, looked upon conversion as a solemn farce, and believed the most of professing Christians were well meaning but deluded people. He was well versed in all the subtle arguments of infidel writers, had studied the Bible quite carefully, and could argue against it in the most plausible manner. Courteous and kind to all, few could be offended at his frank avowal of infidel principles, or resent his keen, half-jovial sarcasms upon the peculiarities of some weak-minded, though sincere members of the church.

But Mr. Lowe saw and acknowledged the saving influence of the morality of Christianity. He had, especially, good sense enough to confess that the Sabbath-school was a noble moral enterprise. He was not blind to the fact, abundantly proved by all our criminal records, that few children trained under her influences ever grow up to vice and crime. Hence his permission for his children to attend the Sabbath school.

Among the many children who kneeled as penitents at the altar in the little vestry, one bright, beautiful Sabbath were Sarah Lowe and her brother and sister. It was a moving sight to see that gentle girl, with a mature thoughtfulness far beyond her years, take that younger brother and sister by the hand, and kneel with them at the mercy seat, a sight to heighten the joy of the angels.

When the children had told their mother what they had done, and expressed a determination to try and be Christians, she, too, was greatly moved. She had been early trained in the principles and belief of Christianity, and had never renounced her early faith. Naturally confiding, with a yielding, conciliatory spirit, she had never obtruded her sentiments upon the notice of her husband, nor openly opposed any of his peculiar views. But now, when her little ones gathered around her and spoke of their new love for the Savior, their joy, and peace, and hope, she wept. All the holy influences of her own childhood and youth seemed breathing upon her heart. She remembered the faithful sermons of the old pastor whose hands had baptized her. She remembered, too, the family altar, and the prayers which were offered morning and evening by her now sainted father. She remembered the councils of her good mother, now in heaven. All these memories came crowding back upon her, and under their softening influence she almost felt herself a child again.

When Mr. Lowe first became aware of the change in his children, he was sorely puzzled to know what to do. He had given his consent for them to attend the Sabbath school and should he now be offended because they had yielded to its influence? Ought he not rather to have expected this? And, after all, would what they call religion make them any worse children? Though at first quite disturbed in his feelings, he finally concluded upon second thought to say nothing to them upon the subject, but to let things go on as usual.

But not so those happy young converts! They could not long hold their peace. They must tell their father also what they had experienced. Mr. Lowe heard them, but he made no attempt to ridicule their simple faith, as had been his usual course with others. They were *his children*, and none could boast of better. Still, he professed to see in their present state of mind nothing but youthful feeling, excited by the peculiar circumstances of the last few weeks. But when they began in their childish ardor to exhort him also to seek the Lord, he checked their simple earnestness with a peculiar sternness which said to them, "The act must not be repeated."

The next Sabbath the father could not prevent a feeling of loneliness as he saw his household leave for church. The three children, with their mother, and Joseph, the hired boy, to drive and take care of the horse, all packed into the old commodious carriage, and started off. Never before had he such peculiar feelings as when he watched them slowly descend the hill.

To dissipate these emotions he took a dish of salt and started up the hill to a "mountain pasture," where his young cattle were enclosed for the season. It was a beautiful day in October, that queen month of the year. A soft melancholy breathed in the mild air of the mellow "Indian summer," and the varying hues of the surrounding forests, and the signs of decay seen upon every side, all combined to deepen the emotions which the circumstances of the morning had awakened.

His sadness increased; and as his path opened out into a bright, sunny spot far up on the steep hillside, he seated himself upon a mossy knoll, and thought. Before him lay the beautiful valley, guarded on either side by its lofty hills, and watered by its placid river. It was a lovely picture; and as his eye rested upon the village, nestling down among its now gorgeous shadetrees and scarlet shrubbery, he could not help thinking of that company who were then gathered in the little church, with its spire pointing heavenward, nor of asking himself the question, "Why are they there?"

While thus engaged, his attention was attracted by the peculiar chirping of a ground sparrow near by. He turned and but a few feet from him saw a large black snake, with its head raised about a foot above its body, which lay coiled upon the ground. Its jaws were distended, its forked tongue playing around its open mouth, flashing in the sunlight like a small lambent flame, while its eyes were intently fixed upon the bird. There was a clear, sparkling light about those eyes that was fearful to behold—they fairly flashed with their peculiar bending fascination. The poor sparrow was fluttering around a circle some few feet in diameter, the circle becoming smaller at each gyration of the infatuated bird. She appeared conscious of her danger, and yet unable to break the spell that bound her. Nearer and still nearer she fluttered her little wings to those open jaws; smaller and smaller grew the circle, till at last, with a quick, convulsive cry, she fell into the mouth of the snake.

As Mr. Lowe watched the bird, he became deeply interested in her fate. He started a number of times to destroy the reptile, and thus liberate the sparrow from her danger, but an unconquerable curiosity to see the end restrained him. All day long the scene just described was before him. He could not forget it or dismiss it from his mind. The last cry of that poor little bird sinking into the jaws of death was constantly ringing in his ears, and the sadness of the morning increased.

Returning to his house, he seated himself in his library and attempted to read. What could be the matter? Usually he could command his thoughts at will, but now he could think of nothing but the scene on the mountain, or the little company in the house of God. Slowly passed the hours, and many times did he find himself, in spite of his resolution not to do so, looking down the road for the head of his dapple gray to emerge from the valley. It seemed a long time before the rumbling of the wheels was at length was heard upon the bridge which crossed the mountain stream, followed in a few moments by the old carry-all creeping slowly up the hill.

The return of the family somewhat changed the course of his thoughts. They did not say anything to him about the good meeting they had enjoyed, and who had been converted since the last Sabbath; but they talked it all over among themselves, and how could he help hearing? He learned all about "how good farmer Haskell talked," and "how humble and devoted Esquire Wiseman appeared," and "how happy Benjamin and Samuel were;" though he seemed busy with his book, and pretended to take no notice of what was said.

It was, indeed, true then that the old lawyer had become pious. He had heard the news before, but did not believe it. Now he had learned it as a fact. The strong minded man, who had been a skeptic all his days, had ridiculed and opposed religion, was now a subject of "the children's revival." What could it mean? Was there something in religion, after all? Could it be that what these poor fanatics, as he had always called them, said about the future world was correct? Was there a heaven, and a hell, and a God of Justice? Were his darling children right, and was he alone wrong? Such were the thoughts of the boasted infidel, as he sat there listening to the half whispered conversation of his happy children.

Little Ella came and climbed to her long accustomed place upon her father's knee, and throwing her arms around his neck, laid her glowing cheek, half hidden by the clustering curls, against his own. He knew by her appearance she had something to say, but did not dare to say it. To remove this fear, he began to question her about her Sabbath school. He inquired after her teacher, and who were her classmates, what she learned, etc. Gradually the shyness wore away, and the heart of the innocent, praying child came gushing forth. She told him all that had been done that day-what her teacher had said of the prayer meeting at noon, and who spoke, and how many went forward for prayers. Then folding her arms more closely around his neck, and kissing him tenderly, she added, "Oh Father, I do wish you had been there!"

"Why do you wish I had been there, Ella?"

"Oh, just to see how happy Nellie Winslow looked while her grandfather was telling us children how much he loved the Savior, and how sorry he was that he did not give his heart to his heavenly Father when he was young. Then he laid his hand on Nellie's head, who was sitting by his side, and said, 'I thank God that he ever gave me a little praying granddaughter to lead me to the Savior.' And Father, I never in all my life saw anyone look so happy as Nellie did."

Mr. Lowe made no reply—how could he? Could he not see where the heart of his darling Ella was? Could he not see that by what she had told him about Esquire Wiseman and his pet Nellie, she meant *he* should understand how happy *she* should be if *her* father was a Christian? Ella had not said so in words—that was a forbidden subject—but the language of her earnest, loving look and manner was not to be mistaken; and the heart of the infidel father was deeply stirred.

He kissed the rosy cheek of the lovely girl, and taking his hat left the house. He walked out into the field. He felt strange. Before he was aware of the fact, he found his infidelity leaving him, the simple, artless religion of childhood winning its way into his heart. Try as hard as he might, he could not help believing that his little Ella was a Christian. There was a reality about her simple faith and ardent love, that was truly "the evidence of things not seen." What should he do? Should he yield to this influence, and be led by his children to Christ? What! Captain Lowe, the boasted infidel, overcome by the weakness of excited childhood! The thought roused his pride and with an exclamation of impatience at his folly, he suddenly wheeled about, and retraced his steps, with altered appearance, he reentered his house.

His wife was alone, with an open Bible before her. As he entered he saw her hastily wipe away a tear. In passing her, he glanced upon the open page, and his eye caught the words, "Ye must be born again!" They went like an arrow to his heart. "Truth," said a voice within, with such fearful distinctness that he started at the fancied sound; and the influence which he had just supposed banished from his heart returned with tenfold power. The strong man trembled. Leaving the sitting room, he ascended the stairs leading to his chamber. Passing Sarah's room, a voice attracted his attention. It was the voice of prayer. He heard his own name pronounced, and he paused to listen.

"Oh Lord, save my dear father. Lead him to the Savior. Let him see that he *must be born again*. Oh, let not *the serpent charm him*! Save, oh, save my dear father!"

He could listen no longer. *"Let not the serpent charm him!"* And was he then like that helpless little bird, who, fluttering around the head of the serpent, falling at last into the jaws of death? The thought shot a wild torrent of newly awakened terror through his throbbing heart.

Hastening to his chamber he threw himself into a chair. He started! The voice of prayer again fell upon his ear. He listened. Yes, it was the clear, sweet accents of his little pet. Ella was praying—*was praying for him.*

"Oh Lord, bless my dear father. Make him a Christian, and may he and dear mother be prepared for heaven!"

Deeply moved, the father left the house and hastened to the barn. He would fain escape from those words of piercing power. They were like daggers in his heart. He entered the barn. Again he hears a voice. It comes stealing down from the hayloft, in the rich silvery tones of his own noble boy. John had climbed up the ladder, and kneeling down upon the hay was praying for his father.

"Oh Lord, save my father!"

It was too much for the poor convicted man, and, rushing to the house, he fell, sobbing, upon his knees by the side of his wife and cried, "Oh Mary, I am a poor, lost sinner! Our children are going to heaven, and I—I—am going to hell! Oh wife, is there mercy for a wretch like me?"

Poor Mrs. Lowe was completely overcome. She wept for joy. That her husband would ever be her companion in the way of holiness, she had never dared to hope. Yes, there was mercy for even them. "Come unto me, and find rest." Christ had said it, and her heart told her it was true. Together they would go to this loving Savior, and their little ones should show them the way.

The children were called in. They came from their places of prayer, where they had lifted up their hearts to that same God who had said, "Whatsoever ye shall ask the Father in my name he will give it to you." They had asked the Spirit's influence upon the hearts of their parents, and it had been granted. They gathered around their weeping, broken hearted father and penitent mother, and pointed them to the cross of Jesus. Long and earnestly they prayed, and wept, and agonized. With undoubting trust in the promises, they waited at the mercy seat, and their prayers were heard. Faith conquered. The Spirit came, and touched those penitent hearts with the finger of love; and then sorrow was turned to joy—their night, dark and cheerless and gloomy, was changed to a blessed day.

REMARKABLE ANSWERS TO PRAYER

They arose from their knees, and Ella sprang to the arms of her father, and together they rejoiced in God.—*Rev. H. P. Andrews, in* Christian Advocate

The stowaway

On board an English steamer, a little ragged boy, aged nine years, was discovered on the fourth day of the voyage out from Liverpool to New York, and carried before the first mate, whose duty it was to deal with such cases. When questioned as to his object in being stowed away, and who had brought him on board, the boy, who had a beautiful sunny face, that looked like the very mirror of truth, replied that his stepfather did it, because he could not afford to keep him, nor pay his passage out to Halifax, where he had an aunt who was well off, and to whose house he was going.

The mate did not believe the story, in spite of the winning face and truthful accents of the boy. He had seen too much of stowaways to be easily deceived by them, he said; and it was his firm conviction the boy had been brought on board and provided with food by the sailors.

The little fellow was very roughly handled in consequence. Day by day he was questioned and re-questioned, but always the same result. He did not know a sailor on board, and his father alone had secreted and given him food which he ate. At last the mate, wearied by the boy's persistence in the same story, and perhaps a little anxious to inculpate the sailors, seized him one day by the collar, and dragged him to the fore, told him that unless he told the truth, in ten minutes from that time he would hang from the yardarm. He then made him sit down under it on the deck. All around him were the passengers and sailors of the mid way watch, and in front of him stood the inexorable mate, with chronometer in his hand, and the other officers of the ship by his side. It was a touching sight to see the pale, proud, scornful face of that noble boy; his head erect, his beautiful eyes, bright through the tears that suffused them.

When eight minutes had fled, the mate told him he had two minutes to live, and advised him to speak the truth and save his life. But he replied with the utmost simplicity and sincerity, by asking the mate if he might pray. The mate said nothing, but nodded his head, and turned as pale as a ghost, and shook with trembling like a reed in the wind. And then all eyes turned on him, the brave and noble fellow—this poor boy whom society owned not, and whose own step father could not care for—knelt with clasped hand and eyes upturned to heaven. There then occurred a scene as of Pentecost. Sobs broke from strong, hard hearts, as the mate sprang forward and clasped the boy to his bosom, and kissed him, and blessed him, and told him how sincerely he now believed his story, and how glad he was that he had been brave enough to face death, and be willing to sacrifice his life for the truth of his word.—*Illustrated Weekly Telegraph.*

The midnight conflict

Shall I repeat a true story told me by the sufferer himself a few weeks ago? And may I repeat it, so far as memory serves me, in his own language? I can never forget the passionate energy of my friend, as he walked again in the darkened chambers of a wrecked life, and recalled the scene when alone he met the tempter. But to the story:

"I left my New England home in boyhood. As I kissed my mother good-bye, she put her hand on either side of my cheeks, and said, 'You are pure now, my son. Ever keep your soul sweet and clean, and never touch a glass of intoxicating liquor.' The pledge I then made to her I kept under strong temptations, and in circumstances that severely tried my good resolutions. Serving throughout the war, I came out with a cough that threatened quick-consumption. My physician recommended cod-liver oil and whiskey. I took his prescription. The former cured me of one disease; the latter brought on one of deeper and deadlier nature. Yet I was not conscious of it, till one day a friend roused me with the words, 'Major, you must be careful. You are bringing disgrace to your family.' I was shocked, and resolved that this should never be said of me again; but I still pursued the vile way.

"A little later, my brother repeated the warning, and I pledged him that I would heed his kindly words. That pledge was broken. I had a delightful home, was blessed with wife and children, and to her wifely pleading I again said, 'I'll drink no more.' And went on to disgrace the name she bore.

"One morning as I passed the open door of my daughter's room, I saw her on bended knees, and heard her sweet voice crying out, 'Oh God, spare my father, and save him from a drunkard's grave.' Then and there I vowed before God that I would never drink again. I was drunk before night! A little later I was summoned to see a loving sister that was sick. I hastened to her bedside only to find in a darkened room her dead body. As I leaned over that marble form, and my tears fell on her cold cheeks, there, with clasped hands, alone with the dead, I told my God that the cup should never again soil my lips. In three days I was as bad as ever! At last, in a fit of desperation, I sent for my father and mother to visit my home, securing for them a palace-car, making their long journey as pleasant as possible. They came to my charming home to meet their drunkard son. The dear mother begged and prayed with and for me, that my purity might be restored.

REMARKABLE ANSWERS TO PRAYER

"After their return, with the echo of her agonizing petition sounding in my ears, I said, 'I will once more take the pledge, and if broken now, I will go to the Pacific coast, leaving wife and children, to hide myself where they shall never hear of me again.' With this came the resolve to invite in a few friends to take one more social glass together, and then to sign the pledge. I sent to Boston for the choicest liquors, and one night when I had been left alone in the house, invited them in. For an hour I waited, and no one came. I paced the floor, and looked out into the moonlight, longing for their presence, that I might satisfy the appetite that began to clamor.

"And the clock struck nine, and no friends came. Then rushed into my soul visions of my childhood, and the voice of my mother sounded out, 'Keep your soul pure and clean, my son;' and her words of tenderness awakened memories that had long been sealed. I opened the Bible, and read, 'No drunkard shall inherit the kingdom of God.' Ah! Does that mean me? Closing the book I paced the room, and longed for companionship, that these busy thoughts might be dispelled, and the clock struck ten. I listened for voices, but there was quiet everywhere save in my own tempest-tossed soul.

"Then it flashed upon me that alone I must meet the tempter, and alone take the promised pledge. I reached out my hand to unseal the bottle that never looked so attractive, when a voice seemed to sound, 'Let it remain untouched—now is the decisive hour;' and again I paced the room, and again with greater force, appetite begged for satisfaction. The struggle began to be more bitter, the tempter made a heavier assault, the hours dragged wearily along, and the clock struck eleven.

"Then I felt that the next hour must be the joint on which my destiny for eternity was poised. For I was impressed by the thought that if I could resist the tempter until midnight, in some way, I knew not how, God would bring to me a way of escape. Oh, how I longed to break the bottle, the contents of which were more attractive than anything on earth; and yet that voice sounded out, 'Touch but a single glass, and you are lost.'

"Then said the tempter, 'Why not drink just once? You have resolved tonight to take the pledge; it will be all right to indulge in a parting farewell to an old friend.'

"I again opened the Bible, and read, 'God so loved the world, that he gave his only begotten Son, that whosoever believeth in him should not perish, but have everlasting life.' I fell on my knees, and with the open Bible before me, and the bottle by my side, implored and prayed for strength to hold on till midnight. Oh! How appetite begged and clamored; and yet I was conscious that if I yielded it would be fatal, and my soul would be lost. The minutes dragged along, oh! so slowly, till eleven thirty o'clock, and the voice cried, 'Only hold on till twelve, and you are safe.'

"Fifteen minutes passed, and then came the sorest, bitterest conflict of soul that man ever experienced. I had been in the midst of great physical peril on the battlefield many a time, when death came on the right and on the left in fearful form, but never had been in such deadly danger as now; for it was a conflict with heaven on one side and hell on the other. One who has never been under the maddening control of a master passion cannot realize the agony that can be concentrated into even a few moments; and so the bitterness of that last fifteen minutes seemed prolonged into hours. Can I hold out? Will this struggle end in life and peace? Will the tempter vanish, a defeated, baffled spirit, and leave me free? Five minutes more and the agony increased, as appetite begged and clamored with tenfold power. There pealed out on the still hour of the night the stroke of the distant clock: one – two – three – four – five – six – seven – eight – nine – ten – eleven – twelve!

"I leaped to my feet and shouted, 'Victory! Saved by the grace of God!' The burden rolled into the open sepulcher, and I felt that I was saved, and saved forever. I went out on my back piazza, and held the bottle up to the moonlight, and looked at it as calmly as a mother would look at a sleeping child; and then, hurling it upon the pavement, fell on my knees in glad thanksgiving, and then and there yielded my soul, my life, my all, to Him who had redeemed me with His precious blood.

"The final stroke of the midnight bell, as it heralded a new day, was the dawn of a new life for me. I was made conscious on the instant, my sins were washed away. From that hour to this I have had no taste or craving for liquor, and my life is devoted to scattering the leaves which shall be for the healing of the nations."

Such is the story of my friend, who, in a Western city, is today doing loyal service for the Master. Years have passed since that midnight conflict, and his life has been one of consecration, and many a soul has been lifted and inspired by his burning, loving words:

"'Touch not, taste not, handle not,' even though it is placed to your lips under the seductive guise of 'only medicine.'"—*Congregationalist.*

Healed through faith. I am the Lord that healeth thee. —*Exodus 15:26*

With a deep sense of gratitude to my Heavenly Father for my restoration to health, I write this testimony. I will begin with extracts from a statement of my condition at the time of my restoration, written by the attending physician; thinking it will be more satisfactory than one of my own.

"Mrs. Claghorn came to me for treatment, first on June 6, 1885, then afterwards during August, 1885, and almost continuously thereafter, until January 26, 1886–

the day of her sudden and marvelous restoration to health. Her symptoms were frequent chills, pains in the bones, pains in the back, inability to sleep, and at times terrible paroxysms of tonic and clonic spasms, strongly marked opisthotones, cramping of limbs, coldness of extremities, intense pain at the base of the brain, intolerance of light, sometimes complete unconsciousness; the paroxysms being frequently followed by partial paralysis of the right side. She also suffered from a large cellulitis tumor. At times the case responded readily to the treatment given; at other times, she grew rapidly worse for several days; the attack culminating in a paroxysm, followed by more or less paralysis.

"Such an attack occurred from the 21st to the 25th of January, 1886, although not so severe as some she had had. The morning of the 26th, she was unable to turn herself in bed, and had not stood upon her feet for five months. The details of her sudden restoration, which occurred that afternoon, she can best give in her own language. She rode about a mile the next evening, in a cutter, to prayer meeting, walked down the aisle like a girl of eighteen, and from a condition of emaciation, rapidly gained in flesh and appearance. I made an examination March 5, 1886, and found the cellulitis tumor gone. More than a year has now passed away, and she is and has been apparently in the most perfect health. There has been no recurrence of her sufferings during the past year.

"–Respectfully, A. M. Hutchinson, M.D., Waseca, Minnesota"

For two weeks before my restoration I was unable to turn myself in bed, or to feed myself. All that time my right side was helpless, and I was rapidly sinking.

On the 25th of January, I was taken with convulsions, though not so severe as on some previous occasions. My physician was with me until midnight, when I grew easier. On the morning of the 26th, I felt better, until about seven o'clock, when I commenced to feel much worse. I suffered intensely, and could feel the terrible convulsions coming back.

While I was in such pain, my husband received some statements of "faith-cure," which an unknown friend had sent, and he commenced reading one; saying it might make the time pass more rapidly if I could bear the reading. I was not at all interested at first, for I knew nothing of such things; I had heard of a few cases, but they were all so far away, I set them aside as something I could not understand. But this was an account of a lady whose disease was just enough like mine to hold my attention, and he read it to a close.

I was too ill to think much, but I could see it was no made-up story, and wondered if God would really do such things.

At 12:40 p.m., my husband went out, leaving me in the care of an attendant, who was in an adjoining room. I began to wonder if it were possible the Lord could have healing for me. I had not, in all my sickness, asked Him for health. But now I seemed to be led to make the request, "Lord, if thou hast this healing for me, give it to me now;" and instantly a voice said, "In the name of Jesus of Nazareth, arise and walk!" And I was thrilled through and through with the sensations impossible to describe. While I was wondering, the command was repeated in the same words. But I did not feel returning strength, and the terrible pain still remained.

So I said aloud, "But I haven't the strength, Lord; give me the strength, and I will get up;" and again the same voice said, "In the name of Jesus of Nazareth, arise and walk!" Then I made an effort to arise; it was more a mental effort than anything else; but I rose like a feather and stood upon my feet. All pain ceased—the first moment for months. It was just one o'clock.

I commenced to say, "Lord, I believe; help thou mine unbelief," and prayed it continually. Then I sat down on the side of the bed, and raising my arms above my head, used the paralyzed side freely.

A swelling the size of an egg was gone, and everything inside of me seemed to be changing position, and recreating sensations impossible to describe were felt through me.

Then I got up and walked a few steps, and turned and looked at the bed, and the medicine beside it, and I commenced to sink to the floor. But I asked for more strength, and received it, and went on around the bed to the center of the room, when I thought I would have my clothes brought, and dress. But when I would have called the nurse, the impression was received, not in an audible voice, "it is enough, you have seen the power of God, go back to bed;" and I obeyed.

Upon returning to bed, I reconsecrated myself to God, and begged Him to complete His will in me; and if He could better use me as a sufferer, to let me suffer, but only glorify Himself in me; and I received the assurance that He would.

Soon after the nurse brought me some food. I surprised her very much by feeding myself, and my stomach, which had previously rejected all food, retained it now with ease.

Now my husband came in, looking so disconsolate, and prepared to find me much worse than when he left me. I need not attempt to tell of his joy and surprise upon hearing what God had done for me in his absence; you can better imagine it. When he had returned thanks, I requested him to go for my physician.

Doctor was not in town, and I did not see him until evening. His first words upon entering my room were, "Glory to God!" And he returned thanks to God for His marvelous work, as only a thoroughly consecrated Christian could; not reserving a particle of credit for the cure, but giving all glory and honor to God. He forbade all medicine.

That night I arose and knelt at the bedside in prayer. I slept that night, as I have every night since, like a babe. I never had such refreshing sleep. I had had no natural sleep during my sickness.

The next morning I arose and dressed, unassisted, and walked out to breakfast; ate heartily, and in the evening I rode nearly a mile to our weekly prayer meeting, and told how great things the Lord had done for me.

My strength returned gradually. For days I could not stand upon my feet without first asking for strength; and if I were standing, and would for an instant take my mind off Christ, I would commence to sink to the floor. All functions were naturally resumed without any pain whatever. Tumors and all inflammation were all dispelled, and I was a well woman. Several times I had severe paroxysms of pain, but I would go right to God, and he would remove them at once.

My right side was much shrunken, and shorter than my other. When I stood upon my left foot, the toes of my right foot touched the floor. That, however, stretched out gradually as I used my limbs. It is now more than a year since I was restored. I have done all my work since the first of June. I ask for strength for a day at a time, and God helps me over all the hard places.

I have not had a sick day since my restoration. I have had severe colds several times, but they have been removed by resorting to my new-found Physician; and I have not taken a drop of medicine since the 26th of January, 1886, neither have I done anything for myself in a medicinal way. God has done it all.

Satan has tried many times to tempt me, but the Sword of the Spirit, when presented, proves too much for him.

I have written this for the glory of God, and trust He will bless it.—Mrs. Alice B. Claghorn, in Michigan Holiness Record

Translation of Bishop Haven

On Saturday morning, January 3, 1880, in Malden, Massachusetts, Bishop Gilbert Haven's physician said that his last day had come, and that it would do him no harm to see his friends. Many were near at hand. Others were summoned by telegram and by messenger, until groups gathered around that couch, touched with the light of immortal glory, to muse over the transition from death unto life. A physician who was present said, "I never saw a person die so before."

A clergyman remarks, "To me it did not seem that I was in the presence of death. The whole atmosphere of the chamber was that of a joyous and festive hour. Only the tears of kindred and friends were suggestive of death. I felt that I was summoned to see a conquering hero crowned." We have preserved some of the Bishop's utterances to different persons, as they were reported in the public prints. As Dr. Daniel Steele entered his chamber, the Bishop lifted up his hand, exclaiming, in his familiar way, "Oh Dan, Dan, a thousand blessings on you! The Lord has been giving you great blessings, and me little ones, and now he has given me a great one. He has called me to heaven before you."

"Do you find the words of Paul true, 'Oh death, where is thy sting?'" inquired Dr. Steele.

"There is no death, there is no death!" interrupted the Bishop; "I have been fighting death for six weeks, and today I find there is no death." Then he repeated again and again John 8:51: "Shall never see death; glory! Glory! Glory!" In life he seldom, if ever, shouted; he certainly had a right to shout in death.

"You have a great Savior," was remarked to him.

"Yes," he answered, "that is the whole of the gospel, the whole of it." With difficulty he repeated,

> *Happy, if with my latest breath*
> *I may but gasp His name;*
> *Preach Him to all, and cry in death,*
> *Behold, behold the Lamb!*

He had an immediate opportunity to preach Christ by witnessing to his saving power, for his counseling physician from Boston had come to bid him farewell. Said the dying man, as he took the doctor's hand, "I am satisfied with your attentions; you have done all that human skill can do to heal me. I die happy. I believe in Jesus Christ."

To Dr. Lindsay he also remarked, "Good night, doctor. When we meet again it will be good morning."

To his old classmate, Dr. Newhall, he said, "I have got the start on you, I thought you would go first. Your mind has been clouded a little, but it is all light over there."

When Dr. Mallalieu approached him he put his arms around his neck and drew him to his face, and exclaimed, "My dear old friend, I am glad to see you. You and I would not have it so if we had our way, but God knows best. It is all right! All right! We have been living in great times, but there are greater times coming. You have been my true friend. You never failed me. You must stand by the colored man when I am gone. Stand by the colored man."

REMARKABLE ANSWERS TO PRAYER

Then he spoke of dying, and said, "Oh, but it is so beautiful, so pleasant, so delightful! I see no river of death. God lifts me up in His arms. There is no darkness; it is all light and brightness. I am gliding away to God, floating up into heaven." As the hour drew near, and death preyed upon him, his faith failed not. His right hand was dead, and black from mortification; but holding up his arm, and gazing at the perishing member for a moment, he said, with triumph, "I believe in the resurrection of the body!" Thus he trampled death under his feet, and Elijah-like, in a flaming chariot of glory, went shouting to his home in the skies.—Golden Dawn

Jessie finding Jesus

A little girl in a wretched tenement in New York stood by her mother's deathbed, and heard her last words, "Jessie, find Jesus."

When her mother was buried, her father took to drink, and Jessie was left to such care as a poor neighbor could give her.

One day she wandered off unmissed, with a little basket in her hand, and tugged through one street after another, not knowing where she went. She had started to find Jesus. At last she stopped, from utter weariness, in front of a saloon. A young man staggered out of the door, and almost stumbled over her. He uttered passionately the name of Him whom she was seeking, "Where is He?" she inquired eagerly. He looked at her in amazement.

"What did you say?" he asked.

"Will you please tell me where Jesus Christ is? For I must find Him," she said, this time with great earnestness.

The young man looked at her curiously for a minute without speaking, and then his face sobered; and he said in a broken, husky voice, hopelessly, "I don't know, child; I don't know where he is."

At length the little girl's wanderings brought her to the park. A woman, evidently a Jewess, was leaning against the railing, looking disconsolately at the green grass and the trees.

Jessie went up to her timidly. "Perhaps she can tell me where He is," was the child's thought. In a low, hesitating voice, she asked the woman, "Do you know Jesus Christ?"

The Jewess turned fiercely to face her questioner, and in a tone of suppressed passion, exclaimed, "Jesus Christ is dead!" Poor Jessie trudged on, but soon a rude boy jostled against her, and snatched her basket from her hand, threw it into the street.

Crying, she ran to pick it up. The horses of a passing streetcar trampled her under their feet—and she knew no more till she found herself stretched on a hospital bed.

When the doctors came that night, they knew she could not live until morning. In the middle of the night, after she had been lying very still for a long time, apparently asleep, she suddenly opened her eyes, and the nurse, bending over her, heard her whisper, while her face lighted up with a smile that had some of heaven's own gladness in it, "Oh Jesus, I have found you at last!"

Then the tiny lips were hushed, but the questioning sprit had received an answer.—*Selected*.

A mob quieted in answer to prayer

In the early part of the summer of 1882, while we were holding a campmeeting at C—, a drunken mob came on the ground and disturbed the meeting by their profanity and quarreling. They came armed with revolvers and were determined to break up the meeting. Not having anticipated any such difficulty, no police force had been provided. Our words of expostulation were unheeded, and they went so far as to yell and blaspheme, and shake their fists in the faces of the leaders of the meeting. So great was the disturbance that for a time the services were entirely suspended and there was certainly imminent danger that the meeting would be completely broken up.

Realizing that God's help alone could give to His children victory, in the midst of the excitement we went to the woods, and in sobs and tears, fell upon our face. God gave us great help of the Spirit in prayer, and we told Him how we were holding the meeting for His glory and the salvation of souls, and unless He came to our rescue great reproach would be brought upon His cause.

We obtained evidence that God would deliver, and hastened back to the camp, called for order, and began to exhort the people in the power of the Spirit. A halo of glory came over the meeting. Wicked men turned pale, and acknowledged the wonderful change. Many began to weep while some of God's children shouted for joy, and many were prostrate under the power of God.

Defeat was changed to almost unthought-of victory, and during all that night the workers were kept busy praying with seekers and many were saved. Not until the light of morning dawned could they find time for rest; and the two remaining days of the meeting were days of triumph.

REMARKABLE ANSWERS TO PRAYER

So great was the conviction and some who repeatedly tried to leave were constrained to return, and yield themselves to God. One man said he was determined not to yield, and for the third time started to leave the grounds; but God showed him that this, if rejected, would be his last chance for salvation. So, at about two o'clock in the morning, he came to the altar, and was gloriously saved.—*Editor.*

Show me the doctor

A man, blind from his birth, a man of much intellectual vigor, and with many engaging social qualities, found a woman who, appreciating his worth, was willing to cast in her lot with him, and become his wife. Several bright, beautiful children became theirs, who tenderly and equally loved both their parents.

An eminent French surgeon, while in this country, called upon them, and, examining the blind man with much interest and care, said to him, "Your blindness is wholly artificial; your eyes are naturally good; and if I could have operated upon them twenty years ago, I think I could have given you sight. It is barely possible that I can do it now, though it will cause you much pain."

"I can bear that," was the reply, "so you but enable me to see."

The surgeon operated upon him, and was gradually successful. First there were faint glimmerings of light; then more distinct vision. The blind father was handed a rose; he had smelled one before but had never seen one. Then he looked upon the face of his wife, who had been so true and faithful to him; and then his children were brought, whom he had so often held, and whose charming prattle had so frequently fallen upon his ears.

He then exclaimed, "Oh, why have I seen all of these before inquiring for the man by whose skill I have been enabled to behold them! Show me the doctor." And when he was pointed out to him, he embraced him, with tears of gratitude and joy.

So, when we reach heaven, and with unclouded eyes look upon its glories, we shall not be content with a view of these. No; we shall say, "Where is Christ—he to whom I am indebted for what heaven is? Show me him, that with all my soul I may adore and praise him through endless ages."—*Selected*

She died for him

A poor emigrant had gone to Australia to "make his fortune," leaving a wife and little son in England. When he had made some money, he wrote home to his wife, "Come out to me here; I send the money for your passage; I want to see you and my boy." The wife took ship as soon as she could, and started for her new home.

One night, as they were all asleep, there sounded the dreaded cry of, "Fire, fire!" Every one rushed on deck, and the boats were soon filled. The last one was just pushing off, when a cry arose, "There are two more on deck!" They were the mother and her son. Alas! "Only room for one," the sailors shouted. Which was to go? The mother thought of her faraway home, her husband looking out lovingly and longingly for his wife. Then she glanced down at the boy, clinging, frightened, to her skirts. She could not let him die. There was no time to lose. Quick! quick! The flames were getting round. Snatching the child, she held him to her a moment.

"Willie, tell father I died for you!" Then the boy was lowered into the sailors' willing arms. She died for him.—*Selected*

Praying for wood

Rev. E. B. Slade tells an interesting instance of answered prayer. One cold winter he was forty miles away from home, holding revival services, when, in the midst of a terrible snowstorm, during which travel was almost wholly impossible, his wife, at home, ran out of wood. To save the little that remained, she put her children to bed, and wrapped them up in blankets. At last baking must be done, and, making a fire of her last wood, she began to pray that help might come, and persevered until her faith won the victory. She then went about her work in perfect peace of mind, assured that relief would come.

In the course of a few hours her nearest neighbor, a lady, waded through the snow, saying that she had been impressed that she must come over and see what was the matter. The facts were stated, and relief promised. Hardly had she gone when another lady came in with the same statement, and the same offer was made. A little while later a gentleman came in, expressing a similar feeling; and when he learned the facts, he took them all to his home, and cared for them until Mr. Slade returned home.

Miraculously healed

We extract the following from the *Methodist Magazine* for July, 1827, being an account of a conversion that occurred in a revival of religion, at Lanjeth, in Cornwell, England. The account is given by Rev. W. Lawry, preacher on the St. Austell circuit.

"The first extraordinary conversion which I remarked was that of old William Morkum, of Lanjeth, who had lived just seventy years without God in the world!

REMARKABLE ANSWERS TO PRAYER

In the month of February, 1826, as he was at work as usual on the high roads, and reflecting on his long life spent in the neglect of religion, his mind became greatly alarmed at the prospect of eternity.

"Night came on; he sought to be refreshed on his bed by sleep, but in vain. His alarm and terror increased so much that his family, consisting of his wife and daughter, were kept up all night. On the next day he proceeded to his labor, but remarked to his companion, with great apparent emotion, 'I believe I am a lost soul.'

"The next night came on, when such was the horror of his mind that his family, at his request, sent for some of their pious neighbors to come and pray with him. They spent the whole night in prayer; but he remained without hope, under the most fearful apprehensions. The third day was spent as the former; but the third night was still more terrible to him than the second.

"The religious friends were again called in, and great was the agony of his mind. Hitherto he could not be persuaded that his prayers would avail; but at this crisis his friends prevailed upon him to join them in prayer to God, in the name of our Lord Jesus Christ. He now poured forth the cry of the publican, 'God be merciful to me, a sinner.'

"During the third night his fears subsided, and he had power to cast his soul on the atonement of the Lord Jesus Christ, through whom he obtained peace with God. For many years he had through infirmity been bowed almost double, and had not been able to lift his hand to his head. His employment had been to break stones on the roads. The moment, however, of his deliverance from his load of guilt and fear, he exclaimed in ecstasy, 'I am made whole both in body and soul!' He accordingly stood perfectly erect and clasped his hands together behind his head.

" 'Now,' said he, 'I will request the parish to buy me a pair of spectacles, that I may learn to read the Bible; and I will myself procure a lantern to light me on the winter evenings to the Methodist chapel.' He joined himself to the society at Lanjeth, and met twice in class. About a month after his conversion he became unwell, and said to his family, 'The time is come that I must die.' He lay down for a few days upon his peaceful bed, without pain or mental conflict, expressing his trust in the adorable Redeemer, and peacefully fell asleep in the Lord."

6

<u>Carletta and the merchant</u>

"IF I COULD HAVE your faith, Hawkins, gladly would I, but I was born skeptic. I cannot look upon God and the future as you do."

So said John Harvey, as he walked with a friend under a dripping umbrella. John Harvey was a skeptic of thirty years standing, and apparently hardened in his unbelief. Everybody had given him up as hopeless. Reasoning ever so calmly made no impression on the rocky soil of his heart. Alas! It was sad, very sad!

But one friend had never given him up. When spoken to about him, "I will talk with and pray for that man until I die," he said; "and I will have faith that he may yet come out of darkness into the marvelous light."

And thus whenever he met him, John Harvey was always ready for a talk, Mr. Hawkins pressed home the truth. In answer, on that stormy night, he said, "God can change a skeptic, John, He has more power over your heart than you, and I mean still to pray for you."

"Oh, I've no objections, none in the world—seeing is believing, you know. I'm ready for any miracle; but I tell you, it would take nothing short of a miracle to convince me. Let's change the subject. I'm hungry, and it's too far to go up town to supper this stormy night. Here's a restaurant. Let us stop here." How warm and pleasant it looked in the long, brilliant dining room!

The two merchants had eaten, and were just on the point of rising, when a strain of soft music came through an open door—a child's sweet voice.

"'Pon my word, that is pretty," said John Harvey; "what purity in those tones!"

"Out of here, you little baggage," cried a hoarse voice and one of the waiters pointed angrily to the door.

"Let her come in," said John Harvey.

"We don't allow them in this place, sir," said the waiter; "but she can go into the reading room."

"Well, let her go somewhere. I want to hear her," responded the gentleman.

All this time the two had seen the shadow of something hovering, backwards and forwards on the edge of the door; now they followed a slight little figure, wrapped in patched cloak, patched hood, and leaving the mark of wet feet as she walked. Curious to see her face—she was very small—John Harvey directed her to the farthest part of the great room, where there were but few gentlemen, and then motioned her to sing. The little one looked timidly up. Her cheek was of olive darkness, but a flush rested there and out of the thinnest face, under the arch of broad temples, deepened by masses of the blackest hair, looked two eyes, whose softness and tender pleading would have touched the hardest heart.

"That little thing is sick, I believe," said John Harvey, compassionately. "What do you sing, child?" he added.

"I sing Italian, or a little English."

John Harvey looked at her shoes. "Why," he exclaimed, and his lip quivered, "her feet are wet to her ankles; she will catch her death of cold."

By this time the child had begun to sing, pushing back her hood, and folding before her little thin fingers. Her voice was wonderful; and simple and common as were both air and words, the pathos of the tones drew together several of the merchants in the reading room. The little song commenced thus:

> *There is a happy land,*
> *Far, far away.*

Never could the voice, the manner, of that child be forgotten. There almost seemed a halo round her head; and when she had finished, her great speaking eyes turned towards John Harvey.

"Look here, child; where did you learn that song?" he asked.

"At the Sabbath school, sir."

"And you don't suppose there is a happy land?" he continued, heedless of the many eyes upon him.

"I know there is; I'm going to sing there," she said, so quietly, so decidedly, that the men looked at each other.

"Going to sing there?"

"Yes, sir. My mother said so. She used to sing to me until she was sick. Then she said she wasn't going to sing any more on earth, but up in heaven,"

"Well—and what then?"

"And then she died, sir," said the child; tears brimming down the dark cheek, now ominously flushed scarlet.

John Harvey was silent for a few moments. Presently he said, "Well, if she died, my little girl, you may live, you know."

"Oh, no, sir! No, sir! I'd rather go there, and be with mother. Sometimes I have a dreadful pain in my side, and cough as she did. There won't be any pain up there, sir; it's a beautiful world."

"How do you know?" faltered on the lips of the skeptic.

"My mother told me so, sir."

Words how impressive! Manner how childlike, and yet so wise!

John Harvey had had a praying mother. His chest labored for a moment—the sobs that struggled for utterance could be heard even in their depths—and still those large, soft, lustrous eyes, like magnets, impelled his glance towards them.

"Child, you must have a pair of shoes." John Harvey's voice was husky.

Hands were thrust in pockets, purses pulled out, and the astonished child held in her little palm more money than she had ever seen before.

"Her father is a poor, consumptive organ grinder," whispered one. "I suppose he's too sick to be out tonight."

Along the soggy street went the child, under the protection of John Harvey, but not with shoes that drank the water at every step. Warmth and comfort were hers now. Down in the deep den-like lanes of the city walked the man, a little cold hand in his. At an open door they stopped. Up broken, creaking stairs they climbed. Another doorway was opened, and a wheezing voice called out of the dim arch, "Carletta!"

"Oh father! Father! See what I have brought you! Look at me! Look at me!" And down went the silver, and, venting her joy, the poor child fell, crying and laughing together, into the old man's arms.

Was he a man? A face dark and hollow, all overgrown with hair black as night, and uncombed—a pair of wild eyes, a body bent nearly double—hands like claws.

"Did he give you all this, my child?"

"They all did, father; now you shall have soup and oranges."

"Thank you, sir—I'm sick, you see—all gone, sir, had to send the poor child out, or we'd starve. God bless you, sir! I wish I was well enough to play you a tune," and he looked wistfully towards the corner where stood the old organ, baize-covered, the baize in tatters.

One month after that the two men met again as if by agreement, and walked slowly down town. Treading innumerable passages they came to the gloomy building where lived Carletta's father.

REMARKABLE ANSWERS TO PRAYER

No—not **lived** there; for, as they paused a moment, out came two or three men bearing a pine coffin. In the coffin slept the old organ grinder.

"It was very sudden, sir," said a woman, who recognized his benefactor. "Yesterday the little girl was took sick, and it seemed as if he drooped right away. He died at six last night."

The two men went silently up stairs. The room was empty of everything save a bed, a chair, and a nurse provided by John Harvey. The child lay there, not white, but pale as marble, with a strange polish on her brow.

"Well, my little one, are you better?"

"Oh, no, sir; father is gone up there, and I am going."

Up there! John Harvey turned unconsciously towards his friend.

"Did you ever hear of Jesus?" asked John Harvey's friend.

"Oh, yes!"

"Do you know who he is?"

"Good Jesus," murmured the child.

"Hawkins, this breaks me down," said John Harvey and he placed his handkerchief to his eyes.

"Don't cry, don't cry, I can't cry, I'm so glad!" said the child, exultantly.

"What are you glad for, my dear?" asked John Harvey's friend.

"To get away from here," she said deliberately. "I used to be so cold in the winter, for we didn't have fire sometimes; but mother used to hug me close, and sing about heaven. Mother told me never to mind, and kissed me, and said if I was His, the Savior would love me, and one of these days would give me a better home; and so I gave myself to Him, for I wanted a better home. And, oh, I shall sing there, and be so happy!" With a little sigh she closed her eyes.

"Harvey, are faith and hope nothing?" asked Mr. Hawkins.

"Don't speak to me, Hawkins; to be as that little child, I would give all I have."

"And to be like her you need give nothing—only your stubborn will, your skeptical doubts, and the heart that will never know rest till at the feet of Christ." There was no answer.

Presently the little girl's hands moved, the arms were raised, the eyes opened—yet, glazed though they were, they turned still upward.

"See!" she cried; "oh, there is mother! And angels and they are all singing." Her voice faltered, but the celestial brightness lingered yet on her face.

"There is no doubting the soul-triumph there," whispered Mr. Hawkins.

"It is wonderful," replied John Harvey, looking on both with awe and tenderness.

He sprang from his chair as if he would detain her; but the chest and forehead were marble now, the eyes had lost the fire of life; she must have died, as she lay looking at them.

"She was always a sweet little thing," said the nurse, softly. John Harvey stood as if spellbound. There was a touch on his arm; he started.

"John," said his friend, with an affectionate look, "shall we pray?"

For a minute there was no answer—then came tears; the whole frame of the subdued skeptic shook as he said—it was almost a cry, "Yes, pray, pray!"

And from the side of the dead child went up agonizing pleadings to the throne of God. And that prayer was answered—the miracle was wrought—the lion became a lamb—the doubter a believer—the skeptic a Christian!—A *tract*

The Golden Rule exemplified

Early one morning while it was yet dark, a poor man came to my door and informed me that he had an infant child very sick, which he was afraid would die. He desired me to go to his home, and, if possible, prescribe some medicine to relieve it. "For," said he, "I want to save its life if possible." As he spoke thus the tears ran down his face. He then added, "I am a poor man; but, doctor, I will pay you in work as much as you ask if you will go."

I said, "Yes, I will go with you as soon as I take a little refreshment."

"Oh, sir," said he, "I was going to try to get a bushel of corn, and get it ground to carry home, and I am afraid the child will die before I get there. I wish you would not wait for me;" and then added, "we want to save the child's life if we can."

It being some miles to his house, I did not arrive there until the sun was two hours high in the morning, when I found the mother holding her sick child, and six or seven little boys and girls around her, with clean hands and faces, looking as their mother did, lean and poor. On examining the sick child, I discovered that it was starving to death! I said to the mother, "You don't give milk enough for this child."

She said, "I suppose I don't."

"Well," said I, "you must feed it with milk."

She answered, "I would, sir, but I can't get any to feed it with."

I then said, "It will be well then for you to make a little water gruel and feed your child."

To this she replied, "I was thinking I would if my husband brings home some Indian meal. He has gone to try to get some, and I am in hopes he will make out."

She said this with a sad countenance. I asked her with surprise, "Why, madam, have you not got anything to eat?"

She strove to suppress a tear, and answered sorrowfully, "No, sir; we have had but little some days."

I said, "What are your neighbors, that you should suffer among them?"

She said, "I suppose they are good people; but we are strangers in this place, and don't wish to trouble any of them, if we can get along without."

Wishing to give the child a little manna, I asked for a spoon. The little girl went to the table drawer to get one, and her mother said to her, "Get the longest handled spoon." As she opened the drawer, I saw only two spoons, and both with handles broken off, but one handle was a little longer than the other.

I thought to myself, *This is a very poor family, but I will do the best I can to relieve them.* While I was preparing the medicine for the sick child, I heard the oldest boy, who was about fourteen, say, "You shall have the biggest piece now, because I had the biggest piece before," I turned around to see who it was that manifested such a principle of justice, and saw four or five children sitting in the corner, where the oldest was dividing a roasted potato among them. And he said to one, "You shall have the biggest piece now," etc. But the other said, "Why, brother, you are the oldest, and you ought to have the biggest piece."

"No," said the other, "I had the biggest piece."

I turned to the mother, and said, "Madam, you have potatoes to eat, I suppose?"

She replied, "We have had, but that is the last one we have left; and the children have now roasted that for their breakfast."

On hearing this, I hastened home, and informed my wife that I had taken the wrong medicine with me to the sick family. I then prescribed a gallon of milk, two loaves of bread, some butter, meat and potatoes, and sent my boy with these; and had the pleasure to hear in a few days that they were all well.—*Selected*

How the prayer of faith reached a family

A day or two after our conversion, we called at a neighbor's, and while there heard the lady of the house say some very hard things against the work of God, which was shaking that whole section of country like an earthquake. We were deeply grieved, but went away without saying much. But scarcely had we reached home before the Holy Spirit spoke to our heart, and told us to go back to that neighbor's and pray. We hesitated a little, but the burden upon our heart became so heavy that we could no longer keep still, and were so strongly drawn to go back to neighbor B——'s that we decided to go, and asked our stepmother to go with us. She wanted to wait to get ready, but our burden was too heavy for delay, and she yielded, and started with us at once. It seemed as we went that we could hardly keep from running; and as soon as we entered the house we fell upon our knees, exclaiming, that God had sent us there to pray.

We scarcely realized our surroundings, and do not know how long or loud we prayed; but when we arose from our knees we could see that all in the house were wonderfully affected, and the one who so short a time before was saying bitter things against the Lord and His work, was wringing her hands, and weeping, and saying, "What have I done? I did not know that I was so wicked that anybody needed to pray like that for me." We shook hands with all present, and left the house.

Soon a Christian young lady, who was at Mr. B——'s when we were there, came over, and in a kind way said that she did not wish to discourage us, but she feared our prayer was too abrupt to do any good. But as she spoke, the Lord gave us the positive assurance of that family's salvation, and we began to praise the Lord. And so it was, for in a very short time the entire family were converted.

Thus did God so early in our Christian experience literally verify his own word, "Likewise the Spirit also helpeth our infirmities, for we know not what we should pray for as we ought, but the Spirit itself maketh intercession for us with groanings which cannot be uttered."–*Editor*

The stone chair

On Thanksgiving morning, six young men stood in quiet conversation, on the corner of Clark and Washington streets, in the great and busy city of Chicago.

"I propose a walk out to Graceland, the beautiful city of the dead." Thus spoke the leader of the company; and all agreeing, they journeyed forth. There are many beautiful monuments in that quiet city; and many a noted one from among the learned and the wealthy, from bank and store, from pulpit and bar, from church and state, has been borne there to rest; but the visit of these six young men at this time to this land of sacred dust, is not for the purpose of seeing the great and grand monuments, or visiting the graves of the rich.

They have reached the beautiful entrance of Graceland, and, passing under the imposing archway through which a stream of sorrow flows day by day and hour by hour, they turn to the right; and following the principal drive for a little more than a block, they reach an elevation where they stop to rest and meditate. And for these young men there is no more appropriate spot on earth to meditate than just here.

REMARKABLE ANSWERS TO PRAYER

Reader, even though you are not interested, yet perhaps you would like to see and know something of this spot. Then draw near, see the place, and hear the words of these young men. It is a small, three-cornered lot, forming an almost perfect equilateral triangle, with three oak trees, one standing near each of the angles. Near the center of the lot is a single grave, that all through the summer months resembled a bed of the richest flowers; but today the flowers are gone, and two well-wrapped rosebushes are all that remain of the summer beauties. When the foliage is full upon the trees, this grave is covered with their mellow shadow all the day. At the head of the grave is a plain low headstone of Italian marble. On the south end of the stone are these letters, *Sec. W. F. M. S.*, on the top of the stone the letters, *S. E. F.*, and just beneath these, in large letters, *Dear Mamma*. On the front of this stone are these words: *Resting in the Everlasting Arms*. Near the head of the grave, and immediately under one of the trees, is a rustic chair, cut out of solid stone, that extends its mute invitation to every weary, sorrowing pilgrim to stop and rest.

Reader, do you ask whose dust lies here? Let these young men answer. The leader of the company says, "Here lies the dust of a holy woman, who found me two years ago, a stranger in the great city of Chicago—a stranger to all the people, but what was much more, a stranger to God. That lady invited me into her Bible class, and though my garments were threadbare, she invited me to her home. She talked with me of Jesus and the better life; she pointed out to me the way up to a noble manhood, and by her leading I was constrained to give my heart to God; and this day Jesus is mine, and I am his."

"And I," says the second of these young men, "well remember the day when I landed in Chicago, a perfect stranger, direct from England. On my first Sabbath in the city, I was invited by a young man whose acquaintance I had made, to visit this lady's Bible class. I had no sooner entered the church than she had me by the hand, inquired of me whence I came, where I lived, and invited me to become a member of her class. Her sweet womanliness, her face of sunshine, and the music of her voice, charmed me into obedience to her wishes. I was constrained first to give my name to the class; afterward I gave my heart to God and my name to the church. Praise God for such a friend."

A third young man speaks, and says, "I came to Chicago from Toronto, Canada. I, too, was homeless and friendless. I heard of this lady, and her work for young men who were strangers in the city. I went to her class, and the first Sabbath took a back seat, and strove to hide myself; but the eyes of this lady missed no young man who appeared to be alone or friendless. At the close of the lesson she came to me, and, as if I were her own son, she sat down beside me, and questioned me concerning my temporal and spiritual condition. I told her I had once been a Christian, and a member of the church, but that I had wandered far away into sin. She looked me in the face and said, while the big tears stood in her eyes, 'My Jesus is anxiously hunting and calling for his wandering sheep; let me lead you back into the fold.' Yes, and she did lead me back into the fold, and this day I am one of the Great Shepherd's flock."

"I will tell you how it was with me," said a fourth.

"I came from my Iowa home, and found myself in Chicago, without friends, without money, and without work. After tramping from early one morning until four o'clock in the afternoon without finding work and without anything to eat, I called at this lady's home, and asked for something to eat. She gave me a little work to do, and while I was doing the work she ordered a dinner prepared for me. While I was eating, she questioned me as to my home, my purpose in the city, and my religious life. She said little at that time about my religious life, but finding me desirous to find work, she exerted herself for me, and through her influence, in two days I had a situation which I have been able to hold from that time to this. After she had found me good work with fair pay, she invited me into her class and her home, and afterwards she led me to Christ."

"And I," said the fifth young man, "have more reason to thank God for this lady than ye all. Two years ago I was a poor drunkard. This lady found me at the Young Men's Christian Association rooms, and asked me to call at her home. She prayed with me, she entreated me for Jesus' sake, for my dear mother's sake, and for my own sake, to reform. She induced me to sign the pledge, placed her hands upon my head, and offered, oh! such a prayer for me. Then and there new strength came into my life, and from that day to this by the grace of God, I have been able to live a sober life. Boys, I tell you, this dear woman was a mother to me."

The sixth young man spoke and said, "Under God, all I am today, or hope to be in the days to come, I owe to this noble woman. No wonder they have cut the name *Dear Mamma* on the headstone, for she was a mother to us all."

The leader said, "You see on the headstone, *Resting in the Everlasting Arms*. This reminds us that she sang *Safe in the Arms of Jesus*. Boys, let us sing that hymn." And they did sing it, with the tears streaming down their cheeks, after which they knelt around the silent grave, and in voiceless prayer gave themselves anew to God.

REMARKABLE ANSWERS TO PRAYER

Reader, would you know whose dust lies here? Over the back of the rustic chair hangs a scroll; draw near and read, *Born July, 1838; Departed, April, 1883.* Read on, *Her work for God and humanity is her monument.* Whose dust lies here? Ah! This is the grave of Sara Houghton Fawcett. And these young men, whom she had led to Jesus, came hither this Thanksgiving day, to offer their tribute of praise and thanksgiving to God for the memory they have of the blessed woman whose dust rests here by the chair of stone. She is not dead—not dead, but departed.

> *There is no death! What seems so is transition,*
>   *This life of mortal breath*
> *Is but a suburb of the life Elysian,*
>   *Whose portal we call Death.* —N. W. *Christian Advocate.*

They are not strangers, mamma

Not long ago I stood by the deathbed of a little girl. From her birth she had been afraid of death. Every fiber of her body and soul recoiled from the thought of it. "Don't let me die," she said. "Don't let me die. Hold me fast. Oh, I can't go!"

"Jennie," I said, "you have two little brothers in the other world, and there are thousands of tenderhearted people over there, who will love you and take care of you."

But she cried out again despairingly, "Don't let me go; they are strangers over there." She was a little country girl, strong limbed, fleet of foot, tanned in the face. She was raised on the frontier, the fields were her home. In vain we tried to reconcile her to the death that was inevitable. "Hold me fast," she cried. "Don't let me go."

But even as she was pleading, her little hands relaxed their clinging hold from my waist, and lifted themselves eagerly aloft; lifted themselves with such straining effort, that they lifted the wasted little body from its reclining position among the pillows. Her face was turned upward, but it was her eyes that told the story. They were filled with the light of Divine recognition. They saw something plainly that we could not see, and they grew brighter and brighter, and her little hand quivered in eagerness to go, where strange portals had opened upon her astonished vision. But even in that supreme moment she did not forget to leave a word of comfort for those who would gladly have died in her place.

"Mamma," she was saying, "Mamma, they are not strangers. I'm not afraid." And every instant the light burned more gloriously in her blue eyes, till at last it seemed as if her soul leaped forth upon its radiant waves. In that moment her trembling form relapsed among its pillows, and she was gone.—*Chicago Woman's World*

A cancer healed, and a withered arm restored

Brother W. B. Bailey wrote us from Hybrid, Missouri, January 7, 1887.

"I had a cancer in my left chest, it pained me very much; had become very bad and tender, and was a running sore. The saints prayed for me, and the Lord answered our prayers. Praise His holy name! The pain left me instantly, but the cancer healed gradually. It healed up without medicine or plaster, or anything but by trusting God alone. Praise the Lord for healing me, both soul and body. See Mark 16:18 and James 5:13-16."

His wife wrote at the same time.

"And all things whatsoever ye shall ask in prayer, believing, ye shall receive (Matthew 21:22). I praise the Lord, prayer was answered for me. I was very much afflicted in body. I went to the doctors. They could not cure me, I only grew worse. Was taken with a pain in my right shoulder. How I suffered none can tell. I could not use my arm without great pain. I could not raise my hand to comb my hair. My arm wasted away until it was less than the other. My hand was cold most all of the time. I was a cripple ten years. The saints prayed for me, and I was healed in answer to prayer. I can use my arm now. My hand is like the other, I can write and work with my right hand. I also had the dyspepsia seventeen years, and am healed in answer to prayer."

Only a vote

A local option contest was going on in W——, and Mrs. Kent was trying to influence her husband to vote *No License*. Willie Kent, six years old, was, of course, on his mamma's side. The night before election, Mr. Kent went to see Willie safe in bed, and hushing his prattle, he said, "Now, Willie, say your prayers."

"Papa, I want to say my own words tonight," he replied.

"All right, my boy, that is the best kind of praying," answered the father.

Fair was the picture as Willie, robed in white, knelt at father's knee and prayed reverently, "Oh dear Jesus, do help papa to vote *No Whiskey* tomorrow. Amen."

Morning came, the village was alive with excitement. Women's hands, made hard by toil, were stretched to God for help in the decision.

The day grew late, and yet Mr. Kent had not been to the polls. Willie's prayer sounded in his ears, and troubled conscience said, "Answer your boy's petition with your ballot."

At last he stood at the polling-place with two tickets in his hand—one *License*; the other *No License*. Sophistry, policy, avarice said, "Vote *License*."

REMARKABLE ANSWERS TO PRAYER

Conscience echoed, "*No License.*" After a moment's hesitation, be threw from him the *No License* ticket and put the *License* in the box.

The next day it was found that the contest was so close that it needed but one vote to carry the town for prohibition. In the afternoon, Willie found a *No License* ticket, and, having heard only one vote was necessary, he started out to find the man who would cast this one ballot against wrong, and in his eagerness he flew along the streets.

The saloon men were having a jubilee, and the highways were filled with drunken rowdies. Little Willie rushed on through the unsafe crowd.

Hark! A random pistol shot from a drunken quarrel, a pierced heart, and sweet Willie Kent had his death wound.

They carried him home to his mother. His father was quickly summoned, and the first swift thought that came to him, as he stood over his lifeless boy was, "Willie will never pray again that I may vote *No Whiskey.*"

With a strange, still grief lie took in his own the quiet little hand, chilling into marble coldness, and there between the fingers, firmly clasped, was the *No License* ballot with which the brave little soul thought to change the verdict of yesterday. Mr. Kent started back in shame and sorrow. That vote in his hand might have answered the prayer so lately on his lips, now dumb, and perhaps averted the awful calamity.

Fathers, may not the hands of the "thousands slain" make mute appeal to you? Your one vote is what God requires of you. You are as responsible for it being in harmony with His law, as if on it hung the great decision.—*The Issue*

Waiting for the angelic convoy

Seldom is the serenely expectant spirit of the dying Christian more graphically portrayed than in the beautiful letter of Rev. J. S. C. Abbott, written shortly before his death, to J. Dewitt Miller and published in the *New York Methodist*. It bears date at Fair Haven, Connecticut, March 3, 1877, and reads as follows:

"I am pillowed upon a sick and dying bed, with a little tablet in my hands. I can, without much difficulty, pencil lines to my friends. I suffer very little pain. My mind, it seems to me, was never more clear and joyous. The physicians assure me that I am liable at any moment to die. I am happy. I do not see how anyone can be more happy out of heaven. I am expecting every hour that a group of loving angels will come and say to me, 'Brother, God has sent us to convey you to heaven—the chariot is waiting.' All the infirmities of flesh and sin will vanish from body and soul. I shall be the congenial companion with the angels in that most wonderful of all conceivable journeys from earth to heaven.

"I have several times taken the tour of Europe. And there was great joy in seeing the wonders of the Old World. But there were sorrows, too, the discomforts of travel, the need of economy, the mind burdened with those earthly cares which never upon earth can be laid aside. But when the angelic summons comes, I shall be an 'heir of God.' He will provide the chariot, and will meet all the expenses. All care, imperfection, pain will be gone. The escort will be glorious—angels loving me with a brother's love, and God will have made me worthy of their love. We shall pass Sirius, the Pleiades, Orion and firmaments, or as Herschel calls them, *other universes of unimaginable splendor*. And then we shall enter heaven! All its glories will burst upon our enraptured view. Angels and archangels, cherubim and seraphim, will gather around us with their congratulations.

"We shall see God, his throne, the splendor of his court, understand all the mysteries of his being, and enter upon blessings inconceivable, forever and forever!

"All this I believe, my dear friend, as fully as I believe in my own existence. And I may enter upon this enjoyment before night shall darken around me. In the religion of the Son of God, and in the atonement He has made for my many sins, I find all that my soul craves. I am indeed happy. But writing these lines has exhausted me. I hope to met you in heaven. There we will clasp hands, and lovingly refer to this correspondence. Yours, affectionately, John S. C. Abbot."—*Golden Dawn*

How a little girl utilized the telephone

A mother, living not very far from the post office in this city, tired with watching over a sick baby, came downstairs for a moment the other day for a few second's rest.

She heard the voice of her little four year old girl in the hall by herself, and curious to know to whom she was talking, stopped a moment at the half open door. She saw that the little thing had pulled a chair in front of the telephone, and stood upon it, with the earpiece against the side of her head. The earnestness of the child showed that she was in no playful mood, and this was the conversation the mother heard, while the tears stood thick in her eyes, the little one carrying on both sides, as if she were repeating the answers:

"Hello."

"Well, who's there?"

"Is God there?"

"Yes."
"Is Jesus there?"
"Yes."
"Tell Jesus I want to speak to him."
"Well?"
"Is that you, Jesus?"
"Yes. What is it?"
"Our baby is sick, and we want you to let it get well. Won't you, now?"

No answer, and statement and question again repeated, finally answered by a "Yes."

The little one put the earpiece back on its hook, clambered down from the chair, and with a radiant face went for Mother, who caught her in her arms.

The baby, whose life had been despaired of, began to mend that day, and got well.—*Elmira Free Press*

Dying in despair

The following certified incident from real life we select from correspondence of the Canada *Christian Advocate*. A man who had indulged the hope of final salvation, regardless of character, was on his deathbed. In the prime of life, his cup of pleasure drained to the dregs, and exhausted nature refused to recruit her wasted energies. Pale and wan, with an awful sense of an uncertain future, the horrors of remorse distracted his inmost soul. The bitter cup of despair persistently held to his lips by the unrelenting hand of an abused and now fully awakened conscience, his hope that all would finally be well with him was forever swept away. No hope; no trust in God. His bed was no bed of roses, although surrounded by every comfort wealth could furnish.

With the dread realities of eternity before his eyes, he cried, "Oh! I can't die; there is no mercy now for me; God can't forgive me now. Oh! How I wish I had lived differently; if I could only live, I would lead a different life." I encouraged him to hope in the mercy of God in Christ Jesus, and earnestly besought him to believe on the Lord Jesus Christ with all his heart, and he should be saved. "Do you think that God will forgive me for Christ's sake, such a sinner as I have been?"

"Yes, oh yes!" said I, "He came to seek and save just such ones as you. Be willing to have Him save you now, just as you are."

"Oh! No," said he, "it is too late now," while the tears streamed down his young face, pallid with disease and suffering. I had never witnessed such a scene before, and I never shall forget the awful expression of that dying sinner's face to my dying breath.

I told him I would pray for him, and that he must pray for himself, and left the room ere my senses forsook me. Horror-stricken almost, and with a feeling as if death's fingers were clutching at my own heart-strings, I could not bear to witness such fearful despair. I went down the stairs, and soon one of his spasms of pain came on; and unable to bear it, with no hope, no peace, no Jesus to sustain him, he gave way to the fiends, as it seemed to me, which possessed him.

With fearful curses, frightful imprecations and horrid oaths, he drove his faithful wife from the room; and he lay there alone to battle with the raging hand of disease, cursing God, and screaming with rage and pain, so that he could be heard in the neighboring houses. I could do nothing for him, and the curses and maledictions of that hour ring in my ears like the wail of the lost in the dark regions of despair. And soon I heard he was dead. Gone to the bar of God, to render up his account at the judgment.

God save us from such a passing away as that; torturing fiends, instead of soothing angels 'round his dying couch. Black despair, in lieu of the overshadowing wing of angelic hope. Death and the judgment staring him in the face, instead of peace in believing and joy in the Holy Ghost. Horrid blasphemies, instead of, "Oh death, where is thy sting? Oh grave, where is thy victory?" A fearful looking forward to the future, in lieu of, "I know that my Redeemer liveth, and because he lives, I shall live also." Too late, too late! Instead of, "Come, Lord Jesus, come quickly." Such is the fearful end of those who trust in the mercy of God out of Christ, for "God out of Christ is a consuming fire."—*Golden Dawn*

A wonderful visitor

I had had a very busy day, and experienced a very delightful feeling of restfulness, as I settled myself in a comfortable armchair, after having said "Good night" to my children. Just before going, they had sung their evening hymn. As their sweet childish voices had joined with that of their mother, one verse had made an impression on my mind. I was familiar with it, but it came to me with a new beauty and force. It was,

> Not a brief glance I beg, a passing word,
>   But as Thou dwell'st with Thy disciples, Lord;
> Familiar, condescending, patient, free,
>   Come not to sojourn, but abide with me.

My wife went away with the little ones to see them to bed, and I was left alone with this verse of the hymn repeating itself in my memory; and the thought came to me,

REMARKABLE ANSWERS TO PRAYER

Supposing He were to come as He came to his disciples, am I altogether prepared to receive Him into my house, to abide with me? And as I meditated on the subject, I fell asleep, and dreamed, and, Lo! The door of the room opened, and in walked one whom I knew at once to be the Christ. Not the glorified Redeemer, as seen by John in the Isle of Patmos. No, he had answered the prayer of our hymn, and had come in humble human form, "familiar, condescending, patient, free" I knelt before Him, but He laid His hand on me and said, "Arise, for I have come to tarry with thee."

My recollection of my dream here grows somewhat confused; but I remember it again when the next morning seemed to have arrived, and I was gathering my children around me, and telling them that Jesus had come to stay with us in the house. The little ones clapped their hands for joy, and my dear wife's face beamed with rapture that seemed to transfigure her.

Just then the Lord Himself entered the room, and we took our seats around the breakfast table. What language can I use to describe the wondrous peace which filled all our souls, or how our hearts burned within us as He talked with us?

But when the meal was over, and we had family worship, which was that day a foretaste of heaven itself, I was filled with perplexity. What should I do with my strange Visitor? It seemed disrespectful to leave Him behind me at home, yet it would mean serious loss to me to stay away from my place of business that day. But I could not take him with me, that was certain; who ever heard of taking Christ to a countinghouse?

The Savior surely knew my thoughts, for he said, "I will go with thee. How did'st thou ask me? Was it not *Come not to sojourn, but abide with me*? So, whatever thou art doing, henceforth I will be beside thee. Lo, I am with you alway, even unto the end of the world."

It seemed rather strange to me, but I could not, of course, question what he said, so I started for my office with the dear Lord by my side.

At my countinghouse I found a man waiting my coming with a good deal of impatience. He was a stock and sharebroker, who transacted considerable business for me. To tell the truth, I was not greatly pleased to see him there, as I was afraid that he might bring forward matters which I would not feel inclined to go into with Jesus listening to our conversation.

It was as I feared. He had come to tell me of a transaction he had arranged, which, whilst perfectly honorable according to the usual code of morals of the stockmarket, meant the saving of myself from the fear of loss by placing another person in the danger of it. He laid the whole scheme before me, without taking the slightest notice of the Lord. I knew not if he even saw Him.

I cannot tell the bitter shame I felt. I saw how impossible it was to square such a transaction with the Golden Rule, but I could not hide from myself the fact that the broker told me of it with a manner and tone that meant that he had no doubt whatever that I would applaud him for his cleverness, and eagerly close with the offer. What must that mean to the Christ? Would it not tell him that I was in the habit of dealing with one thought in my mind—how I could benefit myself?

The broker was astonished when I rejected his proposals, on the ground that they would be prejudicial to the interest of the other party in the transaction and left me abruptly, apparently thinking I had developed a mild species of insanity.

Humbled, I fell at my Savior's feet, and cried to Him for forgiveness for past sinfulness, and strength for time to come.

"My child," said He, in tender accents, "thou speakest as if my presence were something strange to thee. But I have always been with thee. I have seen, and seen with grief, the way thou hast dealt with thy fellows in business, and marveled at thy unbelief of My promise that I would ever be with thee. Have I not said to my servants, *abide in Me, and I in thee?*"

Just as He said these words, another gentleman entered the office. He was a customer whom I could not afford to offend, and I had uniformly shown a cordiality to him which I was far from feeling in my heart. He was vulgar, profane, and often obscene in his talk.

He had not been many minutes in my office before he made use of an expression which brought a hot blush to my check. I had heard him speak in a similar way before and, although I felt repelled by it I had, for fear of offending him, met it with faint laughter. But now I felt as I should have had it been uttered in the presence of a lady, only this feeling was intensified by the realization of the absolute purity of the Divine One who had been a hearer of the speech.

I gave expression to my feeling in a word of expostulation, and he exclaimed, "You seem to have suddenly grown very prudish," and left me in a rage.

Again, I turned to the Christ with a cry for pardon; and again, I learned that he had beheld all my former conversations with this man.

I was now called into the adjoining office, where my clerks were employed, and found that one of them had made a foolish blunder, which would mean a considerable complication, and perhaps loss. I am naturally irritable, and at once lost my temper, and spoke to the delinquent in unmeasured terms. Turning my head, I saw that Jesus had followed me out of my private office, and was standing close beside me. Again I was humbled, and had to cry for mercy.

REMARKABLE ANSWERS TO PRAYER

Through all that strange day, similar incidents occurred and the presence of the Master, which I thought would have been a joy, was a rebuke to me. It showed me, as I had never dreamed before, that I had framed my life on the supposition that He had but little to do with it.

But, on the other hand, there were times during the day when my soul was filled with rapture, times when He smiled on me in loving approval, or when He spoke words of pardon and absolution, or when He opened out before my wondering gaze some fresh beauty of His character and person. Such a time was the moment when, on my return to my home, the children came crowding around Him, and wanted to show Him their toys and pigeons, and a brood of newly hatched chickens, and I rebuked them, and said to them, "Run away, children! Trouble not the Master with such trifles."

And he seated himself and took my curly-headed little boy on His knee, and called my two little girls to His side, and said to me, "Suffer these little children to come unto me, and forbid them not; for of such is the kingdom of heaven."

I awoke, and Lo! It was a dream.—*The Ballarat Christian Union*

The lame healed

Rev. Charles G. Finney, during his lifetime, was familiar with the circumstances connected with the remarkable healing of a sick lady in Oberlin, Ohio, the wife of Rev. R. D. Miller, and these facts were vouched for as unquestionably authentic. Mr. Finney says:

Mrs. Miller is the wife of a Congregational minister, and a lady of unquestionable veracity. However, the fact of her healing is to be accounted for, her story is no doubt worthy of entire confidence, as we have known her for years as a lame, suffering invalid, and now see her in our midst in sound health. This instantaneous restoration will be accounted for by different persons in different ways. Mrs. Miller and those who were present regard the healing as supernatural and a direct answer to prayer. The facts must speak for themselves. Why should not the sick be healed in answer to the prayer of faith? Unbelief can discredit them, but faith sees nothing incredible in such facts as are stated by Mrs. Miller. Her own statement is as follows, and it is fully endorsed by the most reliable citizens and members of the First Church at Oberlin:

"From my parents I inherited a constitution subject to a chronic form of rheumatism. In early life I was attacked with rheumatic weaknesses and pains, which affected my whole system. For nearly forty years I was subject to more or less suffering from this cause, sometimes unable to attend meeting for months at a time. For seven years, until the last three months, I have been unable to get about without the aid of crutch or staff, generally both. I have used many liniments and remedies, but with no permanently good result. I have been a Christian from early life, but last Spring, in our revival, I received a spiritual refreshing from the Lord, which gave a new impulse to my faith. Since then my religion has been a new life to me.

"Last Summer several of us Christian sisters were in the habit of spending short seasons of prayer together, that the Lord would send us a pastor. Some of our number had read the narrative of Dorothea Trudel, and had spoken to me on the subject of healing in answer to prayer. My faith had not then risen to this elevation. I had in fact accepted what I supposed to be the will of God, and made up my mind to be a lame and suffering invalid the rest of my life. I had long since ceased to use remedies for the restoration of my health, and had not even thought of praying in regard to it, for I regarded it as the will of God that I should suffer in silent submission.

"Notwithstanding what had been said to me, I remained in this opinion and in this attitude until the 26th of September, 1872, when several ladies met at our house by appointment for a prayer meeting. I had been growing worse for some time, and was at that time unable to get out to attend a meeting. I was suffering much pain that afternoon; indeed, I was hardly able to be out of my bed. Up to this time, none of the sisters who had conversed with me about the subject of healing by faith had been able to tell me anything from their own experience. That afternoon, one lady was present who could speak to me from her own experience of being healed in answer to the prayer of faith.

"She related several striking instances in which her prayers had been answered in the removal of divers forms of disease to which she was subject. She also repeated a number of passages of Scripture, which clearly justified the expectation of being healed in answer to the prayer of faith. She also said that Jesus had shown her that He was just as ready to heal diseases now as he was when on earth; that such healing was expressly promised in Scripture, in answer to the prayer of faith, and that it was nowhere taken back. These facts, reasonings, and passages of Scripture made a deep impression on my mind and for the first time I found myself able to believe that Jesus would heal me in answer to prayer.

"She asked me if I could join my faith with hers and ask for present healing. I told her I felt that I could. We then knelt and called upon the Lord. She offered a mighty prayer to God, and I followed. While she was leading in prayer, I felt a quickening in my whole being, whereupon my pain subsided and when we rose

REMARKABLE ANSWERS TO PRAYER

from prayer I felt that a great change had come over me, that I was cured. I found that I could walk without my staff or crutch, or any assistance from anyone. Since then my pains have never returned. I have more than my youthful vigor. I walk with more ease and rapidity than I ever did in my life, and I never felt so fresh and young as I now do, at the age of fifty-two.

"Now, the hundred and third psalm is my psalm, and my youth is more than renewed, like the eagle's. I cannot express the constant joy of my heart for the wonderful healing of my soul and body. I feel as if I was every whit made whole."

The testimony of eyewitnesses to this healing is as follows: "We were all present at the time of the healing and know the facts to be true. We are all Christians, and have no interest in deceiving anybody, and would by no means dishonor God by stating more than the exact truth. Since the healing, Mrs. Miller is still with us, and in excellent health. Neither the severe cold of last winter, nor the extreme heat of this summer, has at all injured her health. From our first acquaintance with her, she had been so lame as to be unable to walk, except by the aid of crutches. Since which time she has been able to walk without help, and appears perfectly well."

Her husband, also adding his testimony, says, "She has been unable to walk without crutches for a series of years. A long time ago, we tried many remedies and physicians, with no lasting good results, and were expecting she would remain an invalid. Of late, she had applied no remedy nor taken any medicine. At the time of her cure, she was much worse than for a long while before, being in great pain continually, until the moment she fully believed, and in an instant she was restored to perfect soundness. From that moment to this, she has not felt a particle of her former complaint.

"She can now walk for miles as fast as I wish to, without feeling very much fatigue, does all her own housework, and attends seven meetings during the week. In short, she is stronger, and seems as young and spry as when we were married thirty-two years ago. The work of the dear Savior in her cure seems to be perfect, and she is an astonishment to all who knew her before and see her now. To His name be all the praise.

"Another lady, the same week my wife was healed, a member of the First Congregational Church, confined to her bed with a complicated disease, was prayed for, and restored at once to soundness."—*Wonders of Prayer*.

TOUCHING INCIDENTS AND

7

Prayer for the preacher

JOHN LIVINGSTONE, OF SCOTLAND, once spent a whole night in prayer with a company of his brethren for God's blessing, all of them besieging the throne. The next day, under his sermon, five hundred souls were saved. All the world has heard how the audience of the elder President Edwards was moved by his terrible sermon on *Sinners in the Hands of an Angry God*, some of them even grasping hold of the pillars of the sanctuary, from feeling that their feet were actually sliding into the pit. But the secret of that sermon's power is known to but few. Some Christians in the vicinity—Enfield, Massachusetts—had became alarmed lest while God was blessing other places, He should in anger pass them by. So they met on the preceding evening, and spent the whole night in agonizing prayer.—*Foster's Cyclopoedia*

Prevailing prayer of a child

At the close of a prayer meeting, the pastor observed a little girl about twelve years of age, remaining upon her knees when most of the congregation had retired. Thinking the child had fallen asleep, he touched her, and told her it was time to return home. To his surprise, he found that she was engaged in prayer, and he said, "All things whatsoever ye shall ask in prayer, believing, ye shall receive."

She looked at her pastor earnestly, and inquired, "Is it so? Does God say that?" He took up a Bible, and read the passage aloud. She immediately commenced praying, "Lord, send my father here. Lord, send my father to the church." Thus she continued for about half an hour, attracting by her earnest cry the attention of persons who had lingered about the door.

At last a man rushed into the church, ran up the aisle, and sank upon his knees by the side of his child, exclaiming, "What do you want of me?"

REMARKABLE ANSWERS TO PRAYER

She threw her arms about his neck, and began to pray, "Oh Lord, convert my father!" Soon the man's heart was melted, and he began to pray for himself. The child's father was three miles from the church when she began praying for him. He was packing goods in a wagon, and felt impressed with an irresistible impulse to return home. Driving rapidly to his house, he left the goods in the wagon, and hastened to the church, where he found his daughter crying mightily to God in his behalf, and he was there led to the Savior.—*Foster's Cyclopoedia*

Visions of heaven and hell

In the *Life of William Tennent*, that zealous, devoted minister, and the friend and fellow-laborer of Whitefield, the author of his memoirs gives an account of Tennent being three days in a trance. He became prostrated with a fever, and by degrees sunk under it until, to appearances, he died. In laying him out, one felt a slight tremor under the left arm, though the body was cold and stiff. The time for the funeral arrived, and the people were assembled. But a physician, Tennent's friend, pled that the funeral might be delayed.

Tennent's brother remarked, "What! a man not dead who is cold and stiff as a stake?" The doctor, however, prevailed. Another day was appointed for the funeral. During the interval various efforts were made to discover signs of life, but none appeared save the slight tremor. For three days and nights his friend, the physician, never left him. Again the people met to bury him, but could not even then obtain the doctor's consent. For one hour more he pled. When that was gone, he craved half an hour more. That being expired, he implored a stay of fifteen minutes, at the expiration of which Tennent opened his eyes.

The following brief account is given in Mr. Tennent's own language, and was related to a brother minister: "As to dying, I found my fever increase, and I became weaker and weaker, until all at once, I found myself in heaven, as I thought. I saw no shape as to the Deity, but glory all unutterable. I can say as Paul did, I heard and saw things unutterable. I saw a great multitude before His glory, apparently in the height of bliss, singing most melodiously. I was transported with my own situation, viewing all my troubles ended, and my rest and glory begun, and was about to join the great and happy multitude, when one came to me, looked me full in the face, laid his hand upon my shoulder, and said, 'You must go back.'

"These words went through me. Nothing could have shocked me more. I cried out, 'Lord, must I go back?' With this shock, I opened my eyes in this world. When I saw I was in this world, I fainted, then came to, and fainted again several times, as one probably would naturally have done in so weak a situation.

"For three years the sense of Divine things continued so great, and everything else appeared so completely vain, when compared to heaven, that could I have had the world for stooping down for it, I believe I should not have thought of doing it."

To the writer of his memoirs, Mr. Tennent, concerning this experience, once said, "I found myself, in an instant, in another state of existence, under the direction of a superior being, who ordered me to follow him. I was accordingly wafted along, I know not how, till I beheld, at a distance, an ineffable glory, the impression of which on my mind, it is impossible to communicate to mortal man.

"Such was the effect on my mind of what I had seen and heard, that if it be possible for a human being to live entirely above the world, and the things of it, for some time afterward I was that person. The ravishing sounds of the songs and hallelujahs that I heard, and the very words that were uttered, were not out of my ears, when awake, for at least three years. All the kingdoms of the earth were in my sight as nothing and vanity. So great were my ideas of heavenly glory, that nothing which did not in some measure relate to it, could command my serious attention."

Mr. Tennent lived a number of years after this event, and died in the triumphs of a living faith, March 8, 1777, aged 71 years, his mortal remains being interred at his chapel in Freehold, N.J. He was an able, faithful preacher, and the Divine presence with him was frequently manifested in his public and private ministrations. In personal appearance, be was tall, erect, and of spare visage, with bright, piercing eyes, and grave, solemn countenance.

The following was related and vouched for by the late Robert Young, the missionary. We quote his account of the trance as given in a tract entitled, *A Vision of Hell*, issued by the *Evangelical Publishing Company*, Chicago:

"While residing in a British colony as a Christian missionary, I was called one evening to visit Miss D——, who was said to be dying. Mrs. Young, by whom she was met weekly for religious instruction, feeling a deep interest in her spiritual welfare, accompanied me to her residence. We found her in the chamber of a neat little cottage, exceedingly ill, but confiding in the merits of Jesus. After spending some time with her in conversation and prayer, we commended her to God, and took our departure, without the least hope of seeing her again in this life. Soon after we left she seemed to die; but as the usual signs of death, which so rapidly develop themselves in that country, did not appear, her friends anxiously waited to see the end.

"She was watched with great interest, both night and day, and after having been in this state for nearly a week, opened her eyes and said, 'Mr. C— is dead.' Her attendants, thinking that she was under the influence of delirium, replied that she was mistaken, as he was not only alive but well.

" 'Oh, no!' said she, 'he is dead; for a short time ago, as I passed the gates of hell, I saw him descend into the pit, and the blue flame cover him. Mr. B— is also dead, for he arrived at heaven just as I was leaving that happy place, and I saw its beautiful gates thrown wide open to receive him, and heard the host of heaven shout, 'Welcome, weary pilgrim!'

"Mr. C— was a neighbor, but a very wicked person, and Mr. B— who lived at no great distance, many years had been a member of the Church of God. The parties who heard Miss D—'s startling and confident statements immediately sent to make inquiries about the two individuals alluded to, and found, to their utter astonishment, that the former had dropped down dead about half an hour before, whilst in the act of tying his shoe, and that about the same time the latter had suddenly passed into the eternal world. For the truth of these facts I do solemnly vouch. She then went on to tell them where she had been, and what she had seen and heard.

Visit to heaven

"After being sufficiently recovered to leave the house, she paid us a visit, and Mrs. Young, as well as myself, heard from her own lips the following account of what she had passed through. She informed us that at the time she was supposed to die, a celestial being conducted her into the invisible world, and mysteriously unveiled to her the realities of eternity. He took her first to heaven, but she was told that, as she yet belonged to time, she could not be permitted to enter into that glorious place, but only to behold it, which she represented as infinitely exceeding in beauty and splendor, the most elevated conceptions of mortals, and whose glories no language could describe.

"She told us that she beheld the Savior upon a throne of light and glory, surrounded by the four-and-twenty elders, and a great multitude which no man could number, among whom she recognized patriarchs, prophets, apostles, martyrs. All the missionaries who had died in that colony, besides many others whom she mentioned, and although those parties were not named by the angel that attended her, yet she said that seeing them was to know them.

"She described these celestial spirits as being variously employed, and although she felt herself inadequate to convey any definite idea of the nature of that employment, yet it appeared to be adapted to their respective mental tastes and spiritual attainments. She also informed us that she heard sweet and most enrapturing music, such as she had never heard before, and made several attempts to give us some idea of its melodious character, but found her notes too earthly for that purpose.

"While thus favored, the missionaries already referred to, and other happy spirits, as they glided past her, sweetly smiled and said they knew whence she came, and if faithful to the grace of God she would, in a short time, be admitted into their delightful society. All the orders of heaven were in perfect and blessed harmony, and appeared to be directed in all their movements by a mysterious influence, proceeding from the throne of God.

"She was next conducted to a place whence she had:

A view of hell
"This she described in the most terrific language, and declared that the horrid shrieks of lost spirits still seemed to sound in her ears. As she approached the burning pit, a tremendous effort was made to draw her into it, but she felt herself safe under the protection of her guardian angel. She recognized many in the place of torment whom she had known on earth, and even some who had been thought to be Christians.

"There were princes and peasants, learned and unlearned, writhing together in one unquenchable fire, where all earthly distinctions and titles were forever at an end. Among them she beheld a Miss W—— who had occupied a prominent station in society, but had died during the illness of this young woman. She said that when Miss W—— saw her approach, her shrieks were appalling, beyond the power of language to describe, and that she made a desperate but unsuccessful effort to escape.

"The punishment of lost souls she represented as symbolizing the respective sins which had occasioned their condemnation. Miss W——, for instance, was condemned for the love of money, which I had every reason to believe was her besetting sin, and she seemed robed in a garment of gold, all on fire. Mr. O—— whom she saw, was lost through intemperance, and he appeared to be punished by devils administering to him some boiling liquid.

"She said there was no sympathy among these unhappy spirits, but that unmixed hatred, in all its frightful forms, prevailed in every part of the fiery regions. She beheld parents and children, husbands and wives, and those who had been companions in sin, exhibiting every mark of deep hatred to each other's society, and heard them in fiendish accents upbraiding and bitterly cursing each other. She saw nothing in hell but misery and despair, and heard nothing there but the most discordant sounds, accompanied with weeping, and wailing, and gnashing of teeth.

"While she gazed upon this revolting scene, many souls arrived from earth, and were greedily seized by innumerable devils of monstrous shape, amid horrid shouts of hellish triumph, and tortured according to their crimes."

John Wesley, in his journal of August, 1746, vol. 1, pages 374-376, concerning one he styles "S. T.," says, "About six in the morning she was rising, and inwardly praying to God, when on a sudden, she was seized with a violent trembling. Quickly after she lost her speech, in a few minutes her hearing, then her sight, and, at the same time, all sense and motion.

"Her mother immediately sent for Mrs. Designe, to whom she then went to school. At the same time her father sent for Mr. Smith, apothecary, who lived near. At first he proposed bleeding her immediately, and applying a large blister. But upon examining her further, he said, 'It signifies nothing, for the child is dead.' About twelve o'clock she began to stir, then opened her eyes, and gave the following account:

" 'As soon as I lost my senses, I was in a dismal place. full of briers and pits and ditches; stumbling up and down, and not knowing where to turn, or which way to get either forward or backward. And it was almost quite dark, there being but a little faint twilight, so that I could scarce see before me. I was crying, ready to break my heart; and a man came to me and said, 'Child, where are you going?' I said I could not tell.

" 'He said, 'What do you want?'

" 'I answered, 'I want Christ to be my refuge.'

" 'He said, 'You are the child for whom I am sent. You are to go with me.' I saw it grew lighter as he spoke. I observed his clothes; they reached down to his feet, and were shining, and white as snow.

" 'He brought me through a narrow lane into a vast, broad road, and told me, 'This leads to hell, but be not afraid. You are not to stay there.' At the end of that road a man stood, clothed like the other in white, shining clothes. Turning to the left hand, we went down a very high, steep hill. I could scarce bear the stench and smoke of brimstone. I saw a vast many people that seemed to be chained down, crying and gnashing their teeth. The man told me the sins they delighted in once they are tormented with now. I saw a vast number who stood up, cursing and blaspheming God, and spitting at each other, and many were making balls of fire, and throwing them at one another. I saw many others, who had cups of fire, out of which they were drinking down flames. And others held cards of fire in their hands, and seemed to be playing with them.

" 'We stayed here, I thought, about half an hour. Then my guide said, 'Come; I will now show you a glorious place.' I saw the gate of heaven, which stood wide open; but it was so bright I could not look at it long. We went straight in, and walked through a large place, where I saw saints and angels, and another large place, where were abundance more. They were all of one height and stature; and when one prayed, they all prayed. When one sang, they all sang. And they all sang alike, with a smooth, even voice, not one higher or lower than another.

" 'We went through this into a third place. There I saw God, sitting upon His throne. It was a throne of light, brighter than the sun. I could not fix my eyes upon it. I saw three, but all as one. Our Savior had a pen in His hand. A great book lay at His right side, another at His left, and a third partly behind Him. In the first He set down the prayers and good works of His people. In the second He set down all the curses, and all the evil works of the wicked. I saw that He discerns the whole earth at a glance.

" 'Then our Lord took the first book in His hand, and went and said, 'Father, behold the prayers and the works of my people.' And He held up His hands and prayed, and interceded to His Father for us. I never beard any voice like that but I cannot tell how to explain it.

" 'And His Father said, 'Son, I forgive Thy people, not for their sake, but Thine.' Then our Lord wrote it down in the third book, and returned to His throne, rejoicing with the hosts of heaven.

" 'It seemed to me as if I stayed here several months but I never slept all the while. And there was no night, and I saw no sky or sun, but clear light everywhere. Then we went back to a large door, which my guide opened, and we walked into pleasant gardens, by brooks and fountains. As we walked, I said, 'I did not see my brother here,' who died sometime before.

" 'He said, 'Child, thou canst not know thy brother yet. Thy spirit is to return to the earth. Thou must watch and pray. Thou shalt come again hither, and be joined to these, and know everyone as before.'

" 'I said, 'When is that to be?'

" 'He said, 'I know not, nor any angel in heaven; but God alone.'

" 'While we were walking, he said, 'Sing.'

" 'I said, 'What shall I sing?'

REMARKABLE ANSWERS TO PRAYER

" 'And he said, 'Sing praises unto the King of the place.' I sang several verses.

" 'Then he said, 'I must go.' I would have fain gone with him but he said, 'Your time is not yet. You have more work to do on earth.' Immediately he was gone and I came to myself, and began to speak.'

"She received remission of sins when she was nine years old, and was very watchful from that time. Since this trance she has continued in faith and love."

Again, Mr. Wesley, in his Journal of August 6, 1759, page 42, says, "I talked largely with Ann Thorn, and two others, who had been several times in trances. What they all agreed in was:

"1. That when they went away, as they termed it, it was always at the time they were fullest of the love of God.

"2. That it came upon them in a moment, without any previous notice, and took away all their senses and strength.

"3. That there were some exceptions, but in general, from that moment they were in another world, knowing nothing of what was done or said by all that were round about them.

" 'About five in the afternoon I heard them singing hymns. Soon after Mr. B. came up and told me that Alice Miller was fallen into a trance. I went down immediately, and found her sitting on a stool, and leaning against the wall, with her eyes open and fixed upward. I made a motion as if going to strike but they continued immovable. Her face showed an unspeakable mixture of reverence and love, while silent tears stole down her checks. Her lips were a little open, and sometimes moved, but not enough to cause any sound. I do not know whether I ever saw a human face look so beautiful. Sometimes it was covered with a smile, as from joy, mixing with love and reverence; but the tears fell still, though not so fast.

" 'In about half an hour I observed her countenance change into the form of fear, pity, and distress, then she burst into a flood of tears, and cried out, 'Dear Lord, they will be damned! they will all be damned!' But in about five minutes her smiles returned, and only love and joy appeared in her face. About half an hour after six, I observed distress take place again, and soon after she wept bitterly, and cried out, 'Dear Lord, they will go to hell! The world will go to hell!' Soon after, she said, 'Cry aloud! Spare not!' And in a few moments her look was composed again, and spoke a mixture of reverence, joy, and love. Then she said aloud, 'Give God the glory.' About seven her senses returned.

" 'I asked, 'Where have you been?'

" 'I have been with my Savior.'

" 'In heaven, or on earth?'

" 'I cannot tell; but I was in glory.'
" 'Why then did you cry?'
" 'Not for myself, but for the world; for I saw they were on the brink of hell.'
" 'Whom did you desire to give the glory to God?'
" 'Ministers, that cry aloud to the world; else they will be proud, and then God will leave them, and they will lose their own souls.'"—*The Plumbline.*

The wonderful cure of Mrs. Sherman

Although there are so many cases of healing in answer to prayer, yet the incident of the healing of Mrs. Sherman is so minute, and resulted in such a radical change of the physical constitution, that it is necessary to relate it in full detail. It is too well proven to admit the possibility of a doubt.

"Mrs. Ellen Sherman is the wife of Rev. Moses Sherman, and at the time of this occurrence, in 1873, they were residents of Piermont, New Hampshire. She had been an invalid for many years. In the winter after she was fifteen, she fell on the ice and hurt her left knee, so that it became weak and easy to slip out of joint. Six years after, she fell again on the same knee, so twisting it and injuring the ligaments that it became partially stiff, and, the physician said, incurable.

"The next summer, by very fast walking, one day she brought on special weakness, which no physician was able to cure. From that moment she was subject to severe neuralgia, sick headaches at least monthly, and sometimes even weekly.

"In December, 1859, while stepping out of doors, she slipped, by reason of her stiff joint, and fell, striking near the base of the spine, directly across the sharp edge of the stone step. This caused such a sickness that she was obliged to leave the school she was attending.

"Three years after, in January, 1862, she fell at the top of a stairway, striking just as before, and sliding all the way down to the foot. This nearly paralyzed the spinal cord, and caused deep and permanent spinal disease. After this she was up and down for many years, attended by various physicians, yet nothing bettered, but, rather, growing worse. It may be said, for short, that every organ of the lower body became chronically diseased, and that the headaches increased in violence."

"In September, 1872, through a severe cold, she took her bed, where she lay, except when lifted from it, till the night of August 27, 1873. She was unable to walk a step, or even stand. She could sit up only a short time without great distress. The best medical skill that could be procured gave only temporary relief. The spine grew worse in spite of every appliance, and the nervous sensitiveness and prostration were increasing. During the two or three weeks immediately preceding her cure, she was especially helpless, two persons being required to lift her off and on the bed. On the Monday before, one of her severest neuralgia sick-headaches came on. During Wednesday she began to be relieved, but was still so sick that when, in the evening, she tried to have her clothes changed, she could only endure the change of her nightdress."

It will be seen from this, her utter physical helplessness, and not the slightest hope of any amelioration. During the night of August 27th, she enjoyed a blessed time of communion with her Lord, giving herself, in all her helplessness, wholly to Him to do as he wills.

"With feelings beyond all expression, she felt the nearness of her mighty Savior, and the sense of receiving a new and most delicious pulsation of new life. At last, though she had been bedridden for twelve months, and incapable of any bodily assistance, she felt an uncontrollable impulse to throw off the clothes of the bed with her left arm, and sprang out of bed upon her feet, and started to walk across the room.

"Her husband's first thought was that she was crazed, and would fall to the floor, and he sprang towards her to help her. But she put up her hands against him, saying, with great energy, 'Don't you touch me. Don't you touch me!' and went walking back and forth across the room, speaking rapidly and declaring the work which Jesus had been working upon her.

"Her husband quickly saw that she was in her right mind, and had been healed by the Lord, and his soul was filled with unutterable emotion.

"One of the women of the household was called, also their son, twelve years old, and together they thanked God for the great and blessed wonder he had wrought.

"In the morning, after a sleep of several hours, she further examined herself to see if entirely healed, and found both knees perfectly well; and though for sixteen years she had not been able to use either, now she lifted the left foot and put it upon the right knee, thus proving the completeness of her restoration.

"At the end of two years from her healing, inquiry having been made as to how thorough had been the work, Mrs. Sherman gave full and abundant evidence. 'I cannot remember a summer when I have been so healthy and strong, and able to work hard. I am a constant wonder to myself, and to others, and have been for the two years past. The cure exceeded my highest expectations at the time I was cured. I did not look forward to such a state of vigor and strength. No words can express my joy and gratitude for all this.'

"The parents of Mrs. Sherman also testify of the wonderful change physically which occurred with the cure.

"Before, her appetite was always disordered, but on the very morning of the healing it was wholly changed and her food, which distressed her formerly, she ate with a relish and without any pain following, and she so continues. For years before a natural action of the bowels was rare. From that day since, an unnatural one is equally rare.

"For fifteen years, with few exceptions, she had had severe neuralgic sick-headaches monthly or oftener. From that time she had been natural and without pain, with no return of the headaches, except a comparatively slight one once, from overdoing, and a cold taken through carelessness.

"There was also at that time an immediate and radical change in the action of the kidneys, which had become a source of great trouble before. Moreover, the knee, which had been partially stiff for so many years, was made entirely well. Her body, which had been so full of pain, became at once free from pain and full of health.

"The week after she was healed, she went fifty miles to attend a campmeeting, riding five miles in a carriage, the rest by train. A near neighbor said, 'She will come back worse than ever.' Though the weather was especially bad, she came back better than when she went."

These are but few out of many expressions respecting her extraordinary recovery, which fully satisfy the believing Christian that the Great Physician is with us now, "healing the lame," and curing the sick. It is faith only, unyielding, which the Lord requires, ere he gives his richest blessing. The unbelieving one simply sees in it "something strange," which he cannot understand. But the faith-keeping Christian knows it is the sign of his precious Lord, in whom he trusts and abides forever. —*Wonders of Prayer*

<u>The dying newsboy</u>

In a dark alley in the great city of New York, a small, ragged boy might be seen. He appeared to be about twelve years old, and had a careworn expression on his countenance. The cold air seemed to have no pity as it pierced through his ragged clothes, and made the flesh beneath blue and almost frozen.

This poor boy had once a happy home. His parents died a year before, and left him without money or friends. He was compelled to face the cold, cruel world with but a few cents in his pocket. He tried to earn his living by selling newspapers and other such things. This day everything seemed to go against him, and in despair he threw himself down in the dark alley with his papers by his side.

REMARKABLE ANSWERS TO PRAYER

A few boys gathered around the poor lad, and one asked in a kind way, for a street person, "Say, Johnny, why don't you go to the lodges?" The lodge was a place where almost all the boys stayed at night, costing but a few cents. But the poor little lad could only murmur that he could not stir, and called the boys about him, saying, "I am dying now, because I feel so queer, and I can hardly see you. Gather around me closer, boys. I cannot talk so loud. I can kinder see the angels holding out their hands for me to come to that beautiful place they call heaven. Good-bye, boys. I am to meet father and mother." And, with these last words on his lips, the poor boy died.

Next morning passersbys saw a sight that would soften the most hardened heart. There, lying on the cold stone, with his head against the hard wall, and his eyes staring upward, was the poor little frozen form of the newsboy. He was taken to the church nearby and interred by kind hands. And those who performed this act will never forget the poor forsaken lad.—*Golden Dawn*.

The dying babe

The following extract from an anonymous contribution in the *New York Methodist*, tells a story which many parents could adopt as their own. Few will read it without tears:

All that morning I held the baby in my arms—all that long and weary morning. How hot was that little cheek! How piteous the moaning! How feeble! The cry, how restless! Oh! how sick was my little child! How hard to see it suffer, hour after hour, yet not be able to relieve it! My eyes grew dim with tears, and I could only faintly pray, "God, be merciful, and spare, oh! spare my little, my darling little babe."

In vain, in vain! Again the doctor came, and then he spoke kindly, but we knew there was a depth of meaning in his words. "Your child is very, very sick." Then turning to my husband he added, "You had better not go down to the store this morning," Neither John nor I dared ask him any questions, for we felt there was something in his tone which bade us hope no longer. Something as sad to us as the tolling of the funeral-bell.

"John," I said, after the doctor had left, "bring the baby to me."

Tenderly he raised it up and placed it in my lap, and silently we watched the flame of life decreasing. No words were spoken. The measured ticking of the clock and the restless breathing of the baby alone were heard. An hour it seemed passed away. I gazed upon the face of Willie. The eyes were fixed, the cheek was pale, and the breathing, how quick and short it was! Never had I seen a child so sick before, but I knew—I knew—the dread change was coming.

"Oh John! our darling babe is dying."

"Mary," was all John said, "Mary, the will of God be done."

"Yes, yes, dear husband," I could hardly speak for weeping, "but it is so hard, so very, very hard, to lose a little child."

No more was said, but we wept together. We saw the eyes gently close and open, and close again. The breath came quicker and quicker. Then—then more and more slowly, the little stream of life was ebbing fast away.

Friends came into the room, but I heeded them not. Then someone gently touched me, and said, "Mary." I knew the voice.

"Oh, mother! you have come. Willie is dying."

I can dwell no longer on that scene. Two days after, John said, "In an hour the funeral services will take place. Let us take our last look at the child we loved while we are alone together."

We drew near the coffin. There was the little face we had learned to love, but oh! the eyes were closed, the voice was hushed. There lay the child so still and quiet, the hands together and a wreath of pure white flowers beside them. I kissed the cold face.

"Oh Willie! farewell—farewell—forever."

"No, Mary, not forever," said John. "There is another and a better life."

Then came the solemn funeral services, the journey to the cemetery, the open grave, and all was over. John and I came back to our sad and silent cottage on the hill.

Only a few weeks ago it was that we visited the grave of Willie. We walked through the entrance of Greenwood, along the hard, smooth road to the hillside, near the quiet lake, and there, under the shadow of a wide-branching tree, we stood beside the little mound of earth. I gazed upon the monument which had just been placed there, with a rosebud on a broken stem, engraved upon it the name of our lost child, the date of birth and death, and then the words, *Safe in the Shepherd's arms.*

We gazed and wept, and at last John said, "Mary, life is short. Here beside this grave let us resolve so to live that we shall meet our little one in our true home in heaven." There beside that grave we made the solemn vow, and we shall try to keep it.

I know that I am weak and nervous. As I go to and fro in the daily work of the house, I grieve for the babe that has gone, for I miss it very much. Be patient, oh, my sorrowing spirit, be patient! I think it will not be long—though I dare not tell my husband so—before I shall sleep quietly beside my little babe, not long before I shall meet that gentle spirit in the skies.—*Golden Dawn.*

REMARKABLE ANSWERS TO PRAYER

Little Jennie's sickness and death

(By her mother.) Little Jennie was eight years old, March 30, 1886. The April following, she was taken very sick, and from that time until June 4, she seemed a little suffering angel. Then Jesus, who had so blessedly sustained her during all her sufferings, took her to Himself. She would say, when able to talk, "Mamma, I do not care what I suffer, God knows best." When she was very low, we would often see her dear lips moving, and, listening, hear her praying. She would finish her prayer, and after saying "Amen," having noticed that we were listening to her, would look up into our faces to see if we wanted anything.

This patience and devotion characterized her whole life. Often, when she was at play with her sister, who was the older by five years, when some little trouble would arise, she would take her sister by the hand and say, "Kittie, let's tell Jesus." Then bowing her little head, she would pour out her whole heart in prayer to her God, with the fervency that is always shown by a true Christian.

About three weeks after she was taken ill, her little body was paralyzed, and drawn all out of shape it seemed. Then in a few days her little limbs were so we could almost straighten them. What suffering she endured all that time, no one knows but those who were with her.

May 25th, which was Tuesday, while suffering terribly, she said, "Mamma, play and sing." I took the guitar, and without stopping to think what to sing, began that beautiful song in the *Gospel Hymns*, "Nearer my home, to-day, than I have been before." I could praise God just then, for I was filled with His Spirit. She lay there, looking at me with her little blue eyes, and trying in her weak voice to help me. At last she seemed soothed by the music But we knew that Jesus, in His infinite love, had quieted her for the time, because we were willing to submit to His will. We had said all the time, "Lord, not my will, but thine."

She rested quite well until about three o'clock in the afternoon. Then suddenly she spoke, and her voice sounded quite strong as she said, "Oh mamma, see those people, how funny they look! They look like poles." She was lying so that she could look out of the window, and as she spoke her eyes seemed to rest on some object there. Then she spoke louder, "Oh mamma, come and see the little children! I never saw so many in my life."

I sat down on the front of the bed and said, "Jennie, is there any there that you know?"

She looked them over so earnestly, then said, "No, not one." I asked her how they looked. She said, "Mamma, everyone has a gold crown on its head, and they are all dressed in white." I thought that Jesus was coming for her then. After telling me that there were none there that she knew, she sank back on the pillows as though exhausted. But in a few moments she raised up again and said, "Oh mamma, hear that music! Did you ever hear such grand music? Now, do not shut the windows tonight, will you?" I told her that I would not.

The next morning she called Kittie into the room and said, "Kittie, I want to tell you what I saw last night." She then proceeded to tell her the same as she had told me the evening before. Then she said, "Now, Kittie, you will forgive me for ever being cross to you, won't you?"

Kittie answered, "Little darling, you have never been cross to me. Will you forgive me, sister, for being cross to you?"

"Darling sister," said she, "that is all right."

Thursday night she was paralyzed in her left side, so that she had no use of it. Friday all day she lay unconscious, and that night the same. Saturday, about ten o'clock, she commenced to try and whisper. We could hear her say, "Papa, mamma." We tried to understand her, but at first could not. She kept whispering plainer, and finally we heard her say, "Take me upstairs, I want to lie on my own bed once more." But of course we could not move her.

Suddenly she said aloud, "I am going to die. Kiss me quick, mamma." I bent down and kissed her, and she looked so wretched.

I said, "Jennie, you will not have to go alone; Jesus will take you."

She answered, "I know it. I wish that He would come this minute. Kiss me again, mamma." I did so, then she wished us to sing. Again, without giving one thought, I commenced singing the same words that I sang the Tuesday before. She raised her right hand arm's length, and began to wave it and bow her head. Oh! she was so happy.

Then she said, "Play." They brought the guitar, and she continued to wave her little hand, while I played and sang the whole piece.

One of her aunts, standing near the bed, took hold of her hand to stop it, but it moved—just the same, and I said, "Ollie, let go of her hand, that is the Lord's doings." After I finished, she kissed her father, mother and sister, and bade them good-by. Then called four other very dear friends, and told them good-by after kissing them. She then called for a book and wanted the music teacher, who was present, to play and sing a piece which she dearly loved.

Before she was sick, she would have little prayer meetings, and her sweet little face would shine with happiness. She would say, "Oh mamma! how the Lord has blessed me."

While the dear teacher was playing and singing her favorite, she was waving her little hand. We sang three or four other pieces around her bed. We all thought that Jesus would take her then. Oh, what joy! It was heaven below. Jesus was there and the room was filled with glory on account of His presence. Two of her aunts said that it seemed as though they were in heaven.

She never spoke after that, but would try to make us understand by motioning when she wanted anything. Sometimes it would take us a long time, but she would be so patient. She was ready and waiting. She had peace that the world cannot give, and praise God! that the world cannot take away. The dear little one lived until the next Tuesday afternoon, and went to Jesus about three o'clock. That was the time she saw the vision the Tuesday before.

Tuesday morning before daylight she tried to tell me something. I said, "Sing?" She looked so happy and bowed her head. I began singing, "I am Jesus' little lamb." She bowed her head again. In the forenoon she kept looking at her aunts Ollie and Belle, and pointing up. Oh! it meant so much. It seemed to me that she was saying, that it meant, "Meet me in heaven." Finally she motioned for me to raise the window-curtain. I did so, and she looked out of the window so eagerly, as though she was expecting to see the little children. Then the little blue eyes closed to open no more in this world, but in heaven.—*Mrs. Libbie Jones*

8

There is no rest in hell

ABOUT NINETY YEARS AGO there was in Glasgow a club of gentlemen of the first rank in that city. They met professedly for cardplaying, but the members were distinguished by such a fearless excess of profligacy, as to obtain for it the name of *The Hell Club*. They gloried in the name they had acquired for themselves, and nothing that could merit it was left untried. Beside their nightly or weekly meetings, they held a grand annual festival, at which each member endeavored to "outdo all his former outdoings" in drunkenness, blasphemy, and licentiousness.

Of all who shone on these occasions, none shone half so brilliantly as Archibald Boyle. But, alas! The light that dazzled in him was not "light from heaven" but from that dread abode which gave name to the vile association which was to prove his ruin—ruin for time and eternity!

Archibald Boyle had been at one time a youth of the richest promise, being possessed of dazzling talents and fascinating manners. No acquirement was too high for his ability, but unfortunately, there was none too low for his ambition. Educated by a fond and foolishly indulgent mother, he early met in society with members of *The Hell Club*. His elegance, wit, gaiety, and versatility of talent, united to the gifts of fortune, made him a most desirable victim for them, and a victim and a slave, glorying in his bondage, he quickly became. Long ere he was five-and-twenty, he was one of the most accomplished blackguards it could number on its lists. To him, what were heaven, hell or eternity! Words, mere words, that served no purpose, but to point his blasphemous wit, or nerve his curses! To him, what glory was there, equal to that of hearing himself pronounced "the very life of the club?" Alas! There was none, for as soon as man forgets God, who alone can keep him, his understanding becomes darkened, and he glories in that which is his shame.

Yet, while all within that heart was festering in corruption, he retained all his remarkable beauty of face and person, all his external elegance of manner, and continued an acknowledged favorite in the fairest female society of the day.

One night, on retiring to sleep, after returning from one of the annual meetings of the club, Boyle dreamed that he was still riding, as usual, upon his famous black horse, toward his own house—then a country seat, embowered by ancient trees, and situated upon a hill now built over by the most fashionable part of Glasgow—and that he was suddenly accosted by someone, whose personal appearance he could not, in the gloom of night, distinctly discern, but who, seizing the reins, said, in a voice apparently accustomed to command, "You must go with me."

"And who are you?" exclaimed Boyle, with a volley of blasphemous curses, while he struggled to disengage his reins from the intruder's grasp.

"That you will see bye-and-bye," replied the same voice, in a cold, sneering tone, that thrilled through his very heart. Boyle plunged his spurs into the panting sides of his steed. The noble animal reared, and then suddenly darted forward with a speed that nearly deprived his rider of breath, but in vain. Fleeter than the wind he flew, the mysterious, half-seen guide, still before him!

Agonized by he knew not what, of indescribable horror and awe, Boyle again furiously spurred the gallant horse. It fiercely reared and plunged, he lost his seat, and expected at the moment to feel himself dashed to the earth. But not so, for he continued to fall—fall—fall—it appeared to himself with an ever-increasing velocity. At length, this terrific rapidity of motion abated, and to his amazement and horror, he perceived that this mysterious attendant was close by his side. "Where," he exclaimed, in the frantic energy of despair, "where are you taking me, where am I—where am I going?"

"To hell," replied the same iron voice, and from the depths below, the sound so familiar to his lips was suddenly reechoed.

"To hell," onward, onward they hurried in darkness, rendered more horrible still by the conscious presence of his spectral conductor. At length, a glimmering light appeared in the distance, and soon increased to a blaze. But as they approached it, in addition to the hideously discordant groans and yells of agony and despair, his ears were assailed with what seemed to be the echoes of frantic revelry.

They soon reached an arched entrance, of such stupendous magnificence, that all the grandeur of this world seemed in comparison but as the frail and dingy labors of the mole. Within it, what a scene! Too awful to be described. Multitudes, gnashing their teeth in the hopelessness of mad despair, cursed the day that gave them birth, while memory, recalling opportunities lost and mercies despised, presented to their fevered mental vision the scenes of their past lives. Their fancy still pictured to them the young and lovely, moving up and down in the giddy mazes of the midnight dance; the bounding steed, bearing his senseless rider through the excitements of the goaded race; the intemperate, still drawling over the midnight bowl, the wanton song, or maudlin blasphemy. There the slave of Mammon bemoaned his folly in bartering his soul for *useless* gold, while the gambler bewailed, alas! too late, the madness of his choice.

Boyle at length perceived that he was surrounded by those whom he had known on earth, but were some time dead, each one of them betraying his agony at the bitter recollections of the vain pursuits that had engrossed his time here—time lent to prepare for a far different scene!

Suddenly, observing that his unearthly conductor had disappeared, he felt so relieved by his absence, that he ventured to address his former friend, Mrs. D—— whom he saw sitting with eyes fixed in intense earnestness, as she was wont on earth, apparently absorbed at her favorite game of loo. "Ha, Mrs. D——! Delighted to see you; d' ye know a fellow told me tonight he was bringing me to hell! Ha, ha! If this be hell," said he, scoffingly, "what a devilish pleasant place it must be! Ha, ha! Come, now, my good Mrs. D——, for auld lang syne, do just stop for a moment, rest, and show me through the pleasures of hell," he was going, with reckless profanity, to add.

But, with a shriek that seemed to cleave through his very soul, she exclaimed, 'Rest! There is no rest in hell!" And from interminable vaults, voices, as loud as thunder, repeated the awful, the heart withering sound, "There is no rest in Hell!"

She hastily unclasped the vest of her gorgeous robe, and displayed to his scared and shuddering eye, a coil of fiery living snakes— "the worm that never dies"—*the worm of accusing conscience, remorse, despair*—wreathing, darting, stinging in her bosom. Others followed her example, and in every bosom there was a self-inflicted punishment. In some, he saw bare and throbbing hearts, on which distilled slow drops, as it were, of fiery molten metal, under which consuming, yet ever unconsumed, they writhed and palpitated in all the impotence of helpless, hopeless agony. And many a scalding drop was a tear of hopeless anguish, wrung by selfish, heartless villainy from the eye of injured innocence on earth.

In every bosom he saw that which we have no language to describe, no idea horrid enough even to conceive, for in all he saw the full-grown fruit of the fiend-sown seed of evil passions, voluntarily nourished in the human soul, during it's

mortal pilgrimage here, and in all he saw them lashed and maddened by the serpent armed hand
>*Of despair;*
>>*For hell were not hell*
>>*If hope had ever entered there!*

And they laughed, for they had laughed on earth at all there is of good and holy. And they sang—profane and blasphemous songs sang they! For they had often done so on earth, at the very hour God claims as his own, the still and midnight hour! And he who, in his vision, walked among them in a mortal frame of flesh and blood, felt how inexpressibly more horrible such sounds could be than ever was the wildest shriek of agony on earth.

"These are the *pleasures* of hell," again assailed his ear, in the same terrific and interminable roll of unearthly sound.

He rushed away, but as he fled he saw those whom he knew must have been dead for thousands of years, still absorbed in their recollections of their sinful pleasures on earth, and toiling on through their eternity of woe. The vivid reminiscences of their godlessness on earth inflicted on them the bitterest pang in their doom in hell.

He saw Maxwell, the former companion of his own boyish profligacy, borne along in incessant movement, mocked by the creations of his frenzied mind, as if intent on still pursuing the headlong chase.

"Stop, Harry, stop! Speak to me! Oh, rest one moment!" Scarce had the words been breathed from his faltering lips, when again his terror-stricken ear was stunned with the same wild yell of agony, reechoed by ten thousand voices, "There is no rest in Hell!"

Boyle tried to shut his eyes. He found he could not. He threw himself down, but the pavement of hell, as with a living and instinctive movement, rejected him from its surface and, forced upon his feet, he found himself compelled to gaze with still increasing intensity of horror, at the ever-changing, yet ever-steady torrent of eternal torment. And this was hell—the scoffer's jest—the byword of the profligate!

All at once he perceived that his unearthly conductor was once more by his side. "Take me," shrieked Boyle, "take me from this place! By the living God, whose name I have so often outraged, I adjure thee. Take me from this place."

"Can'st thou still name His name?" said the fiend, with a hideous sneer. "Go, then. But in a year and a day we meet to part no more!"

Boyle awoke, and he felt as if the last words of the fiend were traced in letters of living fire upon his heart and brain. Unable, from actual bodily ailment, to leave his bed for several days, the horrid vision had full time to take effect upon his mind, and many were the pangs of tardy remorse and ill defined terror that beset his vice stained soul, as he lay in darkness and seclusion, to him so very unusual.

He resolved, utterly and forever, to forsake *The Hell Club.* Above all, he determined that nothing on earth should tempt him to join the next annual festival.

The companions of his licentiousness soon flocked around him, and finding that his deep dejection of mind did not disappear with his bodily ailment, and that it arose from some cause which disinclined him from seeking or enjoying their accustomed orgies, they became alarmed with the idea of losing "the life of the club," and bound themselves by an oath never to desist till they had discovered what was the matter with him, and had cured him of "playing the Methodist." Their alarm as to losing "the life of the club" had been wrought up to the highest pitch by one of their number declaring that, on unexpectedly entering Boyle's room, he detected him in the act of hastily hiding a book, which he actually believed was the Bible.

Alas! Alas! Had poor Boyle possessed sufficient true moral courage, and dignity of character, not to have hidden the Bible, how different might have been his future! But like many a hopeful youth, he was ashamed to avow his convictions, and to take his stand for God, and his ruin was the result.

After a time, one of his compeers, more deeply cunning than the rest, bethought himself of assuming an air of the deepest disgust with the world, the club, and the mode of life they had been pursuing. He affected to seek Boyle's company in a mood of congenial melancholy, and to sympathize in all his feelings. Thus he succeeded in betraying him into a much misplaced confidence as to his dream, and the effect it had produced upon his mind. The result may readily be guessed. His confidence was betrayed, his feelings of repentance ridiculed and it will easily be believed, that he who hid the Bible had not nerve to stand the ribald jests of his profligate companions.

We cannot trace the progress, and would not if we could. Suffice it to say that virtuous resolutions once broken, prayers once offered, voluntarily called back by sin from the throne of heaven—*all was lost!* Yet not lost without such a fell struggle between the convictions of conscience and the spirit of evil, as wrung the color from his young cheek, and made him, ere the year was done, a haggard and gray-haired man.

From the annual meeting he shrank with an instinctive horror, and made up his mind utterly to avoid it. Well aware of this resolve, his tempters determined

REMARKABLE ANSWERS TO PRAYER

he should have no choice. How potent, how active, is the spirit of evil! How feeble is unassisted, Christless, unprayerful man! Boyle found himself, he could not tell how, seated at that table on that very day, where he had sworn to himself a thousand and a thousand times nothing on earth should make him sit. His ears tingled, and his eyes swam, as he listened to the opening sentence of the president's address: "Gentlemen, this is leap year. Therefore, it is a year and a day since our last annual meeting."

Every nerve in Boyle's body twanged in agony at the ominous, the well-remembered words. His first impulse was to rise and fly, but then—the sneers! The sneers!

How many in this world, as well as poor Boyle, have sold their souls to the dread of a sneer, and dared the wrath of an almighty and eternal God, rather than encounter the sarcastic curl of a fellow creature's lip?

He was more than ever plied with wine, applause, and every other species of excitement, but in vain. His mirth, his wit, were like lurid flashes from the bosom of a brooding thundercloud, that pass and leave it darker than before, and his laugh sounded fiendish, even to the evil ears that heard it.

The night was gloomy with frequent and fitful gusts of chill and howling wind as Boyle, with fevered nerves and reeling brain, mounted his horse to return home. The following morning the well-known black steed was found, with saddle and bridle on, quietly grazing on the roadside, about halfway to Boyle's country house, and a few yards from it lay the stiffened corpse of its master.—An *authentic narrative, taken from a tract*

The bridal wine cup

"Pledge with wine! Pledge with wine!" cried the young and thoughtless Harry. Pledge with wine ran through the bridal party.

The beautiful bride grew pale. She pressed her hands together, and the leaves of her bridal wreath trembled on her brow. Her breath came quicker, and her heart beat more wildly.

"Yes, Marian, lay aside your scruples for this once," said the judge, in a low tone. "The company expects it. Do not so seriously infringe upon the rules of etiquette. In your own home, do as you please, but in mine, for this once, please me."

Every eye was turned toward the bridal pair. Marian's principles were well known. Harry had been a convivialist, but of late his friends had noticed the change in his manner, and a difference in his habits.

Pouring a brimming cup, they held it with tempting smiles toward her. She was very pale, though now more composed. Smiling, she accepted the crystal tempter and raised it to her lips. But scarcely had she done so, when every hand was arrested by her piercing exclamation of, "Oh, how terrible!"

"What is it?" cried one and all, thronging together, for she had slowly carried the glass at arm's length, and was regarding it as if it were some hideous object.

"Wait," she said, "wait, and I will tell you. I see," she added, pointing her finger at the sparkling liquid, "a sight that beggars all description. And yet, listen, I will paint it for you if I can. It is a lovely spot; tall mountains, crowned with verdure, rise in awful sublimity around. A river runs through, and bright flowers grow to the water's edge. There is a thick, warm mist that the sun seeks vainly to pierce.

"Trees, lofty and beautiful, wave to the motion of the breeze, and in their midst lies a manly form—but his cheeks, how deathly! His eyes, how wildly they glare around him, with the fitful fires of fever! One friend stands beside him—I should say kneels—for see, he is pillowing that poor head upon his breast.

"Genius in ruins, on that high and holy looking brow. Why should death mark it, and he so young? Look, how he throws back the damp curls. See him clasp his hands. How he clutches at the form of his companion, imploring to be saved. Oh, hear him call piteously his father's name. See him twine his fingers together, as he shrieks for his sister, the twin of his soul, weeping for him in a distant native land. See! His arms are lifted to heaven. How wildly he prays for mercy. But fever rushes through his veins. The friend beside him is weeping. Awestricken, the dark men move silently away, and leave the living and the dying together."

There was a hush in that princely parlor, broken only by what seemed a sob from some manly bosom. The bride stood yet upright, with quivering lips, and tears streaming down her pallid cheeks. Her arm had lost its tension, and the glass with its contents came slowly toward the range of her vision. She spoke again. Every lip was mute. Her voice was low, faint, yet distinct. Still she fixed her sorrowful glance upon the wine cup.

"It is evening now. The great white moon is coming up, and her beams fall gently on his forehead. He moves not. His eyes are rolling in their sockets, and are the piercing glances. In vain his friend whispers the names of father and sister. No soft hand and no gentle touch blesses or soothes him. His head shrinks back. One convulsive shudder, and he is dead."

A groan ran through the assembly. So vivid was her description, so unearthly her look, so inspiring her manner, that what she described seemed actually to have taken place then and there. They noticed also that the bridegroom had hidden his face, and was weeping.

REMARKABLE ANSWERS TO PRAYER

"Dead!" she repeated again, her lips quivering faster, as if her heart were broken; "and then they scooped him a grave, and without a shroud, they lay him down in the damp reeky earth, the only son of a proud father, the idolized brother of a fond sister, and he sleeps today in that distant country, with no stone to mark the spot.

"There he lies, my father's son, my own twin brother a victim of this deadly poison! Father!" she exclaimed, turning suddenly, while the tears rolled down her cheeks, "father, shall I drink the poison now?"

The form of the judge was convulsed with agony. He raised not his head, but in a smothered voice he faltered, "No, my child, no!"

She lifted the glittering goblet, and letting it fall suddenly to the floor, it was dashed to pieces. Many a tearful eye watched her movements, and instantaneously every glass was transferred to the marble table. Then, as she looked at the fragments of crystal, she turned to the company, saying, "Let no friend of mine who loves me, hereafter tempt me to peril my soul with wine or any other poisonous venom. Not firmer are the everlasting hills, God helping me, than my resolve never to touch or taste the terrible poison. And he to whom I have given my hand, who watched over my brother's dying form in that land of gold, will sustain me in my resolve. Will you not, my husband?"

His glistening eye, his sad, sweet smile was the answer. The judge had left the room, but when he returned and, with a more subdued manner, took part in the entertainment of the bridal guests, none could fail to see that he, too, had determined to banish the enemy, and at once, from that princely home.

Reader, this is no fiction. I was there, and heard the words which I have penned, as nearly as I can recollect them.

This bride, her husband, and her brother, who died in the gold regions of California, were schoolmates of mine. Those who were present at the wedding of my associates never forgot the impression so solemnly made, and all from that hour forsook the social glass.—*Selected*

A mother's faith—the life of Beate Paulus

In a sketch of the life of Beate Paulus, the wife of a German minister who lived on the borders of the Black Forest, are several incidents which illustrate the power of living faith, and the providence of a prayer-hearing God. Though destitute of wealth, she much desired to educate her children, and five of her six boys were placed in school, while she struggled, and prayed, and toiled, not only in the house, but out of doors, to provide for their necessities.

"On one occasion," writes one of her children, "shortly before harvest, the fields stood thick with corn, and our mother had already calculated that their produce would suffice to meet all claims for the year. She was standing at the window casting the matter over in her mind, with great satisfaction when her attention was suddenly caught by some heavy, black clouds with white borders, drifting at a great rate across the summer sky. 'It is a hailstorm!' she exclaimed, in dismay, and quickly throwing up the window, she leaned out. Her eyes rested upon a frightful mass of wild stormclouds, covering the western horizon, and approaching with rapid fury.

" 'Oh God,' she cried, 'there comes an awful tempest, and what is to become of my corn?' The black masses rolled nearer and nearer, while the ominous rushing movement that precedes a storm began to rock the sultry air, and the dreaded hailstones fell with violence. Half beside herself with anxiety about those fields, lying at the eastern end of the valley, she now lifted her hands heavenward, and wringing them in terror, cried, 'Dear Father in heaven, what art thou doing? Thou knowest I cannot manage to pay for my boys at school, without the produce of those fields! Oh, turn Thy hand, and do not let the hail blast my hopes!'

Scarcely, however, had these words crossed her lips, when she started, for it seemed as if a voice had whispered in her ear, 'Is my arm shortened that it cannot help thee in other ways?' Abashed, she shrank into a quiet corner, and there entreated God to forgive her want of faith. In the meantime the storm passed. And now various neighbors hurried in, proclaiming that the whole valley lay thickly covered with hailstones, down to the very edge of the parsonage fields, but the latter had been quite spared. The storm had reached their border, and then suddenly took another direction into the next valley. Moreover, the whole village was in amazement, declaring that God had wrought a miracle for the sake of our mother, whom he loved. She listened, silently adoring the goodness of the Lord, and vowing that henceforth her confidence should be only in Him."

At another time she found herself unable to pay the expenses of the children's schooling. The repeated demands for money were rendered more grievous by the reproaches of her husband, who charged her with attempting impossibilities, and told her that her self will would involve them in disgrace. She, however, professed her unwavering confidence that the Lord would soon interpose for their relief, while his answer was, "We shall see. Time will show."

In the midst of these trying circumstances, as her husband was one day sitting in his study, absorbed in meditation, the postman brought three letters from different towns where the boys were at school, each declaring that unless the dues were promptly settled, the lads would be dismissed. The father read the letters with growing excitement, and spreading them out upon the table before his wife as she entered the room, exclaimed, "There, look at them, and pay our debt with your faith. I have no money, nor can I tell where to go for any."

"Seizing the papers, she rapidly glanced through them, with a very grave face, but then answered firmly, 'It is all right; the business shall be settled. For He who says, "The gold and silver are mine," will find it an easy thing to provide these sums.' Saying which she hastily left the room.

"Our father readily supposed she intended making her way to a certain rich friend who had helped us before. He was mistaken, for this time her steps turned in a different direction. We had in the parsonage an upper loft, shut off by a trapdoor from the lower one, and over this door it was that she now knelt down, and began to deal with Him in whose strength she had undertaken the work of her children's education. She spread before Him those letters from the study table, and told him of her husband's half scoffing taunt. She also reminded Him how her life had been redeemed from the very gates of death, for the children's sake, and then declared that she could not believe that He meant to forsake her at this juncture. She was willing to be the second whom He might forsake, but she was determined not to be the first.

"In the meanwhile, her husband waited downstairs, and night came on, but she did not appear. Supper was ready, and yet she stayed in the loft. Then the eldest girl, her namesake Beate, ran up to call her, but the answer was, 'Take your supper without me. It is not time for me to eat.' Late in the evening, the little messenger was again dispatched, but returned with the reply, 'Go to bed; the time has not come for me to rest.' A third time, at breakfast next morning, the girl called her mother. 'Leave me alone,' she said. 'I do not need breakfast. when I am ready I shall come.' Thus the hours sped on, and downstairs her husband and children began to feel frightened, not daring, however, to disturb her anymore.

"At last the door opened, and she entered, her face beaming with a wonderful light. The little daughter thought that something extraordinary must have happened; and running to her mother with open arms, asked eagerly, 'What is it? Did an angel from heaven bring the money?'

" 'No, my child,' was the smiling answer, 'but now I am sure that it will come.' She had hardly spoken, when a maid in peasant costume entered, saying, 'The master of the Linden Inn sends to ask whether the Frau Pastorin can spare time to see him?'

" 'Ah, I know what he wants,' answered our mother. 'My best regards, and I will come at once.' Whereupon she started, and mine host looking out of his window saw her from afar, and came forward to welcome her with the words, 'Oh, madame, how glad I am you have come!' Then leading her into his back parlor, he said, 'I cannot tell how it is, but the whole of this last night I could not sleep for thinking of you. For some time I have had several hundred gulden lying in that chest, and all night long I was haunted by the thought that you needed this money, and that I ought to give it to you. If that be the case, there it is. Take it, and do not trouble about repaying me. Should you be able to make it up again, well and good. If not, never mind.'

"On this my mother said, 'Yes, I do most certainly need it, my kind friend, for all last night I too was awake, crying to God for help. Yesterday there came three letters, telling us that all our boys would be dismissed unless the money for their board is cleared at once.'

" 'Is it really so?' exclaimed the Innkeeper, who was a noble hearted and Christian man. 'How strange and wonderful! Now I am doubly glad I asked you to come!' Then opening the chest, he produced three weighty packets and handed them to her with a prayer that God's blessing might rest upon the gift.

"She accepted it with the simple words, 'May God make good to you this service of Christian sympathy, for you have acted as the steward of One who has promised not even to leave the giving of a cup of cold water unrewarded.'

"Husband and children were eagerly awaiting her at home, and those three dismal letters still lay open on the table, when the mother, who had quitted that study in such deep emotion the day before stepped up to her husband, radiant with joy. On each letter she laid a roll of money, and then cried, 'Look, there it is. And now believe that faith in God is no empty madness.' "—*Wonders of Prayer.*

Dying words of Miss Mary Willard

(This devoted young lady was the sister of the well-known Frances E. Willard. She left this vale of tears June 8th, 1862. The record of her life is fully given in *Nineteen Beautiful Years*. We copy the following from *Glimpses of Fifty Years*, her sister's autobiography.—Editor)

On the last day of her life, she was lying with her head in father's lap, and she asked to have the Bible read. He said, "Where shall I read?"

She told him, "Oh, where it makes Christ seem beautiful!" He read a psalm. She said, "Please read where it says, Christ was sorry for sick folks." Father read about the healing of the daughter of Jairus." She liked it, but when he had finished,

REMARKABLE ANSWERS TO PRAYER

her plaintive voice cried out, "Please read where it says he is sorry now." After awhile she added, "We believe that God loves us better than our mothers. Yet mother would have liked me to get well, and God doesn't seem to care. He doesn't seem to see fit to make me well, yet He knows what is right."

In the night she was worse. She wanted everything still; kept moving her hands in a soothing, caressing way, and muttering: "So quiet, so quiet, no noise, so quiet!" At four o'clock, on the morning of the 8th of June, Sabbath morning, we became greatly alarmed, and for the first time father and I decided that she could not get well. I went at his suggestion for Mrs. Bannister and Mary. Father said to our Mary, for the first time coming directly to the subject of her danger, "My child, if God should think it best to take you to Himself, should you be afraid to go?"

She looked quickly at him, with rather a pitiful face. She seemed to consider a moment, and then said, in her low, mournful tone, "I thought I should like to get well, for I am young. But if God wants me to go, I shouldn't be much afraid, but should say, 'Take me, God.'"

We asked if there was anything we could do for her. "Pray," she said, "pray thankful prayers." Mother asked her if she saw Christ, if he was near her.

"Yes, I see him," she said, "but He is not very near. I wish he would come nearer."

I asked her if we should pray. She said, "Yes," and I prayed aloud, that Christ would come close to her, that she might see and feel him plainly; that since she had tried to love and obey Him, He would come right to her now in her great need. She clasped her hands together, and said, so joyfully, "He's come, He's come! He holds me by the hand. He died for me. He died for all this family—father, mother, Oliver, Frank," and Mary Bannister says she added, "my dear sister."

"I'll have Him all to myself," she said, and then seemed to remember and added, "I'll have Him, and everybody may have him, too. There is enough for everybody. He is talking to me. He says, 'She tried to be good, but she wandered; but I will save her;'" and added, "I see Him on the cross. He died for the thief. He didn't die for good people, but for bad people. He died for me."

I said, "I want to ask you to forgive me for all my unkind actions to you, for everything bad I ever did to you."

She answered very earnestly, "Oh! I do, but you never did anything bad. You were always good." Mother asked her if she did not want to leave a message for Oliver. "Don't you think he will be with us in heaven?" she said. "Of course, He is working for God. Tell him to be good, and to make people good." When I asked for a message for her Sunday school class, she said, "Tell them to be good," and then added, with great earnestness, "Tell everybody to be good."

Almost at the last she said, with a bright smile on her face, "Oh! I'm getting more faith!"

Mother questioned, "My darling, you will meet us, won't you, at the Beautiful Gate?"

"Oh, yes! And you will all come, and, father, Christ wants you right off!"

She moved her hand convulsively, and said, "I've got Christ—He's right here!" Then she said to me, "Oh, I'm in great misery," and then, "Dear God, take me quick!" She held out her hands and said, "Take me quick, God. Take me on this side," turning toward the right. She lay still, bolstered up by pillows. I asked her if she knew me, and she repeated my name. Father asked her often if Christ was still near her. She would nod, but did not speak. She seemed troubled. After a few moments father bent over her, and slowly and with difficulty, she told him of her dread of being buried alive, and he promised her over and over again that she should not be. Then she gave some little directions about preparing her bed, as she said, "for those who lay me out," showing her perfect consciousness. She never spoke again, but opened her eyes and looked at us with such intentness, the pupils so wide, the iris so blue. I never saw such soul in human eyes before. She groaned a little then, and for some time, she did not move. Her eyes closed slowly, her face grew white.

Father said, "Lord Jesus, receive her spirit. Lord, we give her back to Thee. She was a precious treasure. We give her back to Thee." Mrs. Bannister closed Mary's eyes. Father and mother went into the sitting room, and cried aloud. I leaned on the railing at the foot of the bed, and looked at my sister—my sister Mary, and knew that she was dead—knew that she was alive! Everything was far off; I was benumbed, and am but waking to the tingling agony.

A cyclone of power and glory in answer to prayer

At a convention of Christian workers, held in April, 1882, we witnessed a spiritual cyclone. Forty or fifty ministers and laymen of different denominations had come together for prayer and counsel concerning the most important doctrines of the Christian church. Great differences of opinion were expressed, and the controversy became so sharp that some seemed offended, and the spiritual influence of the meeting sadly hindered. In fact, the powers of darkness threatened to come in like a flood, and overthrow the good that had already been done.

REMARKABLE ANSWERS TO PRAYER

But some there were in that little company who knew the mighty power of prayer, and in that hour of need went on their faces before God with strong crying and tears. The Spirit interceded with groanings that could not be uttered, and soon an indescribable sacredness came over the meeting. A sister, who is in general opposed to what are termed outward manifestations, was so pressed in spirit that she began to groan aloud, and then to exclaim, "The Lord shall have His way! The Lord shall have His way, the Lord shall have His way." Others began to weep. Then a minister, who had come to the meeting strongly opposed to the views set forth by the leading workers, jumped to his feet and shouted the praise of God, and began to tell of the mighty baptism of the Holy Ghost he had received. And sooner than we can write it, a veritable cyclone of God's power and glory swept over the place, carrying everything before it. Stubborn hearts yielded, and in a very few moments of time, many were saved and filled with the Spirit.

Of this convention and closing service, a minister who is now a presiding elder in the United Brethren Church says, "The interest increased steadily from first to last, closing up in a tornado of Divine power! None who were present the last evening can ever forget how, at the first shout of victory, nearly all of the congregation rushed out of the house, only to return and gaze in speechless wonder, as souls being brought under conviction for sin cried for pardon, or shouted their praises at being brought from nature's darkness to God's marvelous light. Others, groaning under the conviction for holiness, wrestled until the carnal mind was cast out; when some leaped for joy, and others were laid prostrate under the weight of glory. Eternity alone can tell the blessed results of that closing service."

God does not thus reveal himself to the children of men for naught, and already thousands have been influenced for good as a result of that Pentecostal outpouring of His Spirit.—*Editor*

Only a tallow dip

The following was related in an evangelistic meeting: A woman who had been bedridden for years lived near the railroad track, a long way from any other house. Nearby was a deep gully over which the railroad passed on a new, substantial iron bridge, as was supposed. There was a terrible wind one night. This poor woman, as was often the case, was alone.

All at once she beard a fearful crash. She felt sure it was the bridge. She looked at the clock. In ten minutes the through passenger train would be along. What should she do? Her son was away from home. Praying earnestly to God for help, she took the only light in the house, a tallow candle, and began to crawl, for she could not walk, toward the railroad track. How she ever got there she never knew. The track reached, she could hear the roar of the coming train.

She prayed this prayer: "Oh God, help me to light this candle, and keep it burning until the engineer sees it, and make him see it." God heard her prayer. The candle was lighted, there was a lull just when she waved the candle. Would the engineer see it? She heard a grating sound, she knew the brakes were set. She lost consciousness then, but the train came to a standstill a few feet from the yawning chasm. Hundreds of lives were saved. This weak, sick woman did what she could. God used what she had. He will use what you have for the saving of men, if you will do your part.—*Union Gospel News.*

Oh, Christian! If that poor woman felt so deeply the need, and made so great an effort to save the passengers on that train from physical death, how ought you to feel, and what effort ought you to make, in order to rescue the multitudes about you that are hurrying on to eternal ruin, unconscious of their danger and ready to perish, unless someone, who has the light and knowledge, goes to their rescue?

A manifestation of parental love

There are some who reject Christianity because it seems to them incredible that God would have taken so much trouble, as the New Testament represents him to have done, for the salvation of creatures so infinitely beneath Him as we are. They forget that the New Testament teaches also that God is our Father. That being true, I declare to you that it is not surprising that God made such sacrifice to save us. Even a man will not permit a child to perish—any child, it need not be his own—without putting forth mighty effort to save it.

One fact is worth a dozen arguments, and I will therefore ask you to listen to a humble man, as he relates an incident in his otherwise uneventful life. For a little while imagine yourself to be seated around the table of an American boardinghouse, where the inmates are spending an hour or two in the evening relating the more remarkable events that have occurred to them. Imagine that you are listening to one of the guests there, instead of to me:

My name is Anthony Hunt. I am a drover, and I live thirty miles away upon the western prairie. There wasn't a house in sight when we moved there, my wife and I, and now we haven't many neighbors, though those we have are good men.

One day about ten years ago, I went away from home to sell some fifty head of cattle, fine creatures as ever I saw. I was to buy some groceries and dry goods before

REMARKABLE ANSWERS TO PRAYER

I came back and, above all, a doll for our youngest child, Dolly. She never had a shop doll of her own, only the rag babies her mother made her. Dolly could talk of nothing else, and went down to the very gate to call after me to "buy a big one."

Nobody but a parent can understand how my mind was on that toy, and how, when the cattle were sold, the first thing I started off to buy was Dolly's doll. I found a large one with eyes that would open and shut when you pulled a wire, and had it wrapped up in paper, and tucked it under my arm while I had the parcels of calico, and delaine, and tea, and sugar put up. It might have been more prudent to have stayed until the morning, but I felt anxious to get back, and eager to hear Dolly's prattle about the doll she was so eagerly expecting.

I mounted a steady going old horse of mine and, pretty well loaded, started for home. Night set in before I was a mile from town, and settled down dark as pitch while I was in the midst of the wildest bit of road I know of. I could have felt my way through, I remembered it so well, and it was almost like doing that when a storm that had been brewing broke, and the rain fell in torrents. I was five, or maybe six miles from home, too. I rode on as fast as I could, but suddenly I heard a little cry, like a child's voice. I stopped short and listened. I heard it again. I called, and it answered me. I couldn't see a thing. All was dark as pitch. I got down and felt about in the grass; called again and again was answered.

Then I began to wonder. I'm not timid but I was known to be a drover, and to have money about me. I thought it might be a trap to catch me, and there to rob and murder me. I am not superstitious—not very—but how could a real child be out on the prairie in such a night at such an hour? It might be more than human. The bit of coward that hides itself in most men showed itself to me then, and I was half inclined to run away. But once more I heard that piteous cry, and said I, "If any man's child is hereabouts, Anthony Hunt is not the man to let it lie here and die."

I searched again. At last I bethought me of a hollow under the hill, and groped that way. Sure enough, I found a little dripping thing, that moaned and sobbed as I took it in my arms. I called my horse, and he came to me, and I mounted, and tucked the little soaked thing under my coat as best I could, promising to take it home to mamma. It seemed tired to death, and soon cried itself to sleep against my bosom. It had slept there over an hour when I saw my own windows. There were lights in them, and I supposed my wife had lit them for my sake, but when I got into the front yard, I saw something was the matter, and stood still with dead fear of heart five minutes before I could lift the latch. At last I did it, and saw the room full of neighbors, and my wife amid them weeping. When she saw me she hid her face.

"Oh, don't tell him," she said. "It will kill him."

"What is it, neighbors?" I cried and one said, "Nothing now, I hope. What's that in your arms?"

"A poor lost child," said I. "I found it on the road. Take it, will you? I've turned faint." And I lifted the sleeping thing, and saw the face of my own child, my little Dolly. It was my darling, and no other, that I had picked up on the drenched road. My little child had wandered out to meet papa and the doll, while her mother was at work, and for her they were lamenting as for one dead.

I thanked God on my knees before them all. It is not much of a story, neighbors, but I think of it often in the nights, and wonder how I could bear to live now, if I had not stopped when I heard the cry for help upon the road, the little baby cry, hardly louder than a squirrel's chirp.

Is God less pitiful than man? "Like as a father pitieth his children, so the Lord pitieth them that fear him." Did you notice the last sentence in that man's story? "It is not much of a story, neighbors, but I think of it often in the nights, and wonder how I could bear to live now if I had not stopped when I heard that cry for help upon the road, the little baby cry, hardly louder than a squirrel's chirp."

To me that sentence explains the whole story of redemption. That man's love for his child was such that life would have been intolerable to him had he failed to save her.

Sinner! God the Father listened to the cry for help, the piteous wail of misery that ascended to Him from His lost children, and he sent His Son to seek and to save that which was lost. For, be it remembered, He knew not merely that certain children were perishing, but that they were His children.—*Homiletic Cyclopoedia.*

There's the Lord's answer

Many years ago, when in my country charge, I returned one afternoon from a funeral, fatigued with the day's work. After a long ride, I had accompanied the mourners to the churchyard. As I neared my stable door, I felt a strange prompting to visit a poor widow who, with her invalid daughter, lived in a lonely cottage in an outlying part of the parish. My natural reluctance to make another visit was overcome by a feeling I could not resist, and I turned my horse's head toward the cottage.

I was thinking only of the poor widow's spiritual needs, but when I reached her little house, I was struck with its look of unwonted bareness and poverty. After putting a little money into her hand, I began to inquire into their circumstances, and found that their supplies had been utterly exhausted since the night before. I asked them what they had done.

"I just spread it before the Lord!"

"Did you tell your case to any friend?"

"Oh no, sir; naebody kens but Himsel' and me! I kent He would not forget; but I didna ken hoo He wad help me, till I seen you come riding over the brae, and then I said, 'There's the Lord's answer!'" Many a time has the recollection of this incident encouraged me to trust in the loving care of my heavenly Father.— *New Testament Anecdotes*

A lesson for mothers

A little girl once said, "Mother, does God ever scold?" She had seen her mother under circumstances of strong provocation lose her temper, and give way to the impulse of passion, and pondering thoughtfully for a moment, she asked, "Mother, does God ever scold?"

The question was so abrupt and startling, that it arrested the mother's attention almost with a shock, and she said, "Why, my child, what makes you ask such a question?"

"Because, mother, you have always told me that God was good, and that we should try to be like Him, and I should like to know if he ever scolds."

"No, my child, of course not."

"Well, I'm glad he don't, for scolding always hurts me, even if I feel I have done wrong, and it don't seem to me that I could love God very much if he scolded."

The mother felt rebuked before her simple child. Never before had she heard so forcible a lecture on the evils of scolding. The words of the child sank deep in her heart, and she turned away from the innocent face of her little one to hide the tears that gathered to her eyes.

Children are quick observers, and the child, seeing the effect of her words, eagerly inquired, "Why do you cry, mother? Was it naughty for me to say what I said?"

"No, my love, it was all right. I was only thinking that I might have spoken more kindly, and not have hurt your feelings by speaking so hastily, and in anger, as I did."

"Oh mother, you are good and kind, only I wish there were not so many bad things to make you fret and talk as you did just now. It makes me feel away from you so far, as if I could not come near you, as I can when you speak kindly. And, oh, sometimes I fear I shall be put off so far I can never get back again!"

"No, my child, don't say that," said the mother, unable to keep back her tears, as she felt how her tones had repelled her little one from her heart.

The child, wondering what had so affected her parent, but intuitively feeling it was a case requiring sympathy, reached up, and throwing her arms about her mother's neck, whispered, "Mother, dear mother, do I make you cry? Do you love me?"

"Oh, yes! I love you more than I can tell," said the parent, clasping the little one to her bosom, "and I will try never to scold again, but if I have to reprove my child, I will try to do it, not in anger, but kindly, deeply as I may be grieved that she has done wrong."

"Oh, I am so glad. I can get so near to you if you don't scold! And do you know, mother, I want to love you so much, and I will try always to be good?"

The lesson was one that sank deep in that mother's heart, and has been an aid to her for many years. It impressed the great principle of reproving in kindness, not in anger, if we would gain the great end of reproof—that of winning the child to what is right, and to the parent's heart.—*Mother, Home, and Heaven.*

I'm so glad you have come!

I believe it to be a great characteristic of the American heart, that it clings to home and mother. I remember passing over a battlefield, and seeing a man just dying. His mind was wandering. His spirit was no longer on that bloody field. It was at his home far away. A smile passed over his face—a smile, oh, of such sweetness, as looking up he said, "Oh mother! Oh mother! I'm so glad you have come!" And it seemed as if she were there by his side. By and by he said again, "It's cold! It's cold! Won't you pull the blanket over me?" I stooped down, and pulled the poor fellow's ragged blanket closer to his shivering form. And he smiled again. "That will do, mother; that will do!" And so, turning over, he passed sweetly into rest, and was borne up into the presence of God on the wings of a pious mother's prayers.—G. J. *Mingins*

9

A mother's prayer answered

TRAINED RELIGIOUSLY, I HAD reached a young man's years before making a public profession of religion. Prior to my conversion, thoughts of the ministry sometimes flashed across my mind, but it was only a flash. After my conversion, I was earnest for the welfare of others, and wanted to promote the interests of the church and of humanity. The conviction grew upon me that I must preach, yet I tried to put that away, because I feared I could never succeed. I saw the greatness of the work, and the reproachful poverty then connected with the itinerant ministry.

There were two special difficulties in the way. First, I had no gift of speech. My voice was poor, and in school I always shunned declamation. I firmly believed I could never make a speaker, and so chose the profession of medicine, which I studied three years in a professional school.

I think I should have resolutely rejected the idea of the ministry, except that it seemed inseparably connected with my salvation. I fasted, I prayed for Divine direction, but I found no rest until, reading in the Bible one day, I found a passage which seemed especially written for me: "Trust in the Lord with all thy heart; lean not to thine own understanding; in all thy ways acknowledge Him, and He shall direct thy paths." I accepted it, and resolved to do whatever God in his providence should indicate by opening the way. I never lisped to a friend the slightest intimation of my mental agony, but I took a more earnest part in the church services.

One Sabbath I felt a strong impression that I ought to speak to the people at night in prayer meeting, as we had no preaching. I said to myself, "How shall I? For my friends will say I am foolish, as they know I cannot speak with interest." Especially I dreaded an old uncle, who had been a father to me, and superintended my education. While I was discussing this matter with myself in the afternoon, my uncle came into the room, and, after a moment's hesitation said to me, "Don't you think you could speak to the people tonight?" I was surprised and startled. I asked him if he thought I ought. He said, "Yes, I think you can do good."

That night, for some strange reason, the house was crowded, and I made my first religious address to a public congregation. It was not written. It was not very well premeditated. It was simply an outgushing of a sincere and honest heart.

My mother was a widow. I was her eldest son, the only child remaining at home. I feared it would break her heart to leave her, and feared it would be impossible to do so. One day, after great embarrassment, I was induced to speak to my mother on the subject of my mental struggles, and tell her what I thought God required of me. I never shall forget how she turned to me with a smile, and said, "My son, I have been looking for this hour ever since you were born!" She then told me how she and my dying father, who left me an infant, consecrated me to God, and prayed that, if it were His will, I might become a minister, and yet that mother had never dropped a word of intimation in my ear that she ever desired me to be a preacher. She believed so fully in the Divine call, that she would not bias my mind with even a suggestion of it in prayer.

That conversation settled my mind. Oh, what a blessing is a sainted mother! Today I can feel her hands on my head, and I hear the intonation of her voice in prayer.—*Bishop Simpson*

The prodigal

The Rev. Theodore Clapp, for many years a minister of religion in the city of New Orleans, narrates the following incident, which occurred within his experience:

Several years ago there was a lady, a mother, residing in one of the Northern States, distinguished for her wealth, social position, and religious character. She had a favorite son, for whose advancement in life great efforts had been made. But notwithstanding, he became a profligate and vagabond.

I had known the youth in our schoolboy days. The mother addressed to me a letter concerning her lost child. From the latest information she believed that he was wandering in the Southern States. She besought me, if I should meet the hapless fugitive, to acquaint her with the facts, and extend to him such offices of kindness as I might judge expedient.

A few days after the receipt of this letter, the young prodigal made his appearance in New Orleans, and found his way to my study. He was in a most woeful plight, both physically and morally. In manners he was rude, audacious, and grossly profane. He wanted money. "Money will do you no good," said I, "unless you reform your life,"

"Reform!" repeated he. "It is impossible. It is entirely too late. I have no hope. I can never retrieve my steps. I have nothing to live for. I am the curse of all who know me. I have not a friend left in the wide world."

On his saying this I went to my desk, and took out the letter from his mother. Showing him the superscription, I asked him if he knew the handwriting. A change came over his manner. He replied with a thoughtful air, "It is my dear mother's."

I opened the letter, and read to him a single paragraph and this was the sentence I read to him: "Oh my Heavenly Father, I beseech Thee to preserve, forgive, and redeem my poor lost child. In Thy infinite mercy, be pleased to restore him to my embrace, and to the joys of sincere repentance."

In a moment he seemed as if struck by some unseen power. He sank down upon his chair, burst into tears, sobbed aloud, and convulsively exclaimed, "Oh God, forgive my base ingratitude to that beloved mother!"

Yes, the thought of that fond parent, in a far-distant and dishonored home—who cherished for him an undying affection, who overlooked all his baseness, who never failed to mingle his outcast name with her morning and evening prayers—the thought of such tenderness broke his hard heart, and the waters of penitence rushed forth.

From that hour he was a reformed man. He is now an inhabitant of his native place, shedding around him the blessed influence of a sober, useful, and exemplary life.—*Mother, Home, and Heaven*

A great revival in answer to prevailing prayer

During the winter of 1885-86 we were called to hold a revival meeting in New Haven, Shiawassee county, Michigan. During the first few days of the meeting we found many difficulties, and the powers of darkness arrayed against the work. Keenly realizing our need, we went to God in earnest prayer, and soon experienced a wonderful travail of soul for the desolation of Zion. In less than twenty-four hours from the time this wonderful spirit of wrestling prayer was given us, the work commenced to move in earnest. The pastor, in sobs and tears, confessed that he was backslidden, asked pardon of some of his members, and came to the altar seeking forgiveness of God. Many professed Christians followed his example, and in a few days the whole country was in a flame of revival, such as had never been known in that section of the country. The spiritual condition of the community was so changed that for years sinners were converted at almost every public gathering of God's people. Never elsewhere have we witnessed so sweeping and thorough a work of grace, and such wonderful manifestations of God's presence and glory. Over two years after the commencement of that wonderful awakening, at a campmeeting held in the same community, a paper was drawn up endorsing our work, and signed by several ministers of the gospel and forty or fifty others. From that paper we clip the following statement in reference to this glorious revival, known in all that section as "the big revival."

"When Brother Shaw came, great division and lack of harmony existed among the members of the different churches in the neighborhood—Methodist, Episcopal, Free Methodist, Wesleyan Methodist, and German Evangelical. Bible Christianity was at a low ebb, but he preached the truth of God faithfully. He condemned sin of every kind. God honored the message by a mighty outpouring of the Holy Ghost. The truth went home to hearts. The whole county was stirred. Scores who opposed the work bitterly, for a time, were brought under conviction, saved, and became its warmest friends. Under the mighty power of God souls were humbled, confessions were made, wrongs were made right, and sectarian bigotry melted away. Hearts were united. Several ministers of the gospel knelt at the altar as seekers. The work was so thorough that no difference could be discovered among the members of the different churches. All were equally separated from the world, and equally baptized with the Holy Ghost and fire. During the meeting, lasting in all about seven weeks, between two and three hundred souls were gloriously converted, reclaimed or sanctified. Never has there been known in all this community such a revival."—*Editor*

Ship's crew saved in answer to prayer

I had a singular experience, which is very vivid to my mind. The precise year I cannot say, and I may be mistaken in the name of the vessel. But somewhere about the year 1860, the bark *Benjamin Burgess* sailed from Boston for Cienfugos. The crew were mostly from the house of which I had charge. There had been, and there still was, a powerful religious influence pervading our house. I said to the men as they were going on board, "Remember, I shall pray for you every day." I made it a practice, directly after midnight, to retire, and pray, and commune with God.

One day, after the bark had been gone about six weeks, while bringing up before the Lord the different cases, this crew was presented with unusual interest. I was thrown into an agony of feeling before God, and I cried to him to have mercy on that crew. Such were my feelings I noted the time. After the terrible struggle in prayer for God to save that crew, with strong cries and tears, there came into my feeling a great peace, as though prayer were answered, and that crew made safe. Unbeknown to me, the bark was chartered to go to Antwerp, and thence to Boston.

On their arrival back, I said, "Boys, did you have a hard time in either passage?"

"Yes," said they, "a fearful time on the voyage from Cienfugos to Antwerp. We were being driven upon the rocks in a terrible gale and storm. Captain Snow said to us, 'Boys, there is no hope and no deliverance, unless God helps us,' and sure enough, to our great astonishment, there came a wind from off the shore, and we were saved." The day of my agony of prayer before the Lord for that crew, that they might be saved, was the day they were having that terrible experience on the bark. I have no comments to make on that experience. I simply give the facts in the case.—N. Hamilton, in *Christian Witness*

A most miraculous escape

Mrs. C. Chipperfield, of Springfield, Ohio, sent us, in 1887, an account of several very clear and definite answers to prayer for the supply of temporal needs, received during her Christian experience of about ten years, during the greater part of which time she was a widow; and added, "I would like to tell you how the Lord mercifully saved my boy from death.

"While I was on my knees praying for him, I was strongly impressed that some evil was about to happen to him, and while in earnest prayer for him the burden was lifted, and he was saved from a terrible death. In crossing the railroad, where there were many tracks, in trying to avoid one engine he was knocked down by another, and dragged a distance of a block or more. But though his face and hands were terribly lacerated and filled with coal ashes, yet not a bone was broken. This was about eight years ago, and in the morning there was an article in the paper under the heading, *A Most Miraculous Escape*. And when the railroad men tried to explain to me that it was because the road was so smooth that he was dragged along, or if the ties had been above the ground he must have been crushed, I said, 'No, but God heard his mother's prayer.' "

Remarkable experience of C. H. Spurgeon

On his fiftieth birthday, Rev. C. H. Spurgeon was interviewed in reference to his long and eventful ministerial life, especially as to his confidence in the efficacy of prayer. Being asked whether he had in any way modified his views, he replied:

"Only in my faith growing far stronger and firmer than ever. It is not a matter of faith with me, but of knowledge and everyday experience. I am constantly witnessing the most unmistakable instances of answers to prayer. My whole life is made up of them. To me they are so familiar as to cease to excite surprise, but to many they would seem marvelous, no doubt. Why, I could no more doubt the efficacy prayer than I could disbelieve the laws of gravitation. The one is as much a fact as the other, constantly verified every day of my life. Elijah, by the brook Cherith, as he received the daily rations from the ravens, could hardly be a more likely subject for skepticism than I.

"Look at my orphanage. To keep it going entails an annual expenditure of about ten thousand pounds. Only one thousand four hundred is provided for by endowment. The remaining eight thousand six hundred comes to me regularly in answer to prayer. I do not know where I shall get it from day to day. I ask God for it, and he sends it. Mr. Müller, of Bristol, does the same on a far larger scale, and his experience is the same as mine.

"The constant inflow of funds—of all the funds necessary to carry on these works—is not stimulated by advertisements, by begging letters, by canvassing, or any of the usual modes of raising the wind. We ask God for the cash, and he sends it. That is a good, material fact, not to be explained away, but quite as remarkable illustrations of the efficacy of believing faith are constantly occurring in spiritual things.

"Some two years ago a poor woman, accompanied by her neighbors, came to my vestry in deep distress. Her husband had fled the country. In her sorrow she went to the house of God, and something I said in the sermon made her think I was personally familiar with her case. Of course I had known nothing about her. It was a general illustration that fitted a particular case. She told me her story, and a very sad one it was.

"I said, 'There is nothing we can do but to kneel down and cry to the Lord for the immediate conversion of your husband.' We knelt down, and I prayed that the Lord would touch the heart of the deserter, convert his soul, and bring him back to his home. When we rose from our knees, I said to the poor woman, 'Do not fret about the matter. I feel sure that your husband will come home, and that he will yet become connected with our church.' She went away, and I forgot all about it. Some months after she reappeared, with her neighbors, and a man, whom she introduced to me as her husband. He had indeed come back, and he had returned a converted man.

"On making inquiry and comparing notes, we found that the very day on which we had prayed for his conversion, he being at that time on board a ship far away on the sea, stumbled most unexpectedly upon a stray copy of one of my sermons. He read it. The truth went to his heart. He repented, and sought the Lord, and as soon as possible he returned to his wife and to his daily calling. He was admitted a member, and last Monday his wife, who up to that time had not been a member, was received among us. That woman does not doubt the power of prayer. All the infidels in the world could not shake her conviction that there is a God that answereth prayer.

"I should be the most irrational creature in the world if, with a life every day of which is full of experiences so remarkable, I entertained the slightest doubt on the subject. I do not regard it as miraculous. It is a part and parcel of the established order of the universe, that the shadow of a coming event should fall in advance upon some believing soul in the shape of prayer for its realization. The prayer of faith is a Divine decree commencing its operation."—*Faith Made Easy*

Kate Shelly's bravery

Six years ago Miss Shelly won a gold medal from the Iowa Legislature, "and a wealth of admiration from all who read of her act of heroism." The facts are these:

In a fearful thunderstorm and a torrent of falling rain, she looked out of her window in the darkness of the night, and by the vivid flashes of lightning shining on the scene, she saw that a railroad bridge near her home had been swept away by the storm. Just then she saw the headlight of a locomotive swiftly approaching the spot where the bridge had just been swept away. She lighted her lantern, and alone, amidst the thunder and lightning and storm, she crept up a rocky steep, and with her clothes torn to rags, and lacerated flesh, she reached the rails, and on her hands and knees crept out to the last tie of the fallen bridge, swung the lantern back and forth over the abyss, until she heard the faint voice of the engineer, who, though in the greatest peril himself, cried to her to go quickly and give the alarm to save the express train, which was then coming toward that perilous spot, and some help also, to rescue him.

She started for the nearest station, which was a mile away. To reach that station she had to cross a high trestle bridge of five hundred feet in length. She had gone but a few steps when a fearful gust of wind put out her lantern, which she then threw away, knowing that she could not relight it in the storm. She then dropped upon her hands and knees, and crept along from tie to tie over the trestle. Her way was lighted only by frequent flashes of lightning. After crossing the bridge she hastened along the rails by the flashes of lightning to the station, and with what strength she had left told her story, and then fell in a dead faint at the station-agent's feet.

Help went quickly to the poor engineer's rescue, and telegrams flew up and down the line, notifying all that the bridge was gone. While Miss Shelly lay yet unconscious, the express train came rushing into the depot. When the passengers learned what perils the brave girl had passed through to save them, and saw her still lying in an unconscious state, they took her up tenderly, and bathed her torn and bleeding limbs, and soon brought her back to consciousness.

Oh, how the scene beggars description, as the men and women gather about this brave girl of sixteen, looking upon her pale face, her torn and bleeding form. As they think how she went through all this to save their lives, words are too weak to express the deep gratitude of their hearts. They laid a substantial expression of their appreciation at her feet. Then, as the best they could do, they embraced her memory in their warmest affections, while the world placed a wreath of lasting honor on her brow. And Kate Shelly, living or dying, with her approving conscience, can say, "I did what I could."

What an example to all Christians, who see so clearly the dark abyss just a step before unconverted men, and they rushing with great speed towards it. Let us swing the lamp of truth before them, and cry with great earnestness, "Danger ahead! Bridge gone! No crossing but through the bleeding victim of Calvary!" May we all learn a lesson of sacrifice and effort to save others, from this incident, that, in the coming day Christ may say of us, "They have done what they could."–A. B. Earle.

He blesses God for the faith of his little girl
"I came home one night very late," says the Rev. Matthew Hale Smith, in his *Marvels of Prayer*, "and had gone to bed to seek needed rest. The friend with whom I boarded awoke me out of my first refreshing sleep, and informed me that a little girl wanted to see me. I turned over in bed, and said, " 'I am very tired, tell her to come in the morning, and I will see her.'

"My friend soon returned and said, 'I think you had better get up. The girl is a poor little suffering thing. She is thinly clad, is without bonnet or shoes. She has seated herself on the doorstep, and says she must see you, and will wait till you get up.'

"I dressed myself, and opening the outside door I saw one of the most forlorn-looking little girls I ever beheld. Want, sorrows, suffering, neglect, seemed to struggle for the mastery. She looked up to my face, and said, 'Are you the man that preached last night, and said that Christ could save to the uttermost?'

" 'Yes.'

" 'Well, I was there, and I want you to come right down to my house, and try to save my poor father.'

" 'What's the matter with your father?'

REMARKABLE ANSWERS TO PRAYER

" 'He's a very good father when he don't drink. He's out of work and he drinks awfully. He's almost killed my poor mother, but if Jesus can save to the uttermost, He can save him. And I want you to come right to our house now.'

"I took my hat and followed my little guide, who trotted on before, halting as she turned the corners to see that I was coming. Oh, what a miserable den her home was! A low, dark, underground room, the floor all slush and mud—not a chair, table, or bed to be seen. A bitter cold night, and not a spark of fire on the hearth and the room not only cold, but dark.

"In the corner, on a little dirty straw, lay a woman. Her head was bound up, and she was moaning as if in agony. As we darkened the doorway a feeble voice said, 'Oh my child! My child! Why have you brought a stranger into this horrible place?' Her story was a sad one, but soon told. Her husband, out of work, maddened with drink, and made desperate, had stabbed her because she did not provide him with a supper that was not in the house. He was then upstairs, and she was expecting every moment that he would come down and complete the bloody work he had begun. While the conversation was going on the fiend made his appearance. A fiend he looked. He brandished the knife, still wet with the blood of his wife.

"The missionary, like the man among the tombs, had himself belonged to the desperate classes. He was converted at the mouth of a coal pit. He knew the disease and the remedy—knew how to handle a man on the borders of delirium tremens.

"Subdued by the tender tones, the madman calmed down, and took a seat on a box. But the talk was interrupted by the little girl, who approached the missionary, and said, 'Don't talk to father; it won't do any good. If talking would have saved him, he would have been saved long ago. Mother has talked to him so much and so good. You must ask Jesus, who saves to the uttermost, to save my poor father.'

"Rebuked by the faith of the little girl, the missionary and the miserable sinner knelt down together. He prayed as he never had prayed before. He entreated and interceded, in tones so tender and fervent, that it melted the desperate man, who cried for mercy. And mercy came. He bowed in penitence before the Lord, and lay down that night on his pallet of straw a pardoned soul.

"Relief came to that dwelling. The wife was lifted from her dirty couch, and her home was made comfortable. On Sunday, the reformed man took the hand of his little girl and entered the infant class, to learn something about the Savior 'who saves to the uttermost.' He entered upon a new life. His reform was thorough. He found good employment, for when sober he was an excellent workman, and next to his Savior, he blesses God for the faith of his little girl, who believed in a Savior able to save to the uttermost all that come unto God by him."

The greatest revival of the Christian era

Dr. Lyman Beecher said of the great revival in Rochester, N. Y., conducted by Mr. Finney, that it was the greatest revival in the Christian era. During Mr. Finney's evangelistic ministry hundreds of thousands were converted to God through his labors, joined to those of the church. His *Lectures on Revivals* have been most wonderfully blessed in the conversion of sinners, directly and indirectly, not only in this country, but in foreign countries. When they were published in this country, 12,000 of them were sold as fast as they could be printed. They were reprinted in England and France. They were translated into Welsh, French and German. One publisher in London put out 80,000 volumes of them. Great revivals followed wherever they circulated.

But why did such revivals follow Mr. Finney's preaching, and the reading of his lectures? I will let Mr. Finney answer this question himself. Said he, in his autobiography, "Let the reader remember that long day of agony and prayer at sea, that God would do something to forward the work of revivals, and enable me, if He desired to do it, to take such a course as to help forward the work. I felt certain then that my prayers would be answered, and I have regarded all that I have since been able to accomplish, as in a very important sense, an answer to the prayers of that day. The spirit of prayer came upon me as a sovereign grace, bestowed upon me without the least merit, and in despite of all my sinfulness. He pressed my soul in prayer until I was enabled to prevail, and through infinite riches of grace in Christ Jesus. I have been many years witnessing the wonderful results of that day of wrestling with God. In answer to that day's agony, He has continued to give me the spirit of prayer."

Said Dr. N. Murray, "Prayer is the power of the Church, and could I speak as loud as the trumpet which is to wake the dead, I would thus call upon the Church, in all branches and in all lands, 'Awake! Awake! Put on thy strength, O Zion! Put on thy beautiful garments, O Jerusalem! Arise, shine, for thy light is come, and the glory of the Lord is risen upon thee.' Patriarchs, prophets, apostles, martyrs, reformers, were mighty in prayer."—*Prevailing Prayer*, by *Wigle*

The widow and the judge

Sometime about the commencement of the year 1871, a train was passing over the North Western Railroad, between Oskaloosa and Madison. In two of the seats, facing each other, sat three lawyers engaged at cards. Their fourth player had just left the carriage, and they needed another to take his place. "Come, judge, take a hand," they said to a grave magistrate, who sat looking on, but whose face indicated no approval of their play. He shook his head, but after repeated urgings, finally, with a flushed countenance, took a seat with them, and the playing went on.

A venerable woman, gray and bent with years, sat and watched the judge from her seat near the end of the railway carriage. After the game had progressed awhile, she arose, and with trembling hand and almost overcome with emotion approached the group. Fixing her eyes intently on the judge, she said in a tremulous voice, "Do you know me, judge–?"

"No, mother, I don't remember you," said the judge, pleasantly. "Where have we met?"

"My name is Smith," said she, "I was with my poor boy three days, off and on, in the courtroom at Oskaloosa, when he was tried for–for–for robbing somebody, and you are the same man that sent him to prison for ten years, and he died there last June."

All faces were now absorbed, and the passengers began to gather around and stand up all over the car, to listen to and see what was going on. She did not give the judge time to answer her but becoming more and more excited, she went on.

"He was a good boy, if you did send him to jail. He helped us clear the farm, and when father took sick and died, done all the work, and we were getting along right smart. He was a stidy boy until he got to card-playin' an' drinkin', and then, somehow, he didn't like to work after that, and stayed out often till mornin' and he'd sleep so late, and I couldn't wake him when I knowed he'd been out so late the night afore. And then the farm kinder run down, and then we lost the team, one of them got killed when he'd been to town one awful cold night. He stayed late, and I suppose they had got cold standin' out, and got skeered and broke loose, and run most home, but run agin a fence, and a stake run into one of 'em, and when we found it next mornin' it was dead, and the other was standin' under the shed.

"And so, after a while, he coaxed me to let him sell the farm, and buy a house and lot in the village, and he'd work at carpenter work. And so I did, as we couldn't do nothin' on the farm. But he grew worse than ever, and after awhile, he couldn't get any work, and wouldn't do anything but gamble and drink all the time. I used to do everything I could to get him to quit and be a good, industrious boy agin', but he used to get mad after awhile, and once he struck me, and then in the morning I found he had taken what little money there was left of the farm, and had run off. After that time I got along as well as I could, cleanin' house for folks and washin', but I didn't hear nothin' of him for four or five years. But when he got arrested and was took up to Oskaloosa for trial, he writ to me."

By this time there was not a dry eye in the car, and the cards had disappeared. The old lady herself was weeping silently, and speaking in snatches. But recovering herself, she went on. "But what could I do? I sold the house and lot to get money to hire a lawyer, and I believe he is here somewhere," looking around. "Oh, yes, there he is, Mr.——," pointing to a lawyer, who had not taken part in the play. "And this is the man, I am sure, who argued agin' him," pointing to Mr. ——, the district attorney.

"And you, judge, sent him to prison for ten years. 'Spose it was right, for the poor boy told me that he really did rob the bank. But he must have been drunk, for they had all been playin' cards most all the night, and drinkin'. But, oh dear! It seems to me kinder as though if he hadn't got to playin' cards he might a been alive yet. But when I used to tell him it was wrong and bad to play, he used to say, 'Why, mother, everybody plays now. I never bet only for the candy, or the cigars, or something like that.' And when we heard that the young folks played cards down to Mr. Culver's donation party, and that Squire Ring was goin' to get a billiard table for his young folks to play on at home, I couldn't do nothin' with him. We used to think it was awful to do that way, when I was young. But it jist seems to me as if everybody was goin' wrong nowadays into something or other.

"But may be it isn't right for me to talk to you, judge, in this way but it jist seemed to me the very sight of them cards would kill me. Judge, I thought if you only knew how I felt, you would not play on so. And then to think, right here before these young folks! Maybe, judge, you don't know how younger folks, especially boys, look up to such as you, and then I can't help thinking that maybe if them that ought to know better than to do so, and them as are better larnt and all that, wouldn't set sich examples, my Tom would be alive and caring for his poor old mother. But now, there ain't any of my family left but me and my poor granchile, my darter's little girl, and we are going to stop with my brother in Illinoy."

Tongue of man or angel never preached a more eloquent sermon than that gray, withered old lady, trembling with old age, excitement and fear that she was doing wrong. I can't recall half she said, as she, poor, lone, beggared widow, stood before the noble looking men, and pleaded the cause of the rising generation. The look they bore as she poured forth her sorrowful tale was indescribable. To say that they looked like criminals at the bar would be a faint description. I can imagine how they felt. The old lady tottered to her seat, and taking her little grandchild in her lap, hid her face on her neck.

The little one stroked her gray hair with one hand and said, "Don't cry, grandma; don't cry, grandma." Eyes unused to weeping were red for many a mile on that journey. And I can hardly believe that anyone who witnessed that scene ever touched a card again. It is but just to say that when the passengers came to themselves, they generously responded to the judge, who, hat in band, silently passed through her little audience.—Selected

Saved from the flames and waves, and shall be from sins
A Christian wife, whose husband was an officer on a Mississippi steamer, which was burned as she prayed that her husband would be preserved and saved, not knowing of the disaster, was assured that his life would be spared, and that he would be saved. When, the day following, she received a telegram, stating that her husband had perished, she folded it and said, "It is not so. He is saved from the flames and waves, and shall be from his sins." A few days later he arrived at home, and was soon converted. The faith of this Christian wife, after praying earnestly, was of the same nature as the faith of Luther, who, after praying nearly all night, with some of his friends, exclaimed: "Deliverance has come! Deliverance has come!"—*Rev. S. A. Keene, in* Prevailing Prayer

The famous Praying Johnny
This eminent saint of God labored in England during the early history of Methodism. His biographer, Harvey Leigh, says, "Our brother was an extraordinary man in the importunity and prevalence of his prayers. What has been said of the strength and constancy of his faith may be said with equal propriety, of his importunate and prevalent prayers; that is, he was second to none. In fact, we need not be surprised at this, for generally these two excellences walk hand in hand. For some years he was known in the religious world to thousands by the singular name of *Praying Johnny*. This epithet he justified in the whole of his conduct. His prayers were long and very fervent in his own closet.

"Mr. Bottomley, who was stationed with him in the Halifax circuit, says, 'During the time of his stay at Halifax, he was much given up to prayer, and generally spent about six hours each day upon his knees pleading earnestly with God, in behalf of himself, the church and sinners, whose salvation he most ardently desired.'

"Frequently, when harassed by any particular temptation, when concerned about the temporal condition of any person in dangerous affliction, when under engagement to pray for one who was troubled with an evil spirit, when foiled in some late attempt to do good, when travailing in anguish of mind for a revival of religion in the neighborhood in which he was laboring, and when deeply anxious to see the glory of the Lord revealed, he has spent many hours in the most decided abstinence and secluded retirement; and has sometimes in this manner devoted whole days and nights to God. In the public services of the sanctuary John had great influence with God in prayer. In answer to the earnest breathings of his soul, a whole assembly has been moved as the trees of a wood are moved when shaken with a strong wind. A mighty shaking has been felt, and a great noise heard, amongst the dry bones. The breath of Jehovah has been felt, numbers among the slain have been quickened, and a great army has been raised up.

"A strange fact connected with the history of this good man, and strikingly illustrative of his close communion with God in prayer, and of the results of such communion, we shall here relate.

"When in Hull circuit, he visited Burlington Quay, and was rendered eminently useful. When there, his home was with Mr. Stephenson, whose family was one of the most influential in the place. Their mercantile engagements were numerous. At home they carried on a considerable business, and were extensively connected with the shipping department. About the year 1825 Mr. Stephenson had a ship at sea, on a foreign and distant voyage, about the safety of which he and the family began to feel anxious. There had not been any tidings of the vessel extending over a period far beyond what they had expected. And what tended much to increase their solicitude, they had a son on board for whom they feared the worst, feared that they should see him no more. At this time Mr. Oxtoby was sojourning in the family, and was painfully concerned at witnessing their anxiety. Pressed in spirit for them, and desirous to be the instrument of their relief, he fell back upon his usual and safe resort—special fasting and protracted prayer to God in which he besought the Almighty to give him an assurance whether the ship was really lost, or whether it would return home in safety.

"In his protracted travail, he clearly ascertained that the ship, which had been the object of so much solicitude, was not lost, but that it and the son for whose safety the family were so anxious would, in due course, return in safety and that all would be well. This welcome intelligence he communicated to the anxious family, and did it with as much confidence as characterized St. Paul's mind, when he uttered his noble speech to the embarrassed ship's crew, while they drew near to the island of Melita, and, contrary to all human appearance, assured them that not a hair of their heads should perish.

"But high as our brother stood in the estimation of the family, and exalted as was their opinion of his extraordinary piety, and the power and prevalence of his prayers, yet his calm and positive assertions on this subject almost exceeded the powers of their belief, and though they did not distrust them, they staggered at them. But John remained unmoved. He smiled at their doubts, reiterated his expressions of confidence, told them that God had 'shown him the ship while at prayer;' that he was as certain of her safe return as if she were in the harbor then; and that when the vessel returned, though he had never seen her, excepting when revealed to him in prayer, he should know her, and could easily distinguish her from any other.

"Time rolled on, John pursued his work, and the family remained anxious, when news reached them one day that the vessel was safe and on her way home. It soon after arrived, at which time Mr. Oxtoby was about ten miles distant in the country. The Stephenson family were, however, so delighted with the occurrence—with the realization of all their devoted friend had uttered with the accomplishment of what, to them, appeared like a prediction, and from which the good man had never wavered—no, not for a moment—that a gig was immediately sent for him, by which he was to return with the least possible delay. When he reached Burlington Quay, Mr. Stephenson asked him if he should know the ship about which be had sought Divine counsel, providing he could see her.

" 'I should,' said John, 'God so clearly revealed her to me in prayer, that I could distinguish her among a hundred.'

"Then they walked out on the pier, and on their left were many vessels, some near and some remote, floating at anchor in the spacious bay. Among them John looked, and exclaimed, while pointing in a certain direction, 'That's the ship which God showed me while at prayer. I knew she would come home safely, and that I should see her.' We need scarcely add that in this he was correct, and that this last particular of the strange account filled Mr. Stephenson with overwhelming amazement."—*Shining Lights*

How three Sunday school children met their fate

When the Lawrence Mills were on fire a number of years ago—I don't mean on fire, but when the mill fell in—the great mill fell in, and after it had fallen in, the ruins caught fire. There was only one room left entire, and in it were three Mission Sunday-school children imprisoned. The neighbors and all hands got their shovels, and picks, and crowbars, and were working to set the children free. It came on night, and they had not yet reached the children.

When they were near them, by some mischance a lantern broke, and the ruins caught fire. They tried to put it out, but could not succeed. They could talk with the children, and even pass to them some coffee and some refreshments, and encourage them to keep up. But, alas, the flames drew nearer and nearer to this prison. Superhuman were the efforts made to rescue the children. The men bravely fought back the flames, but the fire gained fresh strength, and returned to claim its victims. Then piercing shrieks arose when the spectators saw that the efforts of the firemen were hopeless.

The children saw their fate. They then knelt down and commenced to sing the little hymn we have all been taught in our Sunday school days, oh! how sweet: "Let others seek a home below, which flames devour and waves overflow." The flames had now reached them. The stifling smoke began to pour into their little room, and they began to sink, one by one, upon the floor. A few moments more and the fire circled around them, and their souls were taken into the bosom of Christ. Yes, let others seek a home below if they will, but seek ye the Kingdom of God with all your hearts.—*Moody's Anecdotes*

The dying child's prayer for her drunken father

A child from a poor family had an intemperate father who often used to abuse his wife and children. This child had been to the Sunday school, had become pious. The physician told the father that his little girl would die. No! He did not believe it. Yes, she will, she must die in a few hours. The father flew to the bedside, would not part with her, he said.

"Yes, father, you must part with me, I am going to Jesus. Promise me two things. One is that you won't abuse mother any more, and will drink no more whisky." He promised in a solemn, steady manner. The little girl's face lighted up with joy. "The other thing is, promise me that you will pray," said the child.

"I cannot pray, don't know how," said the poor man.

"Father, kneel down, please. There, take the words after me, I will pray. I learned how to pray in Sunday school, and God has taught me how to pray too. My heart prays, you must let your heart pray. Now say the words."

And she began in her simple language to pray to the Savior of sinners. After a little he began to repeat after her. As he went on his heart was interested, and he broke out into an earnest prayer for himself, bewailed his sins, confessed and promised to forsake them, entered into covenant with God. Light broke out upon him in his darkness, how long he did not know. He seemed to have forgotten his child in his prayer. When he came to himself he raised his head from the bed on which he had rested it. There lay the speaker, a lovely smile was upon the face, her little hand was in that of the father, but she had gone to be among the angels.—*Power of Prayer, by Prime*

REMARKABLE ANSWERS TO PRAYER

A prevailing prayer of Mrs. Van Cott

In 1868, Mrs. Maggie Newton Van Cott held a revival meeting at Stone Ridge, Ulster County, N. Y.

At the opening of the meeting, she announced, under the influence of the Spirit as she believed, that there would be a glorious revival, and that two hundred souls would be converted. Some were shocked at the prediction, and some of the very best people in the church were grieved, for they felt certain that she was doomed to disappointment. She labored for more than a week with little fruit. Her strength began to give way. Her warmest coworkers began to tremble for her.

One morning she remarked to the lady at whose residence she was staying, "I am going into the parlor to settle this church matter with the dear Master. Please do not allow any one to come near me. If I do not come out in time for dinner, do not call me. If I am not with you in time for the afternoon meeting, you may call in the friends. I shall, in the name of God, this day have victory or death."

It was a bitter cold day in February, and no fire had been kindled in that room all winter, and the frost was thick on the windowpanes. She wrapped a large shawl around her, and bowed before God, and presented the promises covered with the blood of the Savior, and in them there could be no failure. "Ask, and ye shall receive," stood before her as in characters of living fire. Also, "If ye abide in Me, and My words abide in you, ye shall ask what ye will, and it shall be done unto you."

"Whatsoever ye shall ask in My name, that I will do, that the Father may be glorified in the Son."

"If ye shall ask anything in My name, I will do it." It was the same voice that awoke slumbering chaos, and new-made worlds teeming with life, glorious and grand. An hour passed—another followed—she had grappled with God's Word, and in the anguish of her spirit, as she afterwards declared, she could in a certain degree understand the Scripture, where it describes the Master's agony in the garden, when He sweat great drops of blood. In those hours of the most intense struggle of spirit, the great drops of sweat rolled from her brow.

The tempter suggested, "Give it up. God will not give the answer today."

"Then today, on this spot, I die," was her answer. The agony increased. The prayer became a struggle as for life. "I will not let Thee go. Thy word is truth. Thou hast said, 'Now is the time.' Oh God, now send the answer. Now, my Father, hear me for the sake of souls—for the two hundred. Christ has paid the price of their redemption. I plead His merits—I will not yield—I will not move—I will not let go my hold—Thou canst not turn me away. Behold, Thine own dear Son pleads—the Spirit intercedes. Give, oh, give the answer."

That moment a sweet ripple of peace floated over her soul, and soon shouts of rapture flooded her spirit.

That night twenty seekers bowed at the altar of prayer. In less than five weeks two hundred and thirty five persons professed faith in Christ.

Thus it ever is, "The fervent, effectual prayer of the righteous availeth much."—*The Harvest and the Reaper*

A great revival in a single night

One of the most remarkable experiences we have had in seventeen years of evangelistic work occurred in the spring of 1890. It will be remembered that at this time the United Brethren Church was sadly divided on the secrecy question, and in many places two pastors were employed—one by the *Liberals* and another by the *Radicals* of the same congregation.

In our travels we stopped to visit an old friend, who was the *Radical* pastor in such a place as these to whom we have referred. We had no thought of stopping only, over the Sabbath, and never did we get into a place where the people had less anticipation of a revival. Much hard feeling had existed, and many unkind, unchristian things had been said and done.

Sunday evening our friend invited us to preach for him. God gave us unusual liberty in prayer and in preaching His word, and opened the very windows of heaven, and showers of blessing fell upon that dry and barren land. In spite of circumstances so utterly forbidding, in one short hour, the people found themselves in the midst of a powerful revival. We never witnessed so much confession in so short a time. Many in tears asked each other's forgiveness, and then came to the altar together, and prayed that they might regain their first love, and God heard and answered their prayers. The *Liberal* pastor was not present, but the *Liberal* Presiding-elder was; and he and the *Radical* pastor had had little confidence in each other. But under the mighty power of the Spirit their hearts were united and they embraced each other in tears.

Thus did God manifest His power, and get to His own name glory, and to Him alone be praise, both now and forever, for in His hands are the hearts of the children of men.—*Editor*

REMARKABLE ANSWERS TO PRAYER

10

William Clowes, the spiritual mountaineer

THIS MAN OF GOD was one of the founders of the Primitive Methodist denomination. Rev. George Lamb, in his memorial of him, says:

"On a certain missionary tour he walked one day twenty-four miles, and while on the road, he says, 'I fell into a profound meditation on the fall of man, his departure from original holiness, the depth of iniquity into which sin had sunk him, and the impossibility for any power but that of God to restore him. These reflections I pursued in my mind until I was brought into great sorrow and distress of soul. I felt the travail in birth, and experienced an internal agony on account of the millions of souls on the earth, who were posting on in the way of death, whose steps take hold on hell. I wept much, and longed for some convenient place on the road, where I might give vent to my burdened soul in prayer. In a short time I arrived on the borders of a wood, and then I gave way to my feelings, poured out my soul, and cried like a woman in the pangs of childbirth. I thought the agony into which I was thrown would terminate my life.

" 'This was a glorious baptism for the ministry. The glory of God was revealed to me in a wonderful manner. It left an unction on my soul which continues to this day and the sweetness which was imparted to my spirit, it is impossible for me to attempt a description of.'

"Space will not allow us to follow this apostolic man as he went through the principal counties, and cities, and towns of England, nor to detail the wonderful displays of Divine power which took place under his ministry. Persecution raged against him, his name was cast out as evil, and he had to endure many and severe hardships. But wherever he went the work of God broke out in power, sinners were converted, believers sanctified, and classes organized. At every session of their Annual Conference, for years, their net increase amounted to four or five thousand, and not infrequently the annual increase was ten thousand.

"Mr. Clowes was very remarkable for his power in prayer. He abounded largely in 'the grace of supplication.' It has never fallen to my lot to experience such baptisms, as I never failed to feel while kneeling with him before the mercy seat. Perhaps it will be seen, in the light of eternity, that much of the success which has crowned the labors of the Connection was graciously vouchsafed in answer to his 'fervent and effectual prayers.' The results of the midnight devotions which he rendered to God, and of his wrestling 'until break of day,' when, 'as a prince, he had power with God and prevailed,' are yet to be revealed. The witness of these holy exercises is in heaven, and their record on high.

"Streaming eyes, broken hearts, cries for mercy, and joyful deliverances, were ordinary effects produced when he drew nigh to God in public prayer. I was present at a love-feast conducted by him and his friend, the Rev. I. Holiday, in Mill Street chapel, Hull, at the conclusion of which about forty souls were professedly converted to God.

"Great as Mr. Clowes was in the pulpit, and mighty as he was in prayer, he was equally conspicuous for his strong and unwavering faith. 'I have believed, I do believe, and I will believe,' he would say, and he soared to what he called the 'mountains of frankincense, and the hills of myrrh,' and regaled himself with fruits and flowers in the garden of the Lord, bathed in its crystal fountains of purity, and basked in its blissful bowers of holy serenity and heavenly joy. His strong faith enabled him to make his constant abode where only a few of even good men pay an occasional visit. He lived at a great spiritual altitude, a sort of Pisgah's mountain-life, on lofty banks of high and holy regions. If ever he pitched his tent, he shifted it higher still. He was a spiritual mountaineer. 'His religious life appears to have been one rapid ascent from grace to grace.' No wonder that one who walked with God in spiritual climes, 'where peace sheds its balm, hope bends its rainbow, and the soul dwells at ease,' should be able to say, as did he—and to the honor of grace and the glory of God, be it recorded—'I have never had a doubt for forty years.'

"In the social circle he was serious without gloom, cheerful without levity, and perhaps no man could have passed half an hour in his fellowship without feeling that he was breathing in an atmosphere of holiness, in contact with a spirit near of kin to 'just men made perfect,' and living for the time on the verge of heaven!

"John Nelson, in describing his introduction to Clowes, says, 'There was a most impressive gravity in his demeanor when he received me. His eyes were devoutly lifted up to heaven, while he implored a blessing upon me. 'Let us pray a minute,' said he, and the next moment he was upon his knees, pouring out the desire of his soul for me, in a manner which I cannot fully describe, nor shall I ever forget. Among other things which he fervently asked, this was one: that the Spirit which used to come upon Samson at times in the camp of Dan, might in all its energy come upon me, and that, aided by that power, I, too, might so smite the Philistines, that they might fall before me, heaps upon heaps. While he thus pleaded, the fire of the Holy Ghost fell upon me, and I was more fully endued with a power which, to a greater extent, prepared me for the work for which I was ill fitted and from which I had shrunk with trembling apprehensions.'

"Mr. Clowes had several prominent characteristics; but the most prominent of all was his constancy and power in prayer. In all things through which he was called to pass, he had one never-failing resource, and that was prayer."—Shining Lights

How Carvosso prevailed with God for his children

Carvosso, noted for the earnestness and faith of his prayers, tells as follows of the conversion of his children:

"I had always prayed for my children, but now I grasped the promise with the hand of faith, and retired daily at special seasons to put the Lord to His word. I said nothing of what I felt or did, to anyone but the Searcher of hearts, with whom I wrestled in an agony of prayer."

About two weeks after he was called from his work to pray with his daughter, who became a seeker of Christ. His oldest son was converted at the same time.

Regarding his younger son he says, "I laid hold by faith on the promise which I had while pleading for my other children. One day while I was wrestling with God, in mighty prayer for him, these words were applied with power to mind: 'There shall not a hoof be left behind.' Soon after he yielded, and obtained the knowledge of salvation by the remission of sins.

"A dull and careless way of praying for our friends will avail nothing. It may conceal hypocrisy, or strengthen deception concerning our own piety, but it will not move God nor convert a single soul. Our friends know that we are not in earnest, and care little for it. But let us take hold of the matter in a spirit corresponding to the magnitude of the object to be secured, and there will be a movement!"—Prevailing Prayer, by Wigle

New England saved in answer to prayer

At an early date in our history, 1746, the French fitted out a powerful fleet for the destruction of New England. This fleet consisted of forty ships of war, and seemed to all human judgment a sufficient force to render that destruction certain. It was put under the command of the resolute and experienced Duke d'Anville, and set sail on its terrible errand, from Chedabucto, in Nova Scotia.

In the meantime, our pious forefathers, apprised of their danger and feeling that their safety was in God, appointed a season of fasting and prayer to be observed in all their churches.

While the Rev. Mr. Prince was officiating in Old South Church, Boston, on this fast day, and praying most fervently to God to avert the dreaded calamity, the wind suddenly rose—the day had till now been perfectly clear and calm—and became so powerful as to rattle violently all the windows in the building. The man of God, startled for a moment, paused in his prayer, and cast a look round upon the congregation. He then resumed his supplications, and besought Almighty God to cause that wind to frustrate the object of their enemies, and save the country from conquest and popery. The wind increased to a tempest, and that very night the greater part of the French fleet was wrecked on the coast of Nova Scotia. The Duke d'Anville, the principal general, and the second in command, both committed suicide. Many died with disease, and thousands were consigned to a watery grave. The small number that remained alive returned to France without health and without spirit. The enterprise was abandoned, and never again resumed.—*Present Conflict of Science with Religion*

The escape of the Spree

Mr. D. L. Moody and others, who were on the disabled steamer *Spree*, believe that the vessel was providentially saved in answer to prayer. In the midst of a severe storm, on November 27, 1892, the main shaft broke, and plunged through the bottom of the ship. The waterlogged vessel rolled fearfully, and the decks were washed by the waves. The passengers became greatly alarmed, the indications being that the vessel would sink before help could reach it. On Sunday, at Mr. Moody's suggestion, a prayer service was organized. Every person on board attended, except the officers and crew, who could not leave their posts.

Gen. O. O. Howard, who was one of the passengers, says, "It was the most impressive religious gathering any of us ever attended. Jews, Catholics, and all others forgot differences in creeds and denominations. There was no room for them in such an hour. Mr. Moody read the ninety-first and one hundred and seventh Psalms, which one of the Germans translated verse by verse for his countrymen. Mr. Moody offered a most fervent prayer, and made a short address. God heard us and answered us. I went to my stateroom to rest after the meeting, and I was asleep when some one touched me. I awoke to find a sweet, fond little German girl, the daughter of one of the passengers, by my cot. She could not understand a word of English, but my daughter had drilled her to speak four English words, which was the message she brought me, 'The steamer is coming,' and then she added her German 'hallelujah.' "

Mr. Moody says of the rescue, "There never was a more earnest prayer to God than that of those seven hundred souls on that helpless, almost sinking ship in mid-ocean, Sunday evening, November 27th, when we met in the saloon to implore God's help, and God answered us, as I knew He would. He sent us a rescuing ship, and He calmed the sea so that for a week it was as smooth as it is in this harbor, though there were storms all around us. It was the grandest test of prayer I ever knew. My son was with me. He is a student in Yale College, and the learned professors there have instilled in him some doubts about God's direct interference in answer to prayer. After we had prayed that Sunday night, I had reached a point where I cared not whether it was God's will that we should go up or down, determined to go to rest as though we were sailing safely on our way. My boy couldn't rest. We were fast drifting out of the track of vessels, and our peril was extreme.

"About 2:15 a.m. he came and woke me, telling me to come on deck. There he pointed out an occasional glimpse of a tiny light that showed over the waves as our ship rolled heavily from side to side. 'It is our star of Bethlehem,' he cried, 'and our prayers are answered.' Before daylight the *Huron*, whose masthead light it was, had reached us, and the waves were stilled and the winds were hushed by Divine command, while we were drawn out of the direst peril to this safe haven."

The *Spree* arrived at Queenstown, December 2, with her stern thirty feet in the water, notwithstanding her pumps had been steadily worked from the moment of the disaster.—*Western Christian Advocate*

The sailor and the picture of Christ
The following is stated by Rev. B. Fay Mills:

"Some of you have seen the great picture that was painted by Muneakszy, of the Christ. That picture was being exhibited in Canada—at Toronto, I think—and there came a wild, rough, wicked sailor to see it. He entered the room, at the time of day when there were no others there and, paying his money to the woman who sat inside the room he came in and stood for a moment looking at the canvas as though he would glance at it and go away.

"But as he looked he could not turn. He stood there with his eyes fixed on the central figure of majesty and love. In a few minutes he took off his hat and let it fall on the floor. After a few minutes more he sat down upon a seat, and there he reached down and picked up a book that described the picture, and began to read, and every few seconds his eyes would turn towards the canvas, and toward the picture of Christ. The lady who sat by the door, saw him lift up his hand and wipe away the tears. Still he sat, till five, ten, fifteen, sixty minutes went away, and still the man sat there, as though he could not stir.

"At last he rose, and coming softly and reverently toward the door, he hesitated, to take one last look, and said to the woman who sat there, 'Madam, I am a rough, wicked sailor. I have never believed in Christ. I have never used His name, except in an oath, but I have a Christian mother, and my old mother begged me today, before I went to sea, to go and look at the picture of the Christ. To oblige her I said I would come. I did not believe that anyone believed in Christ, but as I have looked at that form, and that face, I have thought that some man must have believed in Him, and it has touched me, and I have come to believe in Him, too. I am going out from this time to be a believer in Jesus Christ and a follower of Him.' Oh, that we may be 'changed into the same image from glory to glory.'"—*Prevailing Prayer*

A persecutor's awful end
The following is from the journal of George Fox, the founder of the *Society of Friends*. Fox says of this wonderful occurrence:

"... I came again to Thomas Taylor's, within three miles of Halifax, where was a meeting of about two hundred people, amongst which were many rude people, and divers butchers, several of whom had bound themselves with an oath before they came out that they would kill me, as I was told. One of these butchers had been accused of killing a man and a woman.

"They came in a very rude manner, and made a great disturbance in the meeting. The meeting being in a field, Thomas Taylor stood up, and said unto them, 'If you will be civil, you may stay, but, if not, I charge you to begone off my ground.' But they were the worse, and said they would make it like a common. And they yelled, and made a noise, as if they had been at a bear-baiting. They thrust Friends up and down, and Friends, being peaceable, the Lord's power came over them.

"Several times they thrust me off from the place I stood on, by the crowding of the people together against me; but still I was moved of the Lord to stand up again, as I was thrust down. At last I was moved of the Lord to say unto them, if 'they would discourse of the things of God, let them come up to me one by one, and if they had anything to say or to object, I would answer them all, one after another;' but they were all silent and had nothing to say. And then the Lord's power came so over them all, and answered the witness of God in them, that they were bound by the power of God, and a glorious, powerful meeting we had, and his power went over all. And the minds of the people were turned by the Spirit of God in them to God, and to Christ their teacher.

"The powerful word of Christ was largely declared that day and in the life and power of God we broke up our meeting and that rude company went their way to Halifax. The people asked them why they did not kill me, according to the oath they had sworn, and they maliciously answered, that I had so bewitched them, that they could not do it.

"Thus was the devil chained at that time. Friends told me that they used to come at other times and be very rude, and sometimes break their stools and seats, and make frightful work amongst them, but the Lord's power had now bound them. Shortly after this, the butcher that had been accused of killing a man and a woman before, and who was one of them that had bound himself by an oath to kill me, killed another man, and then was sent to York jail.

"Another of those rude butchers, who had also sworn to kill me, having accustomed himself to thrust his tongue out of his mouth, in derision of Friends when they passed by him, had it so swollen out of his mouth that he could never draw it in again, but died so."—*Shining Lights*

Revival at Harvey, Illinois

During the spring of 1892, we held a five weeks' revival meeting in the Methodist Episcopal Church, in Harvey, the new temperance town near Chicago, Illinois. A series of meetings had closed but a few weeks before, and the church was divided, and some were doing all in their power to undermine and destroy the influence of the godly pastor. From a human standpoint, it looked almost like presumption to commence a protracted effort under such unfavorable circumstances. Yet in spite of the discouragements, we felt the call was from God, and were given an inspiration of prayer for the town. We prayed especially for help, and God sent two devoted sisters from Chicago, and one from Rockford, to our aid.

After a few days of great burden of soul for the work, the Lord moved in power among the people, and from that time they came in great crowds. The work done was thus reported by Evangelist Sarah A. Cooke, one of the workers mentioned above, in the *Highway and Banner of Holiness*.

"'Harvey has never had such a shaking up as this before,' said the janitor of the Methodist church, as we looked on the display of the Lord's power moving on the people. Night after night the altar has been filled with seekers, and deep conviction has taken hold of many, long hardened by the deceitfulness of sin. In one of the factories they have commenced a noonday prayer meeting, and another in the academy, the principal of which has been gloriously sanctified during the revival, and like a fire in his bones the love of God has burned. 'I believe,' he said in a testimony a few nights ago, 'I can claim the whole academy for Christ.' Twenty-three the other afternoon professed they had found the Lord.

"No church is preached, no creed, save the apostles', no dogma, just 'all have sinned and come short of the glory of God;' 'Except ye repent ye shall all likewise perish;' and the faithful saying, 'Jesus Christ came into the world to save sinners, even the chief;' and God, as ever honors His own word.

"Brother S. B. Shaw, of Michigan, is in charge. Weeping between the porch and the altar, realizing the awful responsibility of standing between the living and the dead, and by faith taking hold of God by the mighty arms of faith and prayer, he leads the work on gloriously."

Of the same meeting, Sister Abbie Mills, author of *Quiet Hallelujahs and Whispers of the Comforter*, wrote to the *Christian Witness*:

"I am here beholding the works of the Lord. In this place, known to all that are afar off, as well as to them that are nigh, the people of God are getting clear titles to the reserved inheritance, incorruptible, undefiled, and that will endure when Harvey is no more. I came here on Thursday, thinking to make a very short stay, but found the people engaged in a holiness meeting under the leadership of Brother Shaw, of Michigan. The interest is growing, and some are getting clean hearts, and being filled with the Holy Ghost daily. Yesterday, Sabbath, was a day of much blessing. The class-meeting at the noonhour was glorious. Several crossed over into Beulahland, one aged brother leaving his tobacco behind. At three p.m. Sister Cooke, of Chicago, held a children's meeting. In the evening the church was very full. After the sermon by Brother Shaw, the altar filled twice, while first on one side, then on the other, the cleansed would arise to testify and give their place to others. Far out in the congregation also, there were some on their knees, seeking a God who was not afar off. I had thought my work for the winter about over, but am constrained to tarry here this week, and hope to see an increased outpour or downpour of salvation."

George Müller, of Bristol, England

This mighty man of faith is too well known to the Christian world to need any introduction from us. We quote the following from a brief sketch of his life:

"The support of his orphanage amounts to $230,000 annually. The milk bill amounts to $10,000 yearly! He has sometimes paid out as much as $27,500 in one day. In all, Mr. Müller has received for his orphanage and other works of a Christian and benevolent kind, a total of $4,275,000, and he declares that he never asked a human being for a sixpence! He has made it his uniform rule to go in prayer to Him who has the hearts of all men in His hands, and ask Him for all needed supply, and men have been moved to give it, some giving out of their abundant wealth, and some out of their poverty. He has received as high as $45,000 in one donation, and scores of times $5,000. A principle of his has been never to contract a debt in connection with his orphanage. Often the last sixpence has been spent, and within a few hours either money must come or starvation. But the money came without fail, and never were the children sent hungry to bed.

"Hundreds of times he has held two prayer meetings in a day with his helpers, beseeching God to send them supplies for the next meal of food for the orphans, and in every case the Lord has graciously answered their prayer. In eleven years, he had received five thousand answers to prayer. In the course of his life he has received some thirty thousand answers to prayer within the same day of asking, and that for some things he had been praying every day for over thirty years, and the answer had not come as yet. He mentioned these things to encourage Christians patiently to wait on God. He had received answers after waiting fifteen, twenty, and thirty years. When in the deepest poverty, he never gives any human being the least intimation of his needs either by word or look, but always carries every matter great and small to God, and continually rejoices in the Lord. He declares that his countenance never looks sad or anxious when in need, as he considers that would be dishonoring to God, and inconsistent with a perfect trust in Him.

"He says, 'When I first began allowing God to deal with me, relying on Him, taking Him at His word, and set out, over half a century ago, simply to rely on Him for myself, family, taxes, traveling expenses, and every other need, I rested on simple promises.'

" 'I believed the Word. I rested on it and practiced it. I "took God at His word." A stranger, a foreigner in England, I know seven languages, and might have used them perhaps as a means of remunerative employment, but I had consecrated myself to labor for the Lord. I put my reliance in the God who has promised, and He has acted according to His Word. I've lacked nothing– nothing. I have had my trials, my difficulties, and my empty purse, but my receipts have aggregated tens of thousands of dollars, while the work has gone on all these years."–*Shining Lights*

TOUCHING INCIDENTS AND

John Wesley healed in answer to prayer

An illustrious example of constancy and power in prayer we find in John Wesley:

"It is said that 'as a matter of habit and rule, John Wesley's ordinary private praying consumed two hours a day.' At times he would gather his company and pray all night, or till the power of God came down. Nothing was considered too great or too small to take to the Lord. Seized with a pain in the midst of his preaching, so that he could not speak, 'I know my remedy,' he says, and immediately knelt down. In a moment the pain was gone, and the voice of the Lord cried aloud to sinners.

"Being seized with a pain, fever and cough, so that he could scarcely speak, 'I called on Jesus aloud to increase my faith. While I was speaking my pain vanished, my fever left me, and my bodily strength returned.'

"The elements, as well as sickness, were often in his way, and prayer removed the hindrances. 'Just as I began to preach the sun broke out and shone exceedingly hot on my head. I found if it continued I should not be able to speak long, and I lifted up my heart to God. In a minute or two it was covered with clouds which continued till the service was over.' And he says, 'Let anyone who please call this chance. I call it an answer to prayer.'

"[On another occasion] it was raining, and Wesley and his congregation were crowded out of the church, and the rain ceased the moment they came out. He says in regard to this incident, 'How many proofs must we have that there is no petition too little, any more than too great, for God to grant?'

"Wesley moved things mightily, because he moved God mightily. He became the prince of evangelists, because he was the prince of prayers. He stirred the world with the fire of his zeal, because he had stirred heaven by the fire of his prayers. His pleas had access to men's consciences, because they had access to God. If more men prayed as John Wesley prayed, there would be more of John Wesley's thoroughly spiritual work done."—*Prevailing Prayer, by Wigle*

Prayer answered for a debt of ninety dollars

A few years ago we owed a man ninety dollars. When it came due, we were unable to pay it. We went to him and asked his forgiveness, telling him our circumstances. He was a Christian, and manifested a Christian spirit in telling us not to worry over it, that he was not uneasy. Some time after this, we became greatly burdened on account of the debt, and were led out to pray God to open the way for us to meet the obligation, or to influence him to donate it, as he was a man of means.

REMARKABLE ANSWERS TO PRAYER

Soon after this, a brother minister came to us, and told us how he was impressed to pay the obligation for us. He said he had told his wife of his feelings, and she remarked that she had had the same conviction for some time.

This minister, living in the same neighborhood, went and offered the money, or part of it, which the man took. But a short time after, he was so burdened over it that he could not sleep, and was compelled to take the money back to the minister, Brother K——, in the night. He went to the home of Brother K——, and called him up, and in tears told him how the Lord had appeared to him in the night, and compelled him to return the money. He said it seemed that forks were sticking in him, and he was impressed to donate the money to us, instead of allowing our friend, Brother K——, to pay the obligation. Thus God answered our prayer in a time of special need, as he always does those that call upon Him in the right spirit.—*Editor*

Corn the frost could not kill

By our request, Brother L. G. Whitney, a reliable Christian man, of Hemlock, Michigan, writes us of a remarkable interposition of Providence in reference to his field of corn. This is his story:

"Two years ago, the seedcorn in this part of the country proved poor, not having sufficiently ripened the previous year. I saw an advertisement of a ninety-days corn, and sent to Pennsylvania and obtained enough to plant eleven acres. It grew rapidly, and became tall and stout. When other corn was out of the way of the frost, mine was just beginning to fill. One day as I was walking through it, I realized that it could not come to maturity. I fell on my knees, and talked to my heavenly Father about it. I well remember how I addressed Him, saying, 'Father, I have been deceived in this corn. According to the season and the nature of the corn it cannot ripen. But, Father, it is all in Thy hands. I have given myself and all I have into Thy care. It is only by Thy power that this field of corn can ever ripen. Thy will be done. I will not complain.' While I was thus addressing Him, heavenly peace filled my soul.

"Frost after frost came, and froze ice as thick as a window glass. My neighbors would say, 'What is the matter with Whitney's corn that the frosts do not kill it?' It stood like a green forest through all the frosts till it ripened. I never had such a crop of corn before or since. I know the Lord will answer the prayers of the faithful in heart, and I know no good thing will he withhold from them that walk uprightly.'"

TOUCHING INCIDENTS AND

The dying boy

But I have another anecdote. Ralph Wallace who told me of this one. A certain gentleman was a member of the Presbyterian Church. His little boy was sick. When he went home his wife was weeping, and she said, "Our boy is dying. He has had a change for the worse. I wish you would go in and see him." The father went into the room, and placed his hand upon the brow of his dying boy, and could feel that the cold, damp sweat was gathering there, that the cold, icy hand of death was feeling for the chords of life.

"Do you know, my boy, that you are dying?" asked the father.

"Am I? Is this death? Do you really think I am dying?"

"Yes, my son, your end on earth is near."

"And will I be with Jesus tonight, father?"

"Yes, you will be with the Savior."

"Father, don't you weep, for when I get there I will go right straight to Jesus, and tell Him that you have been trying all my life to lead me to Him." God has given me two little children, and ever since I can remember I have directed them to Christ, and I would rather they carried this message to Jesus—that I had tried all my life to lead them to Him—than have all the crowns of the earth. And I would rather lead them to Jesus than give them the wealth of the world. If you have got a child, go and point the way. I challenge any man to speak of heaven without speaking of children. "For of such is the kingdom of heaven."—*Moody's Anecdotes*

Instances of the power of prayer

The instances in which, in answer to prayer, God has sent remarkable deliverances to people, are numerous and striking. In the days of Queen Elizabeth, the terrible Spanish Armada was scattered or destroyed in answer to fervent prayers offered by the people of God in England. In 1746, the French armament of forty ships, prepared under the Duke d'Anville against the American colonies was, in answer to prayer, totally ruined by a tempest. The leaders of the expedition were so overwhelmed at the suddenness and completeness of their disaster, that both of them committed suicide.

But God can save his beleaguered people without destroying their foes. LeClerc tells us that when, in 1672, the Dutch were expecting an attack from their enemies by sea, "public prayers were ordered for deliverance. It came to pass when their enemies waited only for the tide, in order to land. The tide was retarded, contrary to its usual course, for twelve hours, so that their enemies were obliged to defer the attempt to another opportunity, which they never found, because a storm arose afterwards, and drove them from the coast."

How wonderfully God has answered prayer in behalf of good institutions founded to alleviate human misery. Of this we have a striking instance in the Orphan House, at Halle, founded by Francke. His school was unendowed. In 1696, he had not money to support the school a week longer. When the last morsel was about to be consumed, a thousand crowns were received from an unknown source. At other times of distress he received, in answer to special prayer, twenty, thirty, and fifty crowns. He says, "Another time all our provision was spent, but in addressing myself to the Lord, I found myself deeply affected with the fourth petition of the Lord's prayer, 'Give us this day our daily bread,' and my thoughts were fixed in a more especial manner on the words 'this day,' because on the very same day we had great occasion for it. While I was yet praying, a friend of mine came before my door in a coach, and brought the sum of four hundred crowns!"—*Power of Prayer*, by Prime

Edward Payson, a man who prayed without ceasing

This well-known man of God was for many years pastor of the Congregational Church at Portland, Maine. His remarkable success was, to a very great extent, the result of his prevailing prayers. Oh, that many might follow his example! We clip the following from a sketch of his life in *Shining Lights*:

He prayed without ceasing. Aware of the aberrations to which the human mind is liable, he most earnestly sought the guidance and control of the Holy Spirit. He felt safe nowhere but at the throne of grace. He may be said to have studied theology on his knees. Much of his time he spent literally prostrated, with the Bible open before him, pleading the promises: "I will send the Comforter, and when He, the Spirit of truth, is come, he will guide you into all truth."

To his ardent and persevering prayers must, no doubt, be ascribed, in a great measure, his distinguished and almost uninterrupted success, and next to these, the undoubted sincerity of his belief in the truths which he inculcated. His language, his conversation and whole deportment were such as brought home and fastened on the minds of his hearers the conviction that he believed, and therefore spoke. The revivals of religion which took place under his labors were numerous, and were characterized by a depth and power seldom seen. Nor was his eminent usefulness confined within the narrow sphere of his own congregation. In distant parts of the country, at various special gatherings, his ministry was made a blessing to many thousands, both in the conversion of souls and in raising the tone of piety among believers.

When his body, full of pain, was gradually sinking into the grave, he wrote to his sister, "Were I to adopt the figurative language of Bunyan, I might date this letter from the land of Beulah, of which I have been for some weeks a happy inhabitant. The Celestial City is full in my view. Its glories beam upon me; its breezes fan me; its odors are wafted to me; its sounds strike upon my ears, and its spirit is breathed into my heart. Nothing separates me from it but the river of death, which now appears as an insignificant rill, that may be crossed at a single step, whenever God shall give permission. The Sun of Righteousness has been gradually drawing nearer and nearer, appearing larger and brighter as He approaches, and now He fills the whole hemisphere, pouring forth a flood of glory in which I seem to float like an insect in the beams of the sun, exulting, yet almost trembling, while I gaze on this excessive brightness, and wondering, with unutterable wonder, why God should deign thus to shine upon a sinful worm. A single heart and a single tongue seem altogether too inadequate to my wants. I want a whole heart for every separate emotion, and a whole tongue to express that emotion."

He was asked, "Do you feel reconciled?"

"Oh, that is too cold. I rejoice! I triumph! And this happiness will endure as long as God himself, for it consists in admiring and adoring Him. I can find no words to express my happiness. I seem to be swimming in a river of pleasure, which is carrying me on to the great fountain. It seems as if all the fountains of heaven were opened, and all its fullness and happiness, and, I trust, no small portion of its benevolence, is come down into my heart."

To his wife he said, while dying, "Hitherto I have viewed God as a fixed stare, bright, indeed, but often intercepted by clouds. But now he is coming nearer and nearer, and spreads into a sun so vast and glorious, that the sight is too dazzling for flesh and blood to sustain." This was not a blind adoration of an imaginary Deity, for added he, "I see clearly that all these same glorious and dazzling perfections, which now only serve to kindle my affections into a flame, and to melt down my soul into the same blessed image, would burn and scorch me like a consuming fire, if I were an impenitent sinner."

The angel of mercy

The following pathetic story of our late war is told by a Christian writer:

"At the close of the first bloody day of the battle of Fredericksburg, hundreds of the Union wounded were left lying on the ground and the road ascending Mary's

REMARKABLE ANSWERS TO PRAYER

Heights. All night and most of the next day the open space was swept by artillery shot from both the opposing lines, and no one could venture to the sufferers' relief. All that time their agonized cries went up for 'Water! Water!' But there was no one to help them, and the roar of the guns mocked their distress.

"At length, however, one brave fellow, behind the stone ramparts where the Southern forces lay, gave way to his sympathy, and rose superior to his love for life. He was a sergeant in a South Carolina regiment, and his name was Richard Kirkland. In the afternoon he huried to General Kershaw's headquarters, and finding the commanding officer said to him excitedly, 'General, I can't stand this any longer. Those poor souls out there have been praying and crying all night and all day, and it's more than I can bear. I ask your permission to go and give them water.'

" 'But, do you know,' said the general, admiring the soldier's noble spirit, 'do you know that as soon as you show yourself to the enemy you will be shot?'

" 'Yes, sir, I know it, but to carry a little comfort to those poor dying men, I'm willing to run the risk.'

"The general hesitated for a moment, but finally said, with emotion, 'Kirkland, it's sending you to your death, but I cannot oppose such a motive as yours. For the sake of it I hope God will protect you. Go.'

"Furnished with a supply of water, the brave sergeant immediately stepped over the wall, and applied himself to his work of Christlike mercy. Wondering eyes looked on as he knelt by the nearest sufferer, and tenderly raising his head, held the cooling cup to his parched lips. Before his first service of love was finished, every one in the Union lines understood the mission of the noble soldier in gray, and not a man fired a shot. He stayed there on that terrible field an hour and a half, giving drink to the thirsty and dying, straightening their cramped and mangled limbs, pillowing their heads on their knapsacks, and spreading their army coats and blankets over them, as mother would cover her child. And all the while he was so engaged, until his gentle ministry was finished, the fusillade of death was hushed.

"So it is on life's battlefield. The cannonade of sin and wickedness is hushed and powerless before the fearless Christian soldier who dares to do right, even though his life hangs in the balance."—*N. W. Christian Advocate*

<u>Ivy poison suddenly healed</u>

In answer to our request, Sister S. E. McKeen, of Lake City, Iowa, has furnished us the following account of a wonderful case of physical healing. Her statement is entirely reliable. We give it in her own words:

"Last August, I attended a meeting held at Storm Lake, Iowa, for the promotion of holiness, and while there became acquainted with a young minister and wife from Dakota by the name of Cone. Unfortunately for them, they pitched their tent where poison ivy had grown, and she became sadly poisoned. When I first saw her on Thursday evening, she was suffering from fever, and in great pain. Her face was swollen, her eye bloodshot, and her whole body was covered with the eruption that follows the ivy poison. Her stomach also refused to retain food or medicine, and if she raised her head she became faint.

"Physicians were consulted, and various remedies tried, but still she found no relief. The tent had been moved, and on Sabbath morning, when I called to see her on my way to the tabernacle to morning service, she was no better. That morning her husband had told me that she wanted them to pray that she might be healed. I went on to the service, but the tent was so crowded, and I was feeling so very tired, that I went to our tent to lie down for rest, and read my Bible. I had lain but a few minutes when her sister-in-law came in, and said that Mrs. Cone wanted me. On asking what was wanted, she said, "She wants you to pray that she may be healed." To say that I was surprised does not express it. I was amazed, for "faith-cure" was something I did not know much about, never having given it any serious thought. I did not understand the work of the Holy Ghost, being myself a new convert to holiness, and having come to this place to be established in the doctrine.

"I said, 'I'll go. Oh, Jesus, show me what to say to the dear one, and for her to Thee.' I sat down by her bed a moment, and then asked, 'Do you believe the prayer of faith will save you?'

"She quickly answered, 'Yes.' I knelt down beside her, and prayed, and the Holy Spirit took complete possession of me, for I did not know where I was, or what I said. But when I arose my soul was so full I could not speak. I left her, still in prayer, without a word.

"I was engaged in one of the small tabernacles, and had so completely given her over to Jesus, that the whole thing passed from my mind. It was five o'clock when I returned, and as usual went to see how the sister was when, Lo! I found her sitting outside her door, and dressed for evening service.

"When she saw me she said, 'Praise God! I'm healed. Glory to Jesus!' The Great Physician had been there, and she was restored whole. Her husband had only that morning got permission to leave his tent on the ground, for the Storm Lake physician had said she could not be moved for a week. Hallelujah! How it strengthened my faith, and how strong I felt to do God's will. I have often felt my weakness since then, but it has been a bright spot to look back to ever since.

REMARKABLE ANSWERS TO PRAYER

I am walking in the highway of holiness, and light streaming down from above makes my pathway all clear, going home to Jesus."

Revelations from God in dreams

All dreams that make you better are from God. How do I know it? Is not God the source of all good? It does not take a very logical mind to argue that out. Tertullian and Martin Luther believed in dreams. The dreams of John Huss are immortal. St. Augustine, the Christian father, gives us the fact that a Carthaginian physician was persuaded of the immortality of the soul by an argument which he heard in a dream. The night before his assassination, the wife of Julius Caesar dreamed that her husband fell dead across her lap. It is possible to prove that God does appear in dreams to warn, to convert, and to save men.

My friend, a retired sea-captain and a Christian, tells me that one night, while on the sea, he dreamed that a ship's crew were in great suffering. Waking up from his dream, he put about the ship, tacked in different directions, surprised everybody on the vessel—they thought he was going crazy—sailed on in another direction hour after hour, and for many hours, until he came to the perishing crew, and rescued them, and brought them to New York. Who conducted that dream? The God of the sea.

In 1695, a vessel went out from Spithead for West India, and ran against the ledge of rocks called the Caskets. The vessel went down, but the crew clambered up on the Caskets, to die of thirst or starvation, as they supposed. But there was a ship bound for Southampton that had the captain's son on board. This lad twice in one night dreamed that there was a crew of sailors dying on the Caskets. He told his father of his dream. The vessel came down by the Caskets in time to find and to rescue those two dying men. Who conducted that dream? The God of the rocks, the God of the sea.

The Rev. Dr. Bushnell, in his marvelous book, entitled *Nature and the Supernatural*, gives the following that he got from Captain Yount, in California, a fact confirmed by many families. Captain Yount dreamed twice one night that one hundred and fifty miles away there was a company of travelers fast in the snow. He also saw in the dream rocks of a peculiar formation, and telling his dream to an old hunter, the hunter said, "Why, I remember those rocks. Those rocks are in the Carson Valley Pass, one hundred and fifty miles away." Captain Yount, impelled by this dream, although laughed at by his neighbors, gathered men together, took mules and blankets, and started out on the expedition. He traveled one hundred and fifty miles, saw those very rocks which he had described in his dream, and finding the suffering ones at the foot of those rocks, brought them back to confirm the story of Captain Yount. Who conducted that dream? The God of the snow, the God of the Sierra Nevada.

God has often appeared in dreams to rescue and comfort. You have known people—perhaps it is something I state in your own experience—you have seen people go to sleep with bereavements inconsolable, and they awakened in perfect resignation because of what they had seen in slumber.

Dr. Crannage, one of the most remarkable men I ever met—remarkable for benevolence and great philanthropics—at Wellington, England, showed me a house where the Lord had appeared in a wonderful dream to a poor woman. The woman was rheumatic, sick, poor to the last point of destitution. She was waited on and cared for by another poor woman, her only attendant. Word came to her one day that this poor woman had died, and the invalid of whom I am speaking lay helpless upon the couch, wondering what would become of her. In that mood she fell asleep. In her sleep she said the Angel of the Lord appeared, and took her into the open air, and pointed in one direction, and there were mountains of bread, and pointed in another direction, and there were mountains of butter, and in another direction, and there were mountains of all kinds of worldly supply. The Angel of the Lord said to her, "Woman, all these mountains belong to your Father, and do you think that he will let you, his child, hunger and die?"

Dr. Crannage told me, by some Divine impulse he went into that destitute home, saw the suffering there, and administered unto it, caring for her all the way through. Do you tell me that that dream was woven out of earthly anodynes? Was that the phantasmagoria of a diseased brain? No, it was an all sympathetic God addressing a poor woman through a dream.

Furthermore, I have to say, that there are people in this house who were converted to God through a dream. The Rev. John Newton, the fame of whose piety fills all Christendom, while a profligate sailor on shipboard, in his dream thought that a being approached him and gave him a very beautiful ring, and put it upon his finger, and said to him, "As long as you wear that ring, you will be prospered. If you lose that ring, you will be ruined." In the same dream another personage appeared, and by a strange infatuation persuaded John Newton to throw that ring overboard, and it sank into the sea. Then the mountains in sight were full of fire, and the air was lurid with consuming wrath.

While John Newton was repenting of his folly in having thrown overboard the treasure, another personage came through the dream, and told John Newton he would plunge into the sea and bring the ring up if he desired it. He plunged into the sea and brought it up, and said to John Newton, "Here is that gem, but I think I will keep it for you, lest you lose it again." John Newton consented, and all the fire went out from the mountains, and all the signs of lurid wrath disappeared from the air, and John Newton said that he saw in his dream that that valuable gem was his soul, and that the being who persuaded him to throw it overboard was Satan, and that the one who plunged in and restored that gem, keeping it for him, was Christ. And that dream makes one of the most wonderful chapters in the life of that most wonderful man.

A German was crossing the Atlantic Ocean, and in his dream he saw a man with a handful of white flowers, and he was told to follow the man who had that handful of white flowers. The German, arriving in New York, wandered into the Fulton street prayer meeting, and Mr. Lamphier—whom many of you know, the great apostle of prayer meetings—that day had given to him a bunch of tuberoses. They stood on his desk, and at the close of the religious services he took the tuberoses and started homeward, and the German followed him. Through an interpreter he told Mr. Lamphier that on the sea he had dreamed of a man with a handful of white flowers, and was told to follow him. Suffice it to say, through that interview and following interviews, he became a Christian, and is a city missionary preaching the gospel to his own countrymen. God in a dream!

John Hardock, while on shipboard, dreamed one night that the day of judgment had come, and that the roll of the ship's crew was called except his own name, and that these people, this crew, were all banished. In his dream he asked the reason why his own name was omitted. He was told it was to give him more opportunity for repentance. He woke up a different man. He became illustrious for Christian attainment.

If you do not believe these things, then you must discard all testimony, and refuse to accept any kind of authoritative witness. God in a dream!—*T. DeWitt Talmage*

11

The wonderful results of a little praying band
IN THE YEAR 1874, a little band of humble Christians was formed in Chicago, having for its one object the salvation of souls. Four of the number had been local preachers in England, others were lay workers. But alike, their hearts burned within them to spread abroad the knowledge of redeeming love.

Among them were Charles Cooke, now gone to join the innumerable company around the throne; W. G. Hanmer, now a chairman of the Free Methodist Church in Wisconsin; Mrs. Sarah A. Cooke, still engaged in evangelistic work; Richard S. Martin, at present pastor of Grace Methodist Episcopal Church, Chicago; Thomas Fluck, now preaching on the Pacific coast; Samuel Gittins, now in California; David Andrews, from that time to this out in the great harvest field; and a Brother and Sister Jones, now working in Chicago. James Bird, now in glory, Henry Huck, and others, were engaged in business, but were with the band more or less throughout the great awakening of which we will speak.

They labored for a time in Chicago; but in answer to earnest prayers for God's blessing and guidance, they were led out into Northwestern Indiana.

Their first Macedonian cry from outside the city was from Hessville, a small, neglected place, where the teacher of the dayschool, a Mrs. Price, had been trying amidst much opposition to commence a Sabbath school. In such seemingly unfavorable surroundings the work broke out in great power. Other workers came to their aid, and soon the community was in a flame of revival. Great and glorious were the results. From Hessville the band was called to Gibson, and here as before the work spread in every direction.

They went from Gibson to Ross Station, where we first saw them. At the latter place, the meetings were held in a schoolhouse, but crowds flocked together from the country round. We were then unsaved, and the manifestations of God's presence, and the working of His Spirit on hearts, were beyond anything we had previously witnessed, and were a great mystery to us. Such scenes cannot be described. It is enough to say that sinners wept as if their hearts would break with sorrow for sin, and cried aloud for mercy, until their cries of penitence were changed to songs of praise for deliverance.

Of the experience of the workers, Sister Cooke writes us, "We journeyed from place to place, as surely guided as the children of Israel when led by the pillar of fire. How often as our every want was supplied would the Savior's query come to our minds: 'When I sent you forth without purse or scrip, lacked ye anything?' And they said, 'Nothing.' Our God did supply all our needs. When a call came, we only asked, 'Are we needed in that place? Is this God's call?' These questions satisfactorily answered we went forward, dwelling with unspeakable delight upon the promise, 'Lo! I am with you alway.' "

Merrillville was their fourth point. Here a tent was donated by a Brother Morgan, who had been wonderfully blessed in the meetings. It was afterwards successively pitched at Wood's Mill, Blachley's Corners, Hebron, and other places, and at each place thousands thronged to the services.

Under that tent, while it was located at Wood's Mill, the prayers of our sainted mother, who died when we were but thirteen years old, were answered, and we were gloriously and marvelously converted to God. And since that day God has in His mercy given us thousands of souls.

In spite of opposition, the influence of the work was so great that it was felt in all that part of the state. In each place visited, the revival became the chief topic of conversation among all classes of society. In the very busiest seasons of the year, including the harvest time, farmers might be seen all along the roads for miles, carrying loads of people to the meetings, and singing and praising God as they went. Truly those were days long to be remembered! In many cases people attended regularly who lived eight or ten miles distant, and this interest continued, not only night after night, but week after week, and month after month. Sinners of every grade were saved by scores and hundreds. Many of the converts were called to the ministry, and several labored with the band after their conversion. Many, to this day, are successful laborers in gospel fields.

But we have not space to follow the progress of the work definitely. Hobart, Wheeler, Crown Point, Porter Cross Roads, Valparaiso, North Judson, Knox, and other places, were, in their turn, visited by that little, humble, fire-anointed band. After the weather became too cold for the use of the tent, large halls were used, and in some cases, large tabernacles were built especially for their use. Everywhere the mighty power of God was revealed, and many were rescued from eternal death. No account was kept, but multitudes were numbered among the redeemed, as the direct result of that glorious work, and thousands more are already saved, as the indirect result of the labors.

But what was the secret of such abundant success? Most assuredly the work was not wrought by human might or wisdom, and no dependence was put in the arm of flesh. But it was wrought by the power of the Spirit, and that power was revealed in answer to earnest, constant, humble, prevailing prayer. Well has one of the workers said, "The work was cradled in prayer." In every hour of need, prayer was their one recourse. Truly they lived at the foot of the cross, and so constantly manifested the mind of Christ. To our personal knowledge, it was their custom, before each service, to repair together to some secluded spot, and there pour out their souls to God in pleading for His blessing, and a fresh outpouring of His Spirit. And when they entered the meeting, they were so anointed by the Holy Ghost that revival fires were kindled by their very presence.

Most of their preaching was in the form of burning exhortation. There were no prepared sermons. Just before the service, the question was asked, "Who has the message?" And the one who felt it laid upon his heart read the Word and commented as he was led by the Spirit. They were also eminently given to secret prayer, and everywhere they went were called *The Praying Band*.

The second secret of their success was perfect unity in heart. Though members of different denominations, they never allowed mere differences of opinion to result in prejudice. By prayer and humility they were always able to see eye to eye concerning the work, and all who saw them were compelled to exclaim, "Behold, how these love one another!" To this day, our heart burns within us as we think of what God there wrought through those faithful, humble souls; and we exclaim with Sister Cooke, "I would go all around the world to see another work so glorious."—*Editor*

Triumphant death of three children

Three children of Brother and Sister I. L. Miller, of Sycamore, Ohio, died about the beginning of 1893, of diphtheria. Brother Miller wrote us some of the particulars, and from these an account, though imperfect, is subjoined mostly in his own language

"One was a girl of thirteen years who was converted in our meeting two years ago. Another was a girl of nine years who was converted a short time after the death of the first at family worship. Also a son, eighteen years of age, was converted during his sickness. He rejoiced and praised God until death.

"The first, little Effie, was an earnest Christian worker. Often as we started for prayermeeting, she would say, 'Wait until I go and get a little schoolmate.' She talked much during her sickness about Jesus, although her suffering was great. At one time, a day before she died, she said to me, 'If I could rest a little while.'

"I said, 'Don't you think Jesus would help you, if you would ask Him?'

"'Yes,' she said, 'you ask Him.' She folded her hands and fell asleep, for a full half hour.

"On waking with a smile, I said to her, 'You had good rest.'

"'Yes, I had, and I saw Jesus. He talked with me, and said he was coming for me soon. He showed me heaven. Oh, such a beautiful place!' Soon after she called all, bidding them good-bye, saying, 'I am going to live with Jesus, and I want to meet you in heaven.' As the family was weeping there was not a tear on her cheek, but with smiles and expressions of delight, she said, 'Don't weep. Jesus will let me stay another day.' And so it was.

"The next one was little Vetta, who died about a month later. One day she had been in an apparent stupor. She commenced to call, 'Laurie,' several times. On waking she said that she had seen her aunt Laurie and her sister Effie; that they were together, and she would never come back any more to live here. So she talked freely of leaving, and of heaven. After this she refused to take any more medicine, and said she wanted to die, and go to heaven, where Effie and Jesus were.—*Thomas K. Doty, Editor* Christian Harvester

A guiding voice

A touching story came from Minnesota. A farmer, living on the edge of one of the many lakes of that state, started to cross it in a small sailboat one evening after dark. The wind changed, and a gust overturned the boat when he was in the middle of the lake. The surface of the water was covered with large masses of floating ice. The farmer was an expert swimmer, and he struck out boldly towards the shore, where he thought his house stood, but he grew confused in the darkness. The ice formed rapidly over the whole lake.

He was in a small, quickly narrowing circle, in which he beat about wildly, the chill of death creeping over his body. He gave up at last, and was sinking in the freezing water, when he heard a sound. It was the voice of his little girl calling him "Father! Father!" He listened. The sound of her voice would tell him which way home lay. It put fresh life into him. He thought, "If she would only call once more! But she will be frightened at the dark and cold. She will go in and shut the door.

But just then came the cry, loud and clear: "Father!"

"I turned," said the man afterward, in telling the story, "and struck out in the opposite direction. I had been going away from home. I fought my way. The ice broke before me. I reached the shore and home at last. But if my dear little girl had not persisted in calling me, though hearing no reply, I should have died there alone under the ice."—*Wesleyan Methodist*

What a multitude of souls about us, like that poor man, have lost their balance, and let go their grip on the lifeboat, and are struggling amid the cold, icy waves of sin, soon to sink to the bottomless pit and be forever lost, unless someone goes as near to them as possible and calls them to the right direction. Just one word spoken in Jesus' name may show them the right way, and be the means of their salvation.

Dear brother, the sound of your voice, the words you may speak, the kind action you may do, may show some fallen brother the right way home. Oh, let us not be weary in well-doing, for in due season we shall reap if we faint not.—*Editor*.

A wonderful answer to prayer

Robert Green was born and brought up a slave in Charleston, S. C. His master was a Methodist minister, who owned a large number of slaves, and was consequently very rich, but the Act of Emancipation suddenly reduced him to poverty. This reverse of fortune so overcame him, that he was taken immediately sick, and died soon after. Robert had by this time become a first class cook, and when freed, he went as cook on board a steamship running from Charleston to New York. This position he held for two years, after which he came to New York to live, and found no difficulty in getting and keeping a situation as cook in saloons or hotels. While engaged in this business he was taken sick with a rheumatic disease, which confined him to his bed for six months. After having spent all of his savings for doctors and nurses, he was carried to the Home, a helpless cripple. He could use neither hands nor feet.

One afternoon we were visiting through the wards. Finding him so very sick, we stopped by his bed, and began to talk with him about his soul, warning him to get ready for death. Until this time he had been careless and unconcerned about eternal things, but to find strangers so interested in his soul's welfare, and the solemnity and earnestness with which the exhortation was delivered so deeply impressed him that he could not obliterate the effect from his mind. He slept none that night, for the solemn words kept ringing in his ears, "Get ready for death! Get ready for death!" At one time during the night, he felt quite sure that he saw the same missionary standing by his bedside, repeating the same words, "You better get ready for death!" He heard her voice, and knew it to be the same that warned him in the afternoon.

The following day he would take no food, but said that he must fast and pray until the Lord had forgiven his sins. He was in great distress of soul, praying day and night for mercy.

The next Wednesday he asked if he might be taken into the chapel to the meeting. The doctor said he was not able to go, but he begged so hard that he finally consented; and two of the men helped him into the chapel. After the sermon, an invitation was given for sinners to come to the altar for prayer. Robert said he wanted to go, and the men helped him to the altar, where he began to cry for mercy. The praying ones gathered around him, and carried his case to the Lord in mighty prayer. He had a hard struggle, but came off victorious. The blessing came in overwhelming power. He began to shout the praises of God, and asked to be helped on his feet. They told him he could not stand, and had better remain sitting. But he begged them to help him on his feet, so they raised him from the chair, and held him, while he continued to shout, "Glory to God! Glory to God!"

Soon he told them to let him go, and, breaking away, he walked off a few steps, and stood shouting, "Glory to God!" for a few moments. Then he began walking to and fro in front of the altar, still shouting: "Glory to God! He has converted my soul, and healed my body! I am a well man. Glory to God! He has converted my soul, and healed my body!"

The next day one of the doctors came into the ward, and left him some medicine. He said, "Doctor, I don't want any more medicine. The Lord has converted my soul, and healed my body."

"I heard," said the doctor, "that you walked from the chapel into the ward yesterday. Are you well today? Let me see you walk." Robert rose to his feet and walked across the ward and back. "That will do," said the doctor. "I guess you will be able to leave the Home soon." And he did leave soon after, and engaged in his former business. It is about four years since his conversion. He has enjoyed perfect health ever since. He is a member in good standing in one of the churches, and continues faithfully following the Lord. —*Brands from the Burning.*

TOUCHING INCIDENTS AND

Miss Carrie Webb's story of her restoration to health by prayer

Miss Carrie C. Webb believes that she experienced the faith-cure recently, while sojourning at Northport, Long Island. She has returned to her home, 416 Gold Street, Brooklyn, and many friends and neighbors have called to see her, and hear her remarkable story. She is twenty-three years old, and of slender form. She has been a teacher in the Hanson Place Baptist Church for several years, and her father is a deacon in the Bedford Avenue Baptist Church, whose venerable pastor, the Rev. Dr. Hutchings, with many members of his congregation, are firm believers in the efficacy of prayer in removing disease. Two months ago Miss Webb went to spend the summer at her brother's house, in Northport, and her condition, physically and mentally, was such that her friends never expected to see her come back alive. She has, however, returned, with her mind bright and clear, and her health apparently fully restored. This is Miss Webb's explanation of how the change was brought about:

"I had been declining in health for nearly seven years, suffering constantly from bronchitis and a severe cough. My mind became affected, and I had strange and uncontrollable fancies, and became morbid and despondent. I was at last attacked with neuralgia, and often prayed that I might die, as I became a burden to my family. One day soon after I arrived at Northport, and while I was lying on a lounge in the library, at my brother's house, my eye lighted on a book on the faith cure. I read it.

"That same afternoon my brother asked me if I had ever thought of faith cure, and I told him about the book incident, adding that I had never thought of it in connection with myself. I said I did not think I had sufficient faith to receive such a blessing. He told me to think over and pray about the matter, and three days after I went to him and told him I was ready to be anointed. My brother sent for the Presbyterian minister of the village, and when he arrived we went into the library. The service was very impressive, and I wept all the time it was going on, and when he was pouring oil on my head. I did not feel any better the next day, but rather worse.

"Just one week after the anointing I awoke in unusual pain, and prayed to God to let me die. Then I suddenly thought it would be better for me to pray for health and I prayed and cried for three hours. Finally, when I arose and stood erect, I felt a sensation of health and strength I had not known for seven long years. I realized that I was well again and that my prayers had been answered. Not only had my pains all vanished, but the cloud also disappeared from my mind. The cure was genuine and complete. I have not had a pain or ache since that morning of prolonged prayer."—*New York Sun*

REMARKABLE ANSWERS TO PRAYER

Remarkable prayer of missionary Cox and his brother, for their brother
Melville B. Cox was the first missionary of the Methodist Episcopal Church to Africa. He labored in Liberia but a short time, and died. It was he who, just before his death, uttered those words that have often been reiterated for the purpose of stimulating the endeavors of the missionary cause, as follows: "Let a thousand fall before Africa be given up!"

His memoir was prepared by his brother and published by the Methodist Book Concern. In it is a letter, which will fully explain itself, and at the same time show why we have given it a place in these pages. It is as follows:

"New York, July 25, 1835

"My Dear Sir: There is one circumstance in the life of the late Mr. Cox which, at least to some of his Christian friends, may claim a degree more of attention than he has given to it, and which it is probably out of your own power to give without some additional facts in the case. If I recollect rightly, he has merely recorded the fact, and that rather incidentally. A relation of the circumstances is the more important, as without the detail, the fact may become a subject of ridicule by the semi-infidel, but with this detail may afford him a suggestion, the truth of which he cannot so easily gainsay. I am aware, too, that the occurrence may be passed over, as have been thousands of others of a similar, and even of a more striking character, without acknowledging any supernatural agency. But it must be on the ground of admitting greater mysteries in the explanation than would be found in frankly confessing even the agency of the Deity.

"The following are the facts. They occurred when Mr. Cox was about twenty years of age. At the time of this singular incident his brother James, who, it will be seen, was concerned in the affair, was at sea, being master of the brig *Charles Faucet*, which was then on her passage to New Orleans. This young gentleman, although well fitted for his business in every other respect, and irreproachable in his conduct among men, was destitute of religion.

"From the hour that James sailed for New Orleans, Melville, with another brother of his, and who was alike partner in his 'precious faith,' made the absent brother a constant subject of prayer. Such indeed were their feelings for James, and so absorbing to them was the great question of his soul's salvation, that it became for a few weeks, with them, their first and last thought for the day.

"One evening, just as the sun had fallen the two brothers, as they were sometimes wont to do, visited the edge of the woods back of the village where they then resided, and there knelt down to pray. The first object of interest before them was their absent brother, whose image came up to their view with more than ordinary distinctness, and who, it seemed to them, was not only far away on the sea, tossed upon its waves as the spirit of the storm might drive him, but 'without hope, without God in the world,' and liable to fall into the gulf of woe. As they prayed their own spirits seemed in agony for James, and they poured out their feelings in alternate offerings with a depth of sympathy, of religious fervor, of faith in God never before experienced by them for him. It was given to them to wrestle with God in prayer, and to importune as for their own souls. And thus they did, unconscious of the nightly dews that were falling upon them, until the conflict seemed past and the blessing they sought gained. They both rose from prayer, and without exchanging a word upon the subject of their feelings went to their different homes for the night.

"The next morning, the brothers met, but the feelings of the past night were yet too vivid to be dissipated. Said Melville to the younger, 'What did you think of our feelings last night?'

'I think,' said the younger brother, 'James has experienced religion.'

'Well, I think,' said Melville, '*that he is dead*, and I have put it down in my diary, and you will see if it is not true.' A few weeks passed away, and tidings came that James was dead. He died within a few days' sail of the *Balize*, in the evening and, as the brothers supposed by a comparison of the letter they received with Melville's diary, on the same hour in which they were engaged in prayer for his soul.

"The above letter contained no reference to his religious feelings, so that the correctness of the younger brother's impressions was yet to be determined. On the return of the brig, however, it was ascertained by conversation with the mate that the feelings of both were equally true. It appeared from the mate's testimony, and other circumstances that immediately after his sailing James became serious, abandoned profaneness, to which he had been accustomed for years, and forbade the indulgence of this profitless and degrading crime on board his vessel. This seriousness continued to the hour of his death. He communicated his thoughts, however, to no one excepting to his friends, upon paper, which they received after his death. Yet it does not appear from any of these circumstances, that he found peace to his mind, unless it were in his last hour.

"On the morning of the day on which he died, he said to his mate, 'he thought he should die that day;' and, accordingly, made what arrangements he could for such an event. He gave some directions about the vessel, and requested a lock of hair to be cut from his head; which, with a ring that he took from his finger, was handed to his friends. He then gave himself up to his fate. In the evening, the mate went below, and seeing quite a change had taken place in his appearance, and that death was rapidly approaching, he took his hand, and thus addressed him: 'Captain Cox, you are a very sick man.'

" 'Yes, I know it,' was calmly, though feebly articulated.

" 'You are dying,' continued the mate.

" 'Yes, I know it,' he again whispered.

" 'And you are willing?'

" 'Yes, blessed...' and burst into a flood of tears, and expired.

"To the Christian, I have nothing to say on the above circumstance. To him all is clear as the light of day. But to the infidel, I may propose one question. How was it possible that the event of James' death, and the change which he evidently experienced in his feelings—call it by what name you please, and the consolation of which no one would take from the dying—how is it possible that the event should be so strongly impressed upon the minds of these two brothers, when he to whom they related was thousands of miles distant. And how could it occur, too, on the very hour when the events were taking place?

"Affectionately yours, F."

The heaven-built wall

In the campaign of Napoleon in Russia, while the French army was retreating from Moscow, there lay in a poor, low cottage in a little village, an invalid boy. This village was exactly in the course of the retreating army, and already the reports of its approach had reached and excited the terrified inhabitants. In their turn, they began to make preparations for retreat for they knew there was no hope for them from the hands of soldiers. All seeking their own preservation, and giving no quarter to others, everyone who had the strength to fly, fled, some trying to take with them their worldly goods, some to conceal them. The little village was fast growing deserted. Some burnt their houses or dismantled them. The old were placed in wagons, and the young hurried their families away with them.

But in the little cottage there was none of this bustle. The poor crippled boy could not move from his bed. The widowed mother had no friends intimate enough to spare a thought for her in this time of trouble, when everyone thought only of those nearest to him and of himself. What chance in flight was there for herself and her young children, among whom one was the poor crippled boy?

It was evening, and the sound of distant voices and of preparation had died away. The poor boy was wakeful with terror, now urging his mother to leave him to his fate, now dreading lest she should take him at his word, and leave him behind.

"The neighbors are just going away. I hear them no longer," he said. "I am so selfish, I have kept you here. Take the little girls with you. It is not too late. And I am safe. Who will hurt a poor helpless boy?"

"We are all safe," answered the mother. "God will not leave us, though all else forsake us."

"But what can help us?" persisted the boy. "Who can defend us from their cruelty? Such stories as I have beard of the ravages of these men! They are not men; they are wild beasts. Oh, why was I made so weak—so weak as to be utterly useless? No strength to defend, no strength to fly."

"There is a sure wall for the defenseless," answered his mother. "God will build us up a sure wall."

"You are my strength now," said the boy, "I thank God that you did not desert me. I am so weak, I cling to you. Do not leave me, indeed! I fancy I can see the cruel soldiers hurrying in. We are too poor to satisfy them, and they would pour their vengeance upon us! And yet you ought to leave me! What right have I to keep you here? And I shall suffer more if I see you suffer."

"God will be our refuge and defense still," said the mother, and at length, with low, quieting words, she stilled the anxious boy till he, too, slept like his sisters. The morning came of the day that was to bring the dreaded enemy. The mother and children opened their eyes to find that a "sure wall " had indeed been built for their defense. The snow had begun to fall the evening before. Through the night it had collected rapidly. A "stormy wind, fulfilling His word," had blown the snow into drifts against the low house, so that it had entirely covered it—a protecting wall, built by Him who holds the very winds in his fists, and who ever pities those who trust in Him. A low shed behind protected the way to the outhouse, where the animals were, and for a few days the mother and her children kept themselves alive within their cottage, shut in and concealed by the heavy barricade of snow.

It was during that time that the dreaded scourge passed over the village. Every house was ransacked; all the wealthier ones deprived of their luxuries, and the poorer ones robbed of their necessaries. But the low roofed cottage lay sheltered beneath its wall of snow which, in the silent night, had gathered about it. God had protected the defenseless with a "sure wall."—*Guiding Hand, by H. L. Hastings*

A wonderful experience

In 1890, Sister K. J. Convers, of Stanton, Michigan, wrote us of her remarkable recovery through the faith and prayers of Sister N. G. Fisher, of the same place.

REMARKABLE ANSWERS TO PRAYER

We are well acquainted with these saints of God, and know the circumstances as related to be reliable. Sister Convers' statement is as follows:

"In the year 1885, I was healed by the hand of God, and am still telling of His power, and praising Him for His love to me. At that time I had had poor health for a number of years, but for several weeks previous to my healing was dangerously ill. I went to a great many doctors. They all said I must die. The last one who came said I could not live but a short time.

"But in early life I gave my heart to God, and so was only waiting for Him to take me home. March 1, 1885, I was taken worse. Friends came to see me, expecting it would be the last time. Brother and Sister Honer sat up with me. In the morning, just before they started home, he said, "Sister Convers, at half past two, look to God. We will remember you in prayer for your healing."

"For nearly a year before, every time I saw Sister Fisher she would say that God wanted to cure me. I would answer, "I would like to get well," but that was about all the thought I ever gave it until God fitted me for the work to be done.

"At the time Brother and Sister Honer appointed for special prayer, I was taken very bad. Every time I coughed they had to raise me to keep me from strangling, and that time when I laid down I saw Sister Fisher standing at the foot of my bed, while at the same time she was one mile away praying for me. Just by her side I saw the blessed Savior standing. I saw His hand pointing toward me, and heard Him say, 'If you take that medicine you will surely die at four in the afternoon.'

"God sent Sister Fisher to see me. He came with her, and filled both of us with His blessed faith; praise His name!

"I had consumption. My lungs were so nearly gone that my voice could only be heard in a faint whisper. I had heart disease, and a tumor in my right side, so that I could not touch my feet by bending over. My left side had been struck with paralysis, and my hand was helpless. I had ulcers on my liver, and had not lain on my left side for six months. It was just half past four when Sister Fisher came, and at half past six I was a well woman, and up off from my bed, praising God for what He had done for me.

"I felt God's hand laid on every diseased spot. When the hand was laid on my arm, I felt the hand so plainly I could tell the side the fingers were on. When it passed off from my arm, the Lord said to me, 'Now can you raise clean hands?' My husband said my hand went up. I held it there one hour without even moving a finger.

"Monday evening after God healed me I walked one mile to church and told what God has done for me. It has been five years since God healed me and I keep well by having faith in Him. And when I feel badly I just ask God to keep me well, and I have faith He will, and He does. My faith is strong today. If God can save us from sin, He is able to heal our bodies. I have laid aside medicine and taken God for my physician, and am telling to everybody what God can do, if they will believe His word. Praise His matchless name forever! Oh you of little faith, take God at His word and be healed."

Instances of divine power

1. In the spring of 1858, during the prevalence of the widespread revivals described in Prime's *Power of Prayer*, I was soundly converted to God. At that time I was in mature young manhood, and in business. My health had been poor for a number of years, and when I gave my heart to the Lord Jesus, I appeared to myself to be standing on the very verge of death and hell.

A short time after the mighty change, I was led to pray for "Hezekiah's fifteen years." Hezekiah, the pious king of Judah, was "sick unto death," but "he turned his face to the wall, and prayed unto the Lord," and the Lord was pleased to restore him to health, and made him the promise, "I will add unto thy days fifteen years."

My case occurred long before faith cure received the attention that it does at present. In fact, nothing special appears to have been known or thought about it in those days. The impression upon my mind was doubtless born of the Holy Spirit. I was not led to pray for restored health but simply for fifteen years of continued life. My prayer became very earnest until it resulted in a settled and grounded faith. I most certainly and most devoutly believed that I should yet live fifteen years. But there was a condition in my mind to the promise. This was that I should not backslide. I felt that if I turned from the service of the God who had wonderfully saved me, I should soon die.

The promise of God—the witness, if you please—that my life would be spared was so clear and pronounced that I scarcely ever thought of doubting it. Indeed, in preaching funeral sermons and speaking as one naturally would sometimes of the uncertainty of life in such a way as to include my own, the words would gag my throat and I would have to use language that was more guarded and more in accordance with what I understood to be the facts in my own case.

Of course, my life went on. In fact, nothing could destroy it while I carefully kept the only condition—that of fidelity to God. But at no time was I impressed or permitted to make any public statement of my assurance, or indeed in private, except in possibly a couple of instances, where I thought special good might be the result.

REMARKABLE ANSWERS TO PRAYER

The result was, I not only lived fifteen years—years added to my natural allotment—but also, I am now actually considerably advanced on my third fifteenth year! The last fact indicated is no doubt a result of the many prayers of the people of God, as well as my own, that my days of usefulness might still be lengthened out. To God be everlasting glory!

2. I received my first appointment to a pastoral work by Bishop Simpson, in 1860. It was to a comparatively new work on the northern border of the great North Woods, and not far from the Adirondacks, in the state of New York. It was a lumber region. There were two lakes, the Upper and Lower Chateaugay, and a river, the Chateaugay, running out from them northward until it crossed the frontier, and emptied into the river St. Lawrence. On the east side of the lower lake was an isolated neighborhood, having a schoolhouse. I learned that the gospel was not preached there at all. I was therefore led to send an appointment into the neighborhood for a meeting. It was to be held at a certain hour in the afternoon. This was during the latter part of the summer of 1860.

When the day came for filling the appointment, about a dozen of us started up the river toward the lake in a boat. The most of the company went for the pleasure of going but I went solely to preach the gospel of the Son of God. The boat was moved with oars. There was a sail, but this was useless while we were in the river. It was a considerable distance up the river, perhaps a mile. But there was a boom in it the whole distance up to the lake, and this added to the facts that the river was very narrow, and there were logs on one side of the boom a large part of the way, made our progress very slow.

As we at last emerged from the river into the lake, with two miles of lake between us and my appointment, I looked at my watch and saw at once that by rowing we could not reach the schoolhouse in time. There was no wind, so the sail could not be used. I sat in the stern of the boat and thought. Being late to meeting was particularly obnoxious to me. What should be done? I prayed.

Prayer always brings us out right, praise God! I said nothing to the company, but simply prayed. As I prayed I began to believe. Believe what? That the wind would spring up, so that I could get to the schoolhouse on time. And, sure enough! In a very short time the breeze began—at first very gently, and then increasing, until it became almost a gale. The sail was quickly unfurled, and we scudded through that little lake at a wonderful speed. Arriving at the shore the waves ran so high that it was with some difficulty we could safely land. The result was myself and wife arrived at the schoolhouse before any of the congregation. In due time the people were on hand and I had the pleasure of dealing out to them the saving word of God.

There was no wind, but there was a pressing necessity for it. Prayer was made, faith was exercised, and the wind came. Was it a miracle? That is what I call it—call it what you will. Praise God!

3. In 1882 I received an invitation to assist Brother S. B. Shaw, the editor of this book, in a series of camp meetings in the state of Michigan. I accepted the invitation and was at several of the meetings. I was in those years as now, conducting the *Christian Harvester*, and depended on subscriptions, etc., received during the campmeeting seasons, for the means of buying a stock of paper, which was usually needed in the month of September of each year.

This year, for some reason or other, I received but little money at the meetings—though souls were saved and sanctified—and arrived at my home in Ohio with the usual need of paper, and no money to buy it with. I went to God with my need—his. He inspired my faith that the money should come. At that time of the year comparatively little money was wont to come in through the mails but soon after praying, they began to bring in unusual amounts.

One man in Illinois sent me twenty dollars—a man who was an entire stranger—possibly he had seen me, but I did not remember him. All he asked in return for the money was a year's subscription to the *Harvester*, and that I should pray for him. The unusual inflow of money continued until a sufficient amount was received to pay for the stock of paper, then it immediately stopped. Sammy Hick, the eccentric Yorkshire local preacher, had faith for a wind to grind out his wheat, the flour being needed to feed the people who were coming to the "quarterly-meeting," and the moment Sammy's grist was ground the wind ceased, and none of the neighbors could get any grinding—unless, as the miller said, they had Sammy's faith. So in my case, and showing that it was a matter of pure faith, and not in the usual order of things, when money enough came to supply the need, further supply was immediately withheld. Again, to God be all the glory! Amen.—*Thomas K. Doty*

Persecutors put to silence, and converted

The following is from the autobiography of that wonderful revivalist, Charles G. Finney. The circumstances as related occurred early in his ministry, at Gouverneur, N. Y.

I have said that there was a Baptist church, and a Presbyterian, each having a meetinghouse standing upon the green, not far apart, and that the Baptist church had a pastor, but the Presbyterian had none. As soon as the revival broke out, and attracted general attention, the Baptist brethren began to oppose it. They spoke against it and used very objectionable means indeed to arrest its progress. This encouraged a set of young men to join hand in hand to strengthen each other in opposition to the work. The Baptist church was quite influential and the stand that they took greatly emboldened the opposition and seemed to give it a peculiar bitterness and strength, as might be expected. Those young men seemed to stand like a bulwark in the way of the progress of the work.

In this state of things Brother Nash and myself, after consultation, made up our minds that that thing must be overcome by prayer, and that it could not be reached in any other way. We therefore retired to a grove and gave ourselves up to prayer until we prevailed, and we felt confident that no power which earth or hell could interpose would be allowed permanently to stop the revival.

The next Sabbath, after preaching morning and afternoon myself—for I did the preaching altogether, and Brother Nash gave himself up almost continually to prayer—we met at five o'clock in the church for a prayer meeting. The meetinghouse was filled. Near the close of the meeting, Brother Nash arose, and addressed that company of young men who had joined hand in hand to resist the revival. I believe they were all there, and they sat braced up against the Spirit of God. It was too solemn for them really to make ridicule of what they heard and saw, and yet their brazen facedness and stiff neckedness were apparent to everybody.

Brother Nash addressed them very earnestly, and pointed out the guilt and danger of the course they were taking. Toward the close of his address, he waxed exceedingly warm, and said to them, "Now, mark me, young men! God will break your ranks in less than one week, either by converting some of you, or by sending some of you to hell. He will do this as certainly as the Lord is my God!" He was standing where he brought his hand down on the top of the pew before him, so as to make it thoroughly jar. He sat immediately down, dropped his head, and groaned with pain.

The house was as still as death, and most of the people held down their heads. I could see that the young men were agitated. For myself, I regretted that Brother Nash had gone so far. He had committed himself that God would either take the life of some of them and send them to hell, or convert some of them within a week. However, on Tuesday morning of the same week the leader of these young men came to me in the greatest distress of mind. He was all prepared to submit, and as soon as I came to press him he broke down like a child, confessed, and manifestly gave himself to Christ. Then he said, "What shall I do, Mr. Finney?"

I replied, "Go immediately to all your young companions, and pray with them, and exhort them at once to turn to the Lord." He did so and before the week was out, nearly, if not all, of that class of young men were hoping in Christ.

John Knox's prevailing prayer for Scotland

Among the mighty men of faith and prayer, whose names will stand forth until this world's history is completed, is that of John Knox. The days of turbulence developed their holy zeal and courage. Summoned before the highest of earth's great ones, true everywhere to God, and a man mighty in prayer, Queen Mary of Scotland once said of Knox that she feared his prayers more than an army of ten thousand men. On England's throne sat Mary, the daughter of Henry VIII, who had been brought up by her mother, Catharine of Aragon, in the dark faith of Rome, a complete tool in the hands of the priests, whose one design was to destroy the Protestants.

Soon the jails were filled, the fires kindled in Smithfield, and the whole land was one scene of desolation, and the Protestants were hunted as partridges on the mountains. The great heart of John Knox was stirred. On his knees, on his face for hours together before God, he pleaded for Scotland. "All Scotland for Christ!" was his ceaseless cry

In one of these seasons of mighty taking hold of God he sprang to his feet with the cry, "Deliverance has come! Deliverance has come!" As soon as the courier could speed his way from London to the city where John Knox lived, he made the proclamation, "Mary, Queen of England, is dead!"

Pray ye the Lord of the Harvest to raise up such men in our days, when the tide of worldliness threatens the whole church, and Catholicism is spreading her baneful influence over the free institutions of our land, only waiting for the chance to reenact the scenes of St. Bartholomew's day in France, or the massacre of ten thousand Protestants in one day as in Ireland, to crush out the religion of our fathers, to burn the Bible, and plunge the whole land into papal darkness.—*Sarah A. Cooke*

12

The blind restored to sight

AT THE AGE OF twenty years, a lady in Winchester, Iowa, began to lose her health, and in a short time was confined to her bed. And she writes, "In addition to this, I lost the use of my eyes, and was blind and helpless a greater portion of my time, for five years.

"I enjoyed the blessing of prayer and trust some six months before feeling at liberty to pray for the healing of my body, fearing I should desire it without due submission to God's will. It was with fear and trembling that I first made known this request. Though my pleadings in this direction were earnest, and often agonizing, yet I could say with a fervor as never before, 'Not my will but Thine be done.'

"About the end of November, or early in December, 1873, I realized that my faith was perfect, that I was ready now to be healed, that my faith was momentarily waiting on God, and resting without a doubt on the promises. From this time forward my faith remained fixed with but one exception. During the time between December, 1873, and July, 1874, I was healed to such an extent that I could walk some, and see more or less every day, though sometimes with only one of my eyes. A portion of this time I felt as though in a furnace of fire, but amid the flames, I realized the presence of the Son of God, who said, 'I have chosen thee in the furnace of affliction.'

"This for a time seemed an answer to my petition, and so I thought it my life work to suffer. For a while my faith became inactive and I almost ceased praying for my health. Though I felt submissive, yet somehow I was soon crying, and that most instinctively, 'Thou Son of David, have mercy on me!' After this, my faith did not waver. Oh, the lesson of patience I learned in thus waiting on God's good time! And with what comfort could I present my body an offering to Him, realizing that as soon as at all possible with His will, I should be healed. I had an assurance of this, but did not know whether it would be during life or accomplished only at death.

"In this manner I waited before God until the morning of the 26th of July when, without ecstasy of joy or extra illumination, came a sense of the presence of Jesus, and a presentation of this gift, accompanied with these words: 'Here is the gift for which you have been praying. Are you willing to receive it?'

"I at first felt the incoming of the Divine power at the parts affected, steadily driving out the disease, until death was swallowed up in victory. I at once arose from my bed and proceeded to work about the house, to the great astonishment of my friends, some of whom thought me wild. But I continued my work, assuring them that Jesus had healed me. Realizing the scrutiny and doubt with which I was observed, I said to my father, 'What do you think?'

"He replied, 'It is supernatural power. No one can deny it.'

"My healing took place on Wednesday. On Saturday I was persuaded to lie down, but found the bed was no place for me. I thought of Peter's wife's mother, who 'arose and ministered to them. I knew that to her, strength as well as well as health was instantly given, as in the case of the palsied man who rose, took up his bed, and departed. I returned to my work, backing my experience with those in God's word, and since then have not lain down during the daytime.

"My friends could not realize the completeness of the cure until I read a full hour, and that by lamplight, and until asked to desist, the first opportunity after being healed.

"A week from this time, I discharged the hired girl, taking charge of the household work which I have continued with perfect ease. About four weeks after my healing, I had occasion to walk four miles, which I did with little or no weariness. Let me add, to the praise of God, that I have no disease whatever. Am able to do more hard work with less weariness than at any other period in my life, and faith in the Lord is the balm that made me whole."—*Selected*

Special answers to prayer

Our old friend J. Baker, now preaching at Hartford, Michigan, who has for years trusted the Lord for all things, both temporal and spiritual, sends us the following:

At the Raisin Center campground, August, 1886, a brother came to me on Saturday evening, requesting that I should come to his tent on Sunday morning, and anoint him for the cure of his deafness. He was a man between forty and fifty years of age. He had been deaf ever since a boy, his deafness being caused by scarlet fever. At the time appointed, in company with Clara Rouch and Carrie Kimball, I went to his tent and anointed him with oil, we laying our hands upon his head. He was instantly healed, and shouted and rolled on the ground, calling on those standing around to help him praise the Lord. He declared he could hear the faintest whisper.

When I lived in Detroit, in the winter of 1883, I had a house in view which I desired to use as a home for friendless women. The rent was $20.00 per month. I asked the Lord for the amount to be given me inside of six days, if it was his will I should have the house. In a few days I received a check for $25.00 from Chicago. Some years afterward I met the individual who sent the money, and he told me he was very forcibly impressed to send me the money. He never knew what it was for until I told him the circumstance.

The secret of James Caughey's wonderful success

This wonderful evangelist was known to only a few of the present generation. He died at a good old age in New Brunswick, N.J., but two or three years before the publication of this book.

In one of his books, Mr. Caughey says, "I am now fully persuaded that in proportion as the Spirit of God shall condescend to second my efforts in the gospel message, I shall be successful. No man has ever been signally used in winning souls to Christ without the help of the Spirit. With it, the humblest talent may astonish earth and hell, by gathering into the path of life thousands for the skies, while without it, the finest, the most splendid talents, remain comparatively useless."

Mr. Caughey was called of God to visit England and Ireland, in which countries he labored seven years with the most signal success. During this time, "nearly twenty-two thousand persons professed conversion under his immediate labors, and nearly ten thousand entered into the rest of full salvation." He gives the following account of his call in a letter to a friend, from which we extract as follows:

"You will remember our Conference of 1839 was held in the city of Schenectady, N.Y. That year I was appointed to Whitehall, N.Y. Shortly after, I had my library and study furniture forwarded to my station.

"It was then I began seriously to reflect upon the propriety of choosing a wife, believing that 'marriage is honorable in all men.' I had traveled a number of years, studied hard, and expended all my time and strength in winning souls to Christ. My brethren approved of my intention. But, while indulging in this purpose—for some reasons I could not explain—my heart became very hard. The Lord seemed to depart from me and that countenance, which so often beamed upon me from above, and had daily, for many years, brightened my soul into rapturous joy, appeared now to be mantled in the thickest gloom.

"The more I reflected thus: 'I can see no good reason why I should be singular among my brethren, nor continue to lead this solitary life,' my heart became harder, and my darkness increased. I was soon involved in a variety of evil reasoning. My will seemed to be in a conflict with something invisible. God, who had honored me with such intimate communion with himself since my conversion, apparently left me to battle it out alone. So it appeared to me then, but now I see God himself was contending with me. I was about to step out of the order of his providence, and he was resolved to prevent it, unless I should refuse to understand why he thus resisted me. Had I continued the conflict, I believe he would have let me take my own course, nor would he have cast me off, yet I solemnly feel he would have severely chastised my disobedience.

"My distress and gloom were so great I could not unpack my library nor arrange my study. I began to reflect most solemnly upon my unhappy state of mind, and became more concerned to regain my former peace and joy in God, than to obtain any temporal blessing whatever. The world was a blank, a bleak and howling wilderness to my soul without the smiles of my Savior. In fact, [I felt] that I could not live but must wither away from the face of the earth without his comforting and satisfying presence.

"Like a well chastised son, I came back to the feet of my Heavenly Father, and with many tears. I besought him to reveal his face to my soul; that if my purposes were crossing his, to show me, and whatever was his will. I would at once, by his help, yield my soul unto it. 'Lord God,' I said, 'if my will crosses thy will, then my will must be wrong, for thine cannot but be right.' Now I cared not what he commanded me to do, or to leave undone. I stood ready to obey. I felt assured clear light from God on some points would soon reach my soul, and I was fully prepared for it. But I no more expected such an order as came soon after, than I expected he would command me to fly upward and preach the gospel in another planet.

"During three days I cried to God without any answer. On the third day in the afternoon I obtained an audience with the Lord. The place was almost as lonely as Sinai, where Moses saw the burning bush. It was under open sky, a considerable distance from the habitations of men. Steep rocks and mountains, deep forests, and venomous reptiles surrounded me. Here, and in a moment, the following passage was given me to plead: 'And the Lord descended in the cloud, and stood with him there, and proclaimed the name of the Lord. And the Lord passed by before him, and proclaimed The Lord. The Lord God, merciful and gracious, long-suffering, and abundant in goodness and truth, keeping mercy for thousands, forgiving iniquity, and transgression, and sin, and that will by no means clear the guilty.'—Exodus 34:5-7.

"I took hold of this. Many of the words were as fire, and as a hammer to break the rocks in pieces before the Lord. The fountains of tears were opened, and the great deep of my heart was broken up. I left the place, however, without receiving any light. But my heart was fully softened and subdued, and I felt assured I had prevailed in some way with God. I was confident light and direction were coming, but of what nature I could not tell.

"This was on the 9th of July, 1839. The same evening, about twilight—eternal glory be to God!—when reading in a small room adjoining my study, a light, as I conceived from Heaven, reached me. My soul was singularly calmed and warmed by a strange visitation. In a moment I recognized the change. The following, in substance, was spoken to my heart, but in a manner and with a rapidity I cannot possibly describe. Every ray of Divine glory seemed to be a word that the eye of my soul could read, a sentence which my judgment could perceive and understand: 'These matters which trouble thee must be let entirely alone. The will of God is that thou shouldst visit Europe. He shall be with thee there, and give thee many souls to thy ministry. He has provided thee with funds. Make thy arrangements accordingly, and next Conference, ask liberty from the proper authorities, and it shall be granted thee. Visit Canada first. When this is done, sail for England. God shall be with thee there, and thou shalt have no want in all thy journeying, and thou shalt be brought back in safety again to America.'

"I arose from my knees under a strong conviction that God had called me to take this tour. Letters were written immediately to Canada, etc. The next day my soul was calm and happy. My books were unpacked, and everything in my study arranged with a glad heart and free. Eleven months were before me to criticize the impressions on my soul. With delight I commenced my pastoral work, visited from house to house, and had the pleasure of seeing a most powerful revival of religion in my circuit.

"During this period not the least wish entered my heart to form any connection or engagement whatever that would entangle or hinder me from fulfilling what I conceived to be the high and solemn commission I had received from the Lord. I continued to resign the whole matter to God, entreating him to overrule all to his glory, and to hedge up my way if it were not his will I should leave America."

Let them abide till the morrow

The beautiful valley of Wyoming, on the banks of the Susquehanna river, in Luzerne County, Pennsylvania, has long been known alike to the student of history and the lovers of poetry and song.

Dr. W. H. Van Doren records in *The Evangelist* an incident which recalls the calamities that overwhelmed Wyoming, and illustrates the gracious care of an ever-present God, for those who trust in Him.

It was in the beginning of July, 1778, that an aged saint, who with his four sons lived on a mountain overlooking the valley, found that his barrel of meal was nearly exhausted, and bade his sons fill their sacks with grain, and early in the morning descend the long road to the mill in the valley. As requested, before daylight each of the boys had fed his horse, and they were all prepared by sunrise for their journey. And as the day would be too far spent to have their grain ground, they were accustomed at such times to spend the night near the mill in Wyoming.

As the patriarch came forth in the morning from the closet of prayer, and said to the waiting sons, "Not today," the young men were greatly surprised.

"But, father, our supply is used up, and why should we delay?" they said, as they turned and gazed over the valley, which lay in calm and quiet peacefulness before them.

"Not today, my sons," repeated with emphasis by the man of prayer, satisfied the youths that the father meant what he said. He added, "I know not what it means, but in my prayer my mind was deeply impressed with this word: 'Let them abide till the morrow.'" Without charging their venerated parent with superstition or ignorance, the obedient sons yielded to his word, unladed their beasts, placed them in their stalls, and waited for another morning to come.

That memorable night a horde of savages, with torch and tomahawk, entered Wyoming Valley, and commenced their work of destruction. And it is said that before the bloody drama ended not a house, barn, church, school, or mill escaped the flames, and few of the inhabitants escaped the sudden, deadly blows of the savages. From one end of the valley to the other the settlers were butchered or burned with remorseless fury.

In the morning at sunrise, the father and sons were standing on the highest point, and lo! the valley was filled with volumes of ascending smoke and flames. The awful truth flashed on their minds. The aged saint kneeled down with his sons on the mountaintop, and in humble, adoring prayer thanked God for the promise: "The angel of the Lord encampeth round about them that fear him."– *Guiding Hand*

Behold, I send you forth as sheep among wolves

How continually, as we follow the Lord closely, do His own blessed teachings, His own words, come with full force to our memory, clothed with life and power! One such experience I shall never forget. We were holding tabernacle meetings in Shiawassee County, Michigan. One night, as we gathered to commence, everything looked ominous. The dark countenances of the men gathered on the outside of the congregation soon broke out in murmured words of threatening. God was working and the great adversary, "the devil, and father of lies," had circulated through all the community the report that we were breaking up families as some, contrary to the wishes of relatives, had decided to take the "narrow way," to "forsake all, and follow Jesus." The crowd increased, and soon we found it impossible to carry on the service.

Then came the words of Jesus, "Behold, I send you forth as sheep among wolves." Our little band—as my eye glanced over them, how helpless they looked! Hemming us in was a rough crowd whose teeth gleamed and whose howlings were like those of wolves. The scene of the martyrdom of Stephen came up right before me—how they gnashed on him with their teeth!

Soon our leader, Brother S. B. Shaw, sprang upon a stump of a tree, saying, "Everyone get on his knees, and hold right on to God." In a lower tone he said, "They have got Brother Jenkinson, and will tear him to pieces, if we do not hold on to God for him."

Soon mighty cries went up unto Him who is able to save. For about two hours the scene lasted. While at its very height, the assuring words came to me from the blessed Savior, "There shall not a hair of your head perish." Then the crowd began gradually to disperse, and full of thankful joy we lay down in our little tents to slumber. The angel of the Lord encamped round about us.

"I knew," said Brother Jenkinson, "they could not hurt me while you were holding on to God for me in prayer, and while their fists came down upon me they seemed as soft as pads of velvet." His clothes were much torn, but not one bruise or mark of violence was upon his person. One man, more full of violent hate than the others, had threatened that he would yet take the life of Brother Jenkinson, but the Lord told him to fear him not, for his enemy was no more in his hands than a little stick, and as easily broken.–*Mrs. Sarah A. Cooke*

As this sister has contributed several articles to the pages of this book it will not be amiss to say that we have been acquainted with her ever since the day of our conversion. She helped pray us into the light of salvation. We never knew a person to spend more time than she does in secret player, or to manifest more joy in the Lord's work. She is one of the two sisters so often mentioned in connection with the experience of Mr. Moody. They were so greatly burdened for him that Sister Cooke went to him repeatedly, and told him of his lack of power. He was brought under deep conviction, and requested them to pray for him. The three finally went on their knees, and there wrestled with God, he groaning and agonizing until the baptism of fire fell upon him. The world knows the results of the wonderful experience which under God these humble sisters were there enabled to lead him into, and for which multitudes praise God on earth, and will praise him in heaven.—*Editor*

The secret of John Smith's success

This extraordinary man died at the early age of thirty-seven. He commenced his labors as a Wesleyan minister in England in 1816, and closed them nearly simultaneously with his life on the third of November, 1831. The following, which reveals the secret of his success, is from *Sketches of Wesleyan Preachers*, a very interesting work, by Robert A. West:

"Constant communion with God was at the foundation of Mr. Smith's great usefulness. In this he was surpassed by none of any age. Whole nights were often given up to prayer, and always, when in anything like moderate health—often, too, when wasted by painful disease—he arose at four o'clock in the morning, and throwing himself before the mercy seat, for three hours wrestled with God in mighty prayer. The writer has heard from persons in whose houses he has been temporarily residing that in the coldest winter morning they have heard him at that hour with suppressed voice pleading with God, while his groans have revealed the intensity of his feelings. Immediately after breakfast and family worship he would again retire with his Bible into his study, and spend until near noon in the same hallowed employment. Here unquestionably was the great secret of his power in public prayer and in preaching—the Lord, who seeth in secret, rewarding him openly. Every sermon was thus sanctified by prayer.

"On one occasion when at a country appointment the time for commencing the service had elapsed, and Mr. Smith did not make his appearance. He had left the house where he was a guest about half an hour before, after being some time in his closet. At length he was found in an adjoining barn, wrestling in prayer for a blessing upon the approaching service, having retired thither that unobserved he might pour out his full soul before his heavenly Father. He arose, briefly expressed his regret at not having observed the lapse of time, and on the way to the chapel relapsed into silent prayer.

"During the sermon that evening the fervent prayer of the righteous man proved effectual. The Spirit of God descended upon the congregation. The deep, attentive silence observed at the commencement of the discourse was soon interrupted by sobs and moans, and these ere long were followed by loud and piercing cries for mercy, as one after another the hearers were pricked to the heart. The strongholds of Satan were beaten down until, so universal was the cry of the brokenhearted, that Mr. Smith found it necessary to desist from preaching, and descend into the altar.

"As he had continued his discourse for some time after its remarkable effects first showed themselves, there was considerable confusion for want of a leading and controlling spirit, and the disorder was rapidly increasing. But when he descended from the pulpit and took charge of the meeting his admirable plans and great influence, aided by a voice almost equal to the roar of thunder, soon wrought a change, and in perfect order, though not in silence, the meeting was continued until midnight. Whatever apparent confusion there might be in these meetings, they were actually conducted systematically. Mr. Smith had his method amid all the surrounding excitement, and he never delegated the control to another, but was the last to retire from the scene of the Redeemer's triumphs."—Anecdotes of the Ministry

How William Tennent defeated the powers of darkness
During the great revival of religion in America which took place under Mr. Whitefield, and others distinguished for their piety and zeal at that period, Mr. Tennent was laboriously active and much engaged to help forward the work, in the performance of which he met with strong and powerful temptations. The following is from his own lips:

On the evening preceding public worship he selected a subject for the discourse intended to be delivered and made some progress in his preparations. In the morning he resumed the same subject, with an intention to extend his thoughts further on it, but was presently assaulted with a temptation that the Bible was not of Divine authority but the invention of man. He instantly endeavored to repel the temptation by prayer but his endeavors proved unavailing. The temptation continued and fastened upon him with greater strength as the time advanced for public service. He lost all the thoughts which he had prepared on the preceding evening. He tried other subjects, but could get nothing for the people. The whole book of God, under that distressing state of mind, was a sealed book to him, and to add to his affliction he was "shut up in prayer," a cloud, dark as that of Egypt, oppressed his mind.

Thus agonized in spirit, he proceeded to the church, where he found a large congregation assembled, and waiting to hear the word. Then he was more deeply distressed than ever, and especially for the dishonor which he feared would fall upon religion through him that day. He resolved, however, to attempt the service. He introduced it by singing a psalm, during which time his agitation increased to the highest degree.

When the moment for prayer commenced he arose, as one in the most painful and perilous situation, and with arms extended to heaven, began with this exclamation: "Lord, have mercy upon me!" On the utterance of this petition he was heard. The thick cloud instantly broke away, and light shone upon his soul. The result was a deep solemnity throughout the congregation, and the house, at the end of the prayer, was a place of weeping. He delivered the subject of his evening meditations, which was brought to his full remembrance with an overflowing abundance of other weighty and solemn matter. The Lord blessed this discourse so that it proved the happy means of the conversion of about thirty persons. This day he ever afterwards spoke of as his "harvest-day."—*Anecdotes of the Ministry*

In India—in answer to prayer

The following very interesting account was written by request, expressly for this book. The author was a missionary of the Methodist Episcopal Church in India for a number of years. He is, at the date of our publication, pastor at Huntington, Ohio:

In January, 1888, my devoted wife, since gone to glory, and myself were appointed by Bishop Thoburn to open work in a district of the native state of Hyderabad, India. Our parish embraced more than a thousand towns and villages of over a million souls—a district practically untouched by Christian evangelism.

Full of faith in God, the missionaries cheerfully proceeded to the new field of conflict. Six months later we visited for the third time Kinnal, a village of probably 12,000 souls, sixty miles from our center, for the purpose of supervising a day school and Sunday school recently begun, and preaching the gospel to the people.

REMARKABLE ANSWERS TO PRAYER

We had not a single Christian convert in the village except Andronika, our native teacher, and his young wife, and these were imported for the purpose intimated. Weary from our long bullock-cart ride, we spent an hour in quiet rest and at dinner, after which the school work was looked after.

At five o'clock the people were called together to hear a short gospel talk, and witness the first Christian baptismal service they had probably ever seen. Nearly the entire village, in an amazingly brief time, had congregated in the street just in front of our little mission room, which we had recently purchased for thirty rupees ($10.00).

The village was just being scourged by those deadly diseases, cholera and smallpox, and the deluded natives had sacrificed nearly all their poultry, sheep, goats, and much fruit, to appease the anger of their imaginary deities. Still the scourge went on. For eight months there had been no rainfall, and the people were in a semi-starved condition, and hence a ready prey to these virulent diseases. It is needless to say that our simple discourse upon "Jesus, the all-sufficient sacrifice" had many eager listeners in this sad, spirit-broken assembly.

Then followed a scene we shall never forget. Just in front of the missionary and his companion stood Andronika and his wife presenting their little babe for Christian baptism.

Before the ceremony was finished, a man of the weaver's caste prostrated himself before us, preparatory to the making of an urgent appeal. We beckoned him to wait until the close of the service. Then, after another prostration, the poor fellow advanced to make his request.

With a sad expression on his face and tremulous voice, he proceeded to say, "My wife is dying. For four days I have been breaking coconuts and making poojahs, and my wife has been growing worse all the time. Now I beg of you to pray to your God, to see if he will hear and save my wife!" We were conducted by the sad husband into a little mud hut nearby, followed by the multitude. There lay the poor wife, unconscious and moaning. A brief examination confirmed all the brokenhearted husband had said. It was quite evident that the case was beyond human help.

An indescribable burden came upon my soul while contemplating the situation. I turned to my dear wife and said, "There is no use giving this woman any medicine. It is too late, I can do nothing for her. Only God can help her. And if the purpose of the miracle on Mount Carmel, in answer to the prayer of Elijah, was to vindicate God's cause before the worshipers of Baal, may not the Lord raise this woman to health, to vindicate himself in this province of a million devotees to false gods?

Her answer—I'll never forget it—was, "According to thy faith be it unto thee." Then I said to the husband, "Jesus Christ, who is the only God, can save your wife if he thinks best. Now if he cures her, will you then forever renounce your idols, and worship Jesus Christ only?" A moment of intense anxiety, and his aged mother rushed up to him, and pleaded with him in tears to answer in the negative.

He replied, "I can make better answer after she is cured." But I insisted that I could not feel justified in asking my Savior to interfere in his behalf unless he was willing to answer the question in the affirmative, and worship Jesus if he showed Himself by His superior power to be God. Then there came to the poor tried soul another awful struggle.

All his relatives and the priests gathered around him, and tried to persuade him that it would be better for his wife to die than that he should make such a promise. Another moment of awful suspense, and the brave soul turned and answered, "Houdu, (*Yes*, in the Canarese tongue) if Jesus Christ can save my wife, it shows that what you say is right—my gods are false, and I ought then to worship Jesus Christ."

With eyes uplifted, we prayed the dear Lord to get unto Himself a great name among these benighted souls. And, oh, what a baptism of assurance came into our souls!

We turned immediately to go away, and in less than a minute the excited husband came rushing after us, exclaiming, "Jesus Christ, He is God! My wife is well!" and began in every conceivable way to express his gratitude.

Till nearly midnight the voice of that joyful man, going up and down the narrow streets of the village, was heard crying, "Jesus Christ, He is the only true God!"

Towards morning, a copious shower of rain fell, and the natives said, "It is because the missionary is praying."

At five o'clock next morning we left the village, with hundreds of its grateful people following in procession to do honor to those whom they said brought so much blessing to their village. For miles they followed, and not until we earnestly remonstrated did they turn back. We believe that that event of providence will be blessed to the salvation not only of hundreds in that village, but to many in other places, for among those who witnessed what has been related were more than a score who had been sent from adjoining villages to induce, if possible, the missionary to begin work in their towns. These may for a time continue in heathenism, but they will not forget the strange Power which wrought such wonders before their eyes.

Praise the Lord for His wonderful goodness!—A. E. *Winter*

REMARKABLE ANSWERS TO PRAYER

Can I be saved?

Away on the western coast of England there stands a steep rock that is known to everybody as the *Lady's Rock*. At high water it is surrounded by the sea, but at low water it stands upon a sandy beach and is easily reached.

It gets the name from an accident that occurred years ago. One summer day a lady had walked along the beach as far as this rock, and there sat down and began to read a book that interested her. She read on, never thinking of any danger, when she was suddenly startled by a loud cry from the cliffs. The coastguard had seen her and shouted across the bay. She looked up and in a moment saw her peril. Between herself and the shore there were the curling waves, and the white foam spreading over the sands. Her first look showed her nothing but certain death, for the waves were rising every moment, and as she stood hesitating, a huge breaker dashed its spray over her. Above her frowned the steep, black rock, and even the fisher lads could scarcely climb to get the seabird's eggs. There seemed to be no way of escape there. She looked across to the crowd that were gathering on the shore, but no boat could live in that tumbling sea. Then, as she stood with the waves creeping up after her like wild beasts that chased their prey, she wrung her hands in agony and burst into tears, crying, "Can I be saved? Can I be saved?"

A moment before it was nothing to her. Now it was everything. Wealth, luxury, comfort, pleasure—all thought of these were swept away. Her only anxiety was this: "Oh, to be saved!"

Then across from the shore came the cry from the coastguard again, "You must climb the rock! Your only chance is to climb the rock!" She looked at it hanging over her with jagged sides and steep, slippery front. How could she climb it? But as she delayed, a wave swept up and flung itself over the place where she stood, and close below her the waters surged and hissed. Then she grasped the rock desperately and dragged herself up and hung to the face of it, tremblingly feeling for a higher foothold and rising, little by little, until she reached a ledge from which she looked shudderingly on the waves below.

The tide crept upward until again the spray flew about her. "Climb higher!" rang from the shore, this time from a hundred voices, for the tidings of her peril had spread to the adjoining village. Again she gathered her strength, and hardly knowing how, she crept, little by little, hanging on with bleeding fingers, dragging herself through narrow openings, pressing up the steep, slippery places, until now within her reach lay a tuft of grass. Seizing it she fell fainting on the top, beyond the reach of the waves, while the excited people cried with a shout, "She's saved! Thank Heaven, she's saved!"

A story wild and strange, like the coast, and yet it is true of every life—true of you, reader. Slowly the sea is chasing you from point to point. The sea is rising about you.

You can look back and see how it has driven you from day to day, from year to year, and yet you are unmindful of it. Taken up with a hundred things, you do not see it. It is the last thing you think of. You have time for everything else. You can think of business, of pleasure, of politics, of the markets, of friendships—of everything else but this. And yet the time is coming when you will see the peril, when your own eyes shall look upon the threatening danger, and all of these things of today shall be nothing. Suddenly, all in a moment, you will start up with the cry, "What must I do to be saved?" And it may be too late.—Rev. Mark Guy Pearse

The widow's prayer answered

A captain's widow, whom I knew for many years of our chapel, was much concerned for the conversion of her son, who was a sailor. For a long time he had promised to be a comfort and help to his mother, but through the influence of bad companions he became very wicked and dissolute. Many times have I gone to the public house and other places of temptation to allure him home to his mother's house, and in no instance when his mother's name had been mentioned has he refused to come, for on him the charming name of "mother" seemed to exercise a potent, irresistible spell. I have often taken him up into our Sunday school room, where he used to be a scholar, and have reasoned and prayed with him till the tears ran down his cheeks, and he would promise to get on "a better tack."

On one of these occasions I gave him a pocket Bible, in which he engaged to read one verse a day until the ship returned from Sidney. I mentioned this to his mother, and shall not soon forget her look, as she said, "Thank God! Thank God! I now have hopes of his conversion."

He was gone many months, and but little was heard of him and the mother prayed for him daily at a fixed time. It pleased the Lord to visit her with a painful disease, which terminated in her death, but her faith, joy and peace were marvelous and delightful to witness. I do not remember paying her a single visit in which she did not mention her son, and express her belief that she would meet him in glory.

One evening she remarked, "I am near the grave. I feel my time here is very short. I will leave a message for my boy, which you must deliver to him." Observing her extreme weakness, I prayed with her a few moments, and promised to see her early the next day. Accordingly I called, and saw that she was indeed dying. She desired to be propped up in bed and to sing a hymn, and in order to support her in this final effort, her two daughters knelt on the bed and upheld her as well as they could. She spoke to them of her funeral and her property.

When this business had been transacted she said to me, "I know that I am dying, but I have no fear. All is light and beautiful. Christ is here. Christ is mine, and I am his." Her voice became stronger and clearer, and she bade us sing. Her daughters could sing but little. Their hearts were too full. However, we all did our best in singing her favorite verse:

> *Fearless of hell and ghastly death,*
>   *I'd break through every foe;*
> *The wings of love and arms of faith,*
>   *Would bear me conqueror through.*

While we were singing, a loud knocking was heard. The servant having gone for the doctor, I went to the door and to my surprise found the sailor boy just returned from the sea. I explained to him his mother's condition, and got him to remain in the parlor till I broke the news to her. When I returned to her bedside, she said, "Oh, I thought it was my dear boy. Oh, how I should like to see him once more, and to give him my blessing,"

"Are you able," I inquired, "to hear him, or to see him?"

With a smile, she replied, "I can bear anything, through Christ."

I went for the sailor and when I brought him into the room we found her praying, with her eyes closed, for her only son. In a few moments she looked around and saw her long-absent child. He threw his arms around his mother's neck and tried to speak, but could not. But the mother cried, "Hallelujah! Jesus is faithful and true," and after one kiss, she added, "My dear boy, I am dying and going to Jesus. I have prayed every day for you, my dear Frank. What shall I tell Jesus about you? Your father is there," pointing upwards, "your sisters are on the way. Oh, what shall I tell my blessed Savior?"

"You can tell Him what you like, mother. I am a Christian, converted to God, mother, and he knows all about it."

The mother's heart was full. The good news overcame her strength, and she exclaimed, "Let me go, Lord, I have seen thy salvation! My prayers are all answered! My son is saved—clothed, and in his right mind! Glory! Glory! Glory!"

After sleeping a few minutes she awoke with a beautiful smile on her face, and said, "I see the angels, harps, crowns—bright, golden crowns! Let me go!" Raising her hand above her head, she exclaimed, "Victory, through faith in His blood!" Then her arm fell, her eyes closed, and her spirit returned to God who gave it.—*T. G. Garland*

Prayers answered for rain

Within two blocks of the Pacific Mission in Chicago, is one of our large depots, the *Rock Island and Lake Shore Railroad*. Here is a good field for labor. One night, when inviting one and another to the mission, a lady answered, "We are on our way to Oberlin."

"The place," I asked, "where Charles Finney lived?"

"Yes."

"And did you know him?"

"Yes," she answered, "and my husband, who is here, was a member of his church." Soon he joined us, much crippled and out of health, at first but little inclined to talk. I told him how precious the memory of Mr. Finney was, and asked if he could tell us any personal reminiscences of him. Soon the fire began to burn in his heart, and his lips began to speak.

He said, "We had been long without rain. All vegetation was drying up. Everything looked parched. In the prayer preceding the sermon one Sabbath Mr. Finney began to pour out his full heart to God for rain. He laid the whole case before Him. 'Lord, the cattle in the fields are lowing for water. There will be no food for them for winter unless thou sendest rain. The harvest will fail—no food for man—unless Thou sendest rain. The little squirrels in the woods are panting for rain.' On and on the petitions rose, faith rising as he prayed, until he felt they had entered into the ear of the Lord of Sabaoth, and, that 'as a prince, he had power with God, and prevailed.' His closing words were, 'Lord, we want rain, and we want it now!'

"The service proceeded, the text was chosen, and for about half an hour Mr. Finney preached. When the rain began to dash against windows he stopped, and gave out a hymn:

> When all thy mercies, Oh my God,
>   My rising soul surveys;
> Transported with the view, I'm lost
>   In wonder, love, and praise.

"The whole congregation rose to their feet, and I don't think in that assembly of three thousand people there was one dry eye. I never can tell it," said the stranger, "but it melts me right up."

Yea, we are all melted, while "heaven came down our souls to greet, and glory crowned the Mercy-Seat."

> God, who lived in Elijah's time,
>   Is just the same today.

"Elijah was a man subject to like passions as we are and he prayed earnestly"—when the sins of the people were hurrying them on to destruction—"that it might not rain; and it rained not on the earth for the space of three years. And again he prayed, and the heavens gave rain." Are not all these scriptures given to encourage and strengthen the faith of God's people in all ages? Yea, verily!

Two sisters had left the Taylorville, Illinois, campground on their way to visit a sick woman. The earth had become its dustiest. All nature was parched and drying up under the hot beams of the sun. It was Saturday and looking forward to the Sabbath, bringing its multitudes from all the surrounding country, they thought of the suffering and discomfort there would be.

The elder of the two asked, "Is not God the same today as in the days of Elijah?" The dry bed of a spring seemed a good place for prayer, and there they knelt together. Soon their united faith took hold, and the assurance was given that their prayers were heard, and their petitions should be granted.

Rev. L. B. Kent, of Jacksonville, the leader of the meeting, proposed at the close of the afternoon service that a meeting should be held for prayer for rain.

"And shall I hide what the Lord has already promised?" was the query whispered by the Spirit. "No." And rising to her feet, one of the sisters told how the Lord had promised the rain.

Night came. The moon, in her glorious brightness, shone forth, and there was no indication in the heavens of rain. Hour after hour passed, while every now and then, as faith held on for the promised blessing, the assuring words of Jesus would come, "If ye abide in me, and my words abide in you, ye shall ask what ye will, and it shall be done unto you." Three o'clock came, and the rain began to fall, and the hallelujahs and praises to God went up from many a waiting heart. It fell copiously until seven o'clock, when the clouds dispersed, and the people gathered, and the work of God moved on blessedly.—*Sarah A. Cooke*

The widow's shoes

A poor woman, a widow with an invalid son, a member of the church, could not attend church, or the neighborhood prayer meetings, for the want of shoes. She asked the Lord for the shoes. That very day the village schoolmaster called in to see her son. Meanwhile, he noticed that the boy's mother had very poor shoes. He said nothing but felt impressed, and inwardly resolved to purchase the poor woman a pair of shoes forthwith. He accordingly hired a horse, rode two miles on horseback to a shoestore, bought the shoes, and requested them sent to the widow's cottage without delay. They proved a perfect fit, and that very night the overjoyed woman hurried to the prayer meeting to announce that in answer to prayer the Lord had sent her the shoes.

The young schoolmaster who, I suspect, was my informant himself, now a venerable, white-haired man, heard the poor woman's testimony. His pillow that night was wet with tears of gratitude and joy, because God had used him thus to bless the poor widow, and to answer her prayers.—*Answers to Prayer*

Instantaneously healed

Brother E. B. Williams, of Warren, Illinois, writes us of the instantaneous recovery of a woman in answer to prayer, as follows:

"In the year 1830, in the town of Shelby, Orleans county, New York, a woman of middle age lay very sick for a long time under the doctor's care without any benefit, and pronounced by all as incurable. As I was praying one Sabbath morning in church, without thinking of the case, there came a voice to me from some source which was as distinct as man could speak, saying, 'Go, and pray with and for that woman.'

"I went to her home the next week, and tried to make her comfortable. She was apparently in a dreamy state. I left the house without prayer, and thought no more of it until a day or two after, when father and I went to the same place on business. She saw me and beckoned me to come to her, and I did so.

"She whispered to me, asking why I did not pray for her the other day, and added, 'Something told me thee came to pray for me.' She was a Quaker. I told her I was sent to do so, but diffidence and timidity prevented at that time. I felt no call to pray then but a day or two after, while I was alone and going by the place, without thought on the subject, the words came to me again, as plain as man could speak them: 'Go, and pray for that woman.' I went in, and called the family together, and while we engaged in prayer, an invisible power was felt by all in the house, and that woman was healed at once, and was well."

The Lord's way of sending help

A few years ago we were led out to pray for means to make a payment on our home in Grand Rapids, Michigan. The amount was one hundred dollars, and it was due in two weeks. We had no way of getting the money and, realizing the promises of God to be reliable, we laid the matter before the Lord in prayer.

At the time we were holding meetings in the southern part of Michigan. When the answer to prayer came, we wrote home to wife, telling her that we had the evidence beyond every possibility of a doubt, that the Lord would send the money in time.

In a few days we received a letter from a brother in Texas, whom we had only met but once, saying that he was impressed to send us fifty dollars which was enclosed in the letter. In a short time twenty-five dollars were received from a friend in our own state. The balance came in smaller sums. At the time the obligation was due, the money was on hand, and we praised God for his special help in a time of need.—*Editor*

REMARKABLE ANSWERS TO PRAYER

Redfield in a hard place

John W. Redfield was a remarkable revivalist among the Methodists and Free Methodists. He died not many years ago. From his memoir, prepared by J. G. Terrill, we take the following:

"The Sabbath came, and I went to church. A goodly number had come, probably from curiosity, to see the new preacher. I had resolved to deliver my own soul regardless of persons or conditions by declaring the whole counsel of God. But I saw no favorable indications. After a few efforts during the week following to bring about a change, and finding it all in vain, I went to sinners and exhorted them to flee from the wrath to come. The response from them was, 'Go look after your ungodly members.'

"Sabbath came again, and I delivered my message in view of the judgment. When I was leaving the church, I met the principal member of the official board, who accosted me thus: 'We don't like your preaching here at all, nor the chapters you read from the pulpit. Hell is not very popular here.'

"I inquired, 'Will you tell me, brother, what I have preached that is not Bible truth?'

" 'Well,' said he, 'I believe it is true.'

" 'Do you want me to preach lies?' I asked.

"I went home, weeping along the street. I now saw if I was going to accomplish anything, I must do it with my might. So Monday morning I went to the grove and knelt before the Lord in prayer. It seemed as though the powers of darkness were all about me. The sensations I experienced were as if by the hardest effort I was overcoming great obstacles and rising higher and higher, until my head struck against a rock and I sank back overcome.

"I arose and sought another place to plead with God, and there experienced the same. Thus I continued day after day through the week. I would go to the house once in a while and get something to eat, and then return to the struggle. Sometimes my agony was such that it seemed to me I could rend the heavens with my cries for the salvation of sinners. It seemed to me that if I could hold on until the victory came I should see them saved.

"When Saturday night came my very brain seemed sore, and the jar of my step gave me pain. I felt a kind of bewilderment coming on but I had received no answer. I had resolved, in the name of God, to see a break and salvation come to the church on the next Sabbath, or an end put to its standing as a stench in the nostrils of the Almighty and the world.

"Sunday morning came, and with eyes sore from weeping, and my brain tender from the continual struggle of the week, I walked softly and carefully to the church and into the pulpit. In opening the service, I said to the membership, 'This day ends my labors in this place. You do not want me here, and I do not want to stay, for I am heartily tired of pouring water onto rocks. But if God will help me, I will either see a break today or see this ungodly apology for Methodism annihilated. I have asked no man's money. I go at my own expense, but I shall go straight for God.' Nothing seemed to move in the morning.

"In the evening I went into the pulpit again and announced that I should redeem my pledge. Of course, this aroused their hate to a high pitch. As God helped, I pointed out the track of an acceptable disciple, and the only one that could possibly pass the gates of Paradise. At the close of the sermon, I asked those—and only those who meant it and would take this track and where needed go to their neighbors and confess to them and pray with them, and who would seek for the blessing of holiness until they knew they had it—to rise. I didn't believe I could get them to come forward. Two only arose, and they were of the most lowly.

" 'Well,' I said, 'there seem to be three of us, counting myself as one, and God besides. But I think we will try and have a prayer meeting.' Those two and myself were all that would kneel, I in the altar and they at their seats, about halfway down the church. I opened with a short prayer, and began to rise in spirit until I struck that rock again. I then asked someone else to pray, but no one responded, and I tried again with the same experience and result, and the third time, and the fourth, and fifth, until the sixth time, in immediate succession.

"I now felt that this is the last time, and that if I did not get the victory, God would say to me, 'Let them alone.' The case was a desperate one, and I knew the world and the devil were against me, and the churchmembers who would not kneel.

"But I said in my prayer, 'O God, I'll go as far as I can.' Again in spirit I began to rise, and soon I struck that rock again, and it seemed to shiver to atoms. Instantly the house was filled with the Divine glory. The two who were kneeling with me fell, and their shouts and screams were so loud that they alarmed the village.

"The people came running in to see what was the matter, and as they crowded up the aisles and saw the two prostrate under the power of God, tears chased each other down their faces, and the poor tempted members began one after another to confess their hostility and ask for pardon, and promised to take the track pointed out to them. I stayed one more week, and forty-five sinners were converted. The preacher who had abandoned the work returned, and the revival went on in power for some time. Ten or fifteen years afterward, I heard from that society, and it still was doing well."

REMARKABLE ANSWERS TO PRAYER

13

Prayer answered for one hundred missionaries and money to support them
MAJOR O.M. BROWN, PRESIDENT of the Ohio Christian Alliance of Cleveland, Ohio, furnishes us the following:

In the spring of 1890, Rev. A. B. Simpson, President of the International Christian Alliance, was burdened in prayer for the heathen who were perishing without the knowledge of the true God. And as he prayed, he began to inquire, "Lord, what can I do about it?" Then he began to ask the Lord to give him that year one hundred missionaries for the foreign work, and money enough to pay their transit, and support them one year on the field, which would be about one hundred thousand dollars.

At the New York State Convention of the Alliance, held at Round Lake in July of that same year, Mr. Simpson gave a very stirring address on the subject and the people pledged $1,800 in a few minutes. At the Ohio Convention at Beulah Park, near Cleveland a few days later, $2,200 was pledged. And at the Old Orchard Convention in Maine, in the month of August, $35,000 was pledged. Afterward, the pledges kept coming in until there was upwards of $100,000 pledged. Before the year was out, the one hundred missionaries were, many of them, in the field, or on the way thither. A few of them had not yet departed but were ready to sail.

The work nearly doubled during the year 1892. These missionaries are scattered over large portions of the heathen world—in India, China, Japan, Africa, Palestine, South America, and the islands of the sea. None of this great force of Christian workers receive any stated salary for their service, and no member of the Mission Board receives any remuneration for his service. God will honor those who ask large things of Him.

Testimony of a saved infidel

He had been given up by some as a hopeless case. One man, however, prayed for him until he prevailed and the infidel was saved.

A revival was in progress, and in the midst of a melting meeting he arose and to the surprise of many, "with face shining as did the face of Moses when he saw God," he gave the following striking and suggestive testimony:

"I stand," said Mr. R——, "to tell you the story of my conversion." His lips trembled slightly as he spoke, and his chest heaved with suppressed emotion. "I am as a brand plucked out of the burning. The change in me is an astonishment to myself, and all brought about by the grace of God, and that unanswerable argument.

"It was a cold morning in January and I had just begun my labor at the anvil in my shop when I looked out and saw Mr. B—— approaching. He dismounted quickly and entered. As he drew near I saw he was agitated. His look was full of earnestness. His eyes were dimmed with tears. He took me by the hand; his chest heaved with emotions and with indescribable tenderness he said, 'Mr. R——, I am greatly concerned for your salvation—greatly concerned for your salvation,' and he burst into tears. He stood with my hand grasped in his. He struggled to regain self-possession. He often tried to speak, but not a word could he utter. Finding that he could say no more, he turned, went out of the shop, got on his horse, and rode slowly away.

" 'Greatly concerned for my salvation,' said I, audibly, and I stood and forgot to bring my hammer down. There I stood with it upraised. 'Greatly concerned for your salvation.' Here is a new argument for the truth of religion, which I have never heard before, and which I know not how to answer. Had the aged man reasoned with me I could have confounded him, but here is no threadbare argument for the truth of religion. Religion must be truth or this man would not feel as he does. 'Greatly concerned for my salvation.' It rang through my ears like a thunderclap in a clear sky. 'Greatly concerned I ought to be for my own salvation,' said I. 'What shall I do?'

"I went to my house. My poor pious wife, whom I had always ridiculed for her religion, exclaimed, 'Why, Mr. R——, what is the matter with you?'

" 'Matter enough,' said I, filled with agony and overwhelmed with a sense of sin. 'Old Mr. B—— has rode two miles this cold morning to tell me he was greatly concerned for my salvation. What shall I do? What shall I do?'

" 'I do not know what you can do,' said my astonished wife. 'I do not know what better you can do than to get on your horse, and go and see him. He can give you better counsel than I, and tell you what you must do to be saved.'

"I mounted my horse, and pursued after him. I found him alone in that same little room where he had spent the night in prayer for my poor soul, where he had shed many tears over such a reprobate as I, and had besought God to have mercy upon me.

" 'I am come,' said I to him, 'to tell you that I am greatly concerned for my own salvation.'

" 'Praised be God,' said the aged man. 'It is a faithful saying, and worthy of all acceptation, that Jesus Christ came into the world to save sinners, even the chief,' and he began at that same scripture, and preached to me Jesus. On that same floor we knelt, and together we prayed—and we did not separate that day till God spoke peace to my soul.

"I have often been requested to look at the evidence of the truth of religion, but blessed be God, I have evidence for its truth here," laying his hand upon his heart, "which nothing can gainsay or resist. I have often been led to look at this and that argument for the truth of Christianity, but I could overturn, and, as I thought, completely demolish and annihilate them all. But I stand here tonight, thankful to acknowledge that God sent an argument to my conscience and heart which could not be answered or resisted when a weeping Christian came to tell me how greatly concerned he was for my salvation. God taught him that argument when he spent the night before him in prayer for my soul. Now I can truly say I am a happy man. My peace flows like a river. My consistent, uncomplaining wife, who so long bore with my impiety and unbelief, now rejoices with me that, by the grace of God, I am what I am—that whereas I was blind, now I see. And here permit me to say, if you would wish to reach the heart of such a poor sinner as I, you must get your qualifications where he did, in your closet and on your knees. So it shall be with me. I will endeavor to reach the hearts of my infidel friends through the closet and by prayer."

He sat down overcome with emotion, amid the tears and the suppressed sobs of the assembly. All were touched, for all knew what he once was. All saw what he had now become.—*Tract*

I don't love you now, mother

A great many years ago I knew a lady who had been sick for two years, as you have seen many a one, all the while slowly dying with consumption. She had one child, a little boy named Henry.

One afternoon I was sitting by her side, and it seemed as if she would cough her life away. Her little boy stood by the post of the bed, his blue eyes filled with tears to see her suffer so. By and by the terrible cough ceased. Henry came and put his arms around his mother's neck, nestled his head in his mother's bosom, and said, "Mother, I do love you. I wish you wasn't sick."

An hour later, the same loving, blue-eyed boy came in all aglow, stamping the snow off his feet. "Oh, mother, may I go a-skating? It is so nice—Ed and Charley are going."

"Henry," feebly said the mother, "the ice is not hard enough yet."

"But, mother," very pettishly said the boy, "you are sick all the time—how do you know?"

"My child, you must obey me," gently said his mother.

"It is too bad," angrily sobbed the boy, who an hour ago, had so loved his mother.

"I would not like to have my little boy go," said his mother, looking sadly at the little boy's face, all covered with frowns. "You said you loved me—be good."

"No, I don't love you now, mother," said the boy, going out and slamming the door.

Again the dreadful coughing came upon her, and I thought no more of the boy. After the coughing had commenced, I noticed tears falling thick upon her pillow, but she sank from exhaustion into a light sleep.

In a little while muffled steps of men's feet were heard coming into the house, as though carrying something, and they were carrying the almost lifeless body of Henry.

Angrily had he left his mother and gone to skate, disobeying her, and then broken through the ice, sunk under the water, and now saved by a great effort, was brought home barely alive to his sick mother.

I closed the doors, feeling more danger for her life than the child's, and coming softly in, drew back the curtains from the bed. She spoke, "I heard them. It is Henry. Oh, I knew he went. Is he dead?" But she never seemed to hear the answer I gave her. She commenced coughing—she died in agony—strangled to death. The poor mother! The boy's disobedience killed her.

After a couple of hours I sought the boy's room. "Oh, I wish I had not told mother I did not love her. Tomorrow I will tell her I do," said the child sobbing painfully. My heart ached. Tomorrow I knew we must tell him she was dead. We did not till the child came fully in the room, crying, "Mother, I do love you." Oh! May I never see agony like that child's, as the lips he kissed gave back no kiss, as the hands he took fell lifeless from his hand, instead of shaking his hand as it always had, and the boy knew she was dead.

"Mother, I do love you now," all the day he sobbed and cried, "Oh mother, mother, forgive me." Then he would not leave his mother. "Speak to me mother!" But she could never speak again, and the last words she had ever heard him say were, "Mother, I don't love you now."

That boy's whole life was changed. Sober and sad he was ever after. He is now a gray-haired old man, with one sorrow over his one act of disobedience, one wrong word embittering all his life, with those words ever ringing in his ears, "Mother, I don't love you now."

Will the little ones who read this remember, if they disobey their mother, if they are cross and naughty, they say every single time they do so, to a tender mother's heart, by their actions, if not in the words of Henry, the very same thing, "I don't love you now, mother?"

How a blacksmith prevailed with God for a revival

A story related by Mr. Finney will illustrate the power of the mighty prayer of faith, even when every human aid seems withheld. Nothing remains but the burning, throbbing heart, breathing out its longings, and pouring out its groans and tears before the Lord.

In a certain town there had been no revival for many years. The church was nearly run out, the youth were all unconverted, and desolation reigned unbroken. There lived in a retired part of the town an aged man, a blacksmith by trade, and of so stammering a tongue that it was painful to hear him speak. On one Friday, as he was at work in his shop alone, his mind became greatly exercised about the state of the church and of the impenitent. His agony became so great that he was induced to lay aside his work, lock the shop door and spend the afternoon in prayer.

He prevailed, and on the Lord's Day called on the minister and desired him to appoint a conference meeting. After some hesitation the minister consented, observing, however, that he feared but few would attend. He appointed it the same evening at a large private house.

The people gathered from far and near, doubtless to the surprise of the unbelieving and fainthearted. A solemn sense of the presence of God seemed to oppress the assembly, and feelings too deep for speech were welling up in many hearts. All was silent for a time until one sinner broke out in tears, and said if any one could pray, he begged him to pray for him. Another followed, and still another, until it was found that persons from every quarter of the town were under deep conviction. And what was remarkable was that they all dated their conviction at the hour when the old man was praying in his shop. A powerful revival followed. Thus this old stammering man prevailed and as a prince had power with God.—*Records of Prevailing Prayer*

Result of Rev. John S. Inskip's prayer

From the life of that devoted and noted evangelist, Rev. J. S. Inskip, we quote the following incident, which occurred while he was pastor at Springfield, Ohio, January, 1851. A few days before its occurrence he recorded in his journal that he felt unusually encouraged to look unto God for a revival of religion in his own heart and among the members of his church, and that he was favored with much freedom in discoursing upon the duty and encouragements to prayer. We give the account in his own words:

"This has been one of the greatest days I have ever seen. In the morning I went into the high school and conducted the opening exercises. I then went into the church and attended to some items of business, intending to go subsequently into the country. As I passed along the street I received a message from Brother Howard requesting me immediately to repair to the high school. I went without delay and found in one of the rooms of the institution such a scene as I never witnessed before. There were over thirty of the young ladies and smaller children weeping and crying aloud for mercy. The exercises of the institution were suspended. We held a meeting for the benefit of the students in the afternoon. I presume during the day there were some eighteen converted.

"At night we held a society meeting. There were some eight or ten more converted, making in all some thirty conversions during the day. Twenty joined the society. I never knew such a work. To God be all the glory, glory, glory in the highest! My soul is unspeakably happy." From this manifestation of Divine power, the work spread into the town. It was a time of great excitement.

The winds controlled in answer to John Wesley's prayer

In Dr. Adam Clarke's record of his life and early ministry he relates the following instance of prevailing prayer:

John Wesley, with some of his co-workers, had been laboring in the Norman Islands and had appointed a day to be at Bristol. Taking passage with Dr. Clarke, Dr. Coke, and Joseph Bradford, in an English brig which had touched at Guernsey on its voyage from France, they left Guernsey with a fine, fair breeze, and every prospect of making a quick passage.

In a short time the wind died away and a contrary wind arose and blew with great force. Mr. Wesley was in the cabin reading, and hearing the bustle on deck, occasioned by putting the vessel about, he put his head above deck and inquired the cause. Being told that the wind was contrary and they were obliged to tack ship, he said, "Let us go to prayer." At his request, Coke, Clarke, and Bradford prayed.

As they concluded, Mr. Wesley broke out into fervent supplication, which seemed, says Dr. Clarke, to be more the offspring of strong faith than mere desire. He said, "Almighty and everlasting God, thou hast thy say everywhere, and all things serve the purposes of thy will. Thou holdest the winds in thy fists, and sittest upon the waterfloods, and reignest a king forever. Command these winds and these waves, that they obey **Thee**, and take us speedily and safely to the haven where we would be," etc.

The power of his petition was felt by all. He rose from his knees, made no kind of remark, but took up his book and continued his reading. Dr. Clarke went on deck and to his surprise found the vessel standing on her course with a steady breeze, which did not abate but carried them at the rate of nine or ten miles an hour until they were safely anchored at their desired port. Mr. Wesley made no remark on the sudden change of the wind.

"So fully," says Dr. Clarke, "did he expect to be heard, that he took it for granted he was heard. Such answers to prayer he was in the habit of receiving, and therefore to him the occurrence was not strange.

He who hath "gathered the wind in his fists," (Proverbs 30: 4) and who rules the raging of the sea, bends low to hear his children cry, and deigns to hear their prayer. "Oh that men would praise the Lord for his goodness, and his wonderful works to the children of men!"

The clouds stayed in answer to prayer

In his *Memorials of Methodism in Virginia*, Dr. W. W. Bennett relates the following incidents in the life of John Easter, one of the pioneer ministers who labored there nearly one hundred years ago. He is represented as being the most powerful exhortatory preacher of his day. His faith was transcendent, his appeals irresistible, his prayers like talking to God face to face. Perhaps no man has ever been more signally honored of God as an instrument in the conversion of souls. On one of his circuits eighteen hundred members were added to the church in a single year. Many thrilling scenes under his preaching yet linger in the memory of the people in those counties where he principally labored.

A most extraordinary display of his faith was witnessed in Brunswick. At Merritt's meetinghouse a quarterly meeting was in progress, and so vast was the concourse of people from many miles around that the services were conducted in a beautiful grove near the church. In the midst of the exercises, a heavy cloud arose and swept rapidly towards the place of worship. From the skirts of the grove the rain could be seen coming on across the fields.

The people were in consternation. No house could hold one-third of the multitude, and they were about to scatter in all directions. Easter rose in the midst of the confusion, "Brethren," cried he at the top of his voice, "be still while I call upon God to stay the clouds, till his word can be preached to perishing sinners."

Arrested by his voice and manner, they stood between hope and fear. He kneeled down and offered a fervent prayer that God would stay the rain that the preaching of his word might go on, and afterward send refreshing showers. While he was praying the angry cloud, as it swiftly rolled up to them, was seen to part asunder in the midst, pass on either side of them, and close again beyond, leaving a space several hundred yards in circumference perfectly dry. The next morning a copious rain fell again and the fields that had been left dry were well watered.—*Records of Prevailing Prayer*

Results of a life of prevailing prayer

William Taylor, now Methodist Episcopal Bishop to Africa, and one of the greatest of living men, was converted in 1841, when about twenty years old. He soon entered the ministry and spent seven years in the Baltimore Conference, and a second seven years in California. While there he became known the world over as the *California Street Preacher*. At the end of that time God clearly called him to general evangelistic work and for nearly forty years he has proved himself one of the most mighty men in Christian faith and labor that the church of God has ever known. In every continent on the globe and many of the islands of the sea he has proclaimed to listening multitudes the unsearchable riches of Christ, and untold thousands have been converted to God.

His first field, outside of the United States and Canada, with the exception of a few months in England and Ireland, was Australia, where God gave him six thousand souls as the result of the labor of two and one-half years. But still more wonderful victories awaited him. From Australia God led his servant to Africa, and there among the heathen, speaking what was to him an unknown tongue, God wrought so mightily, so gloriously, that the record is one of the most remarkable that can be found in all the history of the Christian Church. In the short space of seven months nearly 8,000 souls were converted. Out of this number 1,200 were colonists and the rest were Kaffirs, Fingoes and Hottentots.

The following account of a meeting held at Heald Town is quoted from the *Life of William Taylor*, by Rev. E. Davies, and is a fair illustration of the victories of that seven months' tour in Africa.

"The Wesleyan Chapel will hold about eight hundred. The first service was to the natives but Charles Pamla was not there to interpret. They found a Kaffir boy who, after private instruction from Mr. Taylor, answered a good purpose. His name was Siko. He put the sentences into Kaffir very rapidly. An extraordinary power rested upon the audience. Silence reigned, except the suppressed sobs. After the sermon the simplicity of the gospel was explained and the way of salvation by faith. When they were invited, about three hundred rushed forward to take the kingdom by storm. They all prayed audibly and the floor was wet with their tears, yet none seemed to be crying louder than their neighbors. The pastor was afraid, but God was in the movement.

"Fourteen whites were among the seekers. As soon as anyone was converted he was placed in a seat on the side of the pulpit and had an opportunity to testify for Christ. One hundred and thirty-nine natives and seven whites gave their names as converted in one service, which lasted five hours. In a few days after he held another service in the same place, at which God's power was manifested almost as on the Day of Pentecost. It surpassed anything Mr. Taylor ever saw. It was as the Spirit of God moving upon the waters, yea, as the Spirit that moved in the valley of dry bones and raised them up an exceeding great army.

"At this second service at Heald Town there were one hundred and sixty-seven converted, making a total for two services of three hundred six natives and ten whites saved.

"Many will wonder what kind of preaching could produce such marvelous results. He remarks:

"1. He preached the law as proclaimed from the burning Mount of Sinai, the law that is holy, just and good, the law that is our schoolmaster to bring us to Christ. He sought to kill before he made alive, to convict before he sought to point out Christ.

"2. He preached the gospel in all its wonderful and glorious provisions of justification, regeneration, adoption and the witness of the Spirit, and that no professor of religion should live without this grace.

"3. He preached purity of heart and the baptism of fire to all true believers, and his speech and his preaching was not with enticing words of man's wisdom, but in demonstration of the Spirit and of power.

"4. He spent much time in wrestling with God for divine guidance and power to win souls. At one place he could not succeed in starting a school until he had spent a whole night in prayer. All the most important movements of his life were the result of prevailing prayer.

"As a result of his faith and devotion, self-supporting missions have been established, not only in Africa, but also in India and South America, that are a wonder to the world. Christlike in his devotion, strong in faith and mighty in prayer, his life with its results must prove a never-failing inspiration to the church till time shall be no more."

Protected by angels

A good clergyman was once sent to a wild and dangerous part of Australia on some errand of duty and mercy. He traveled up to the place too poor to be in any great danger from bushrangers or robbers, but as he came back he had to bring in his saddlebags a large sum of money, not of his own, but belonging to the dying man he had been sent for to comfort.

He knew that a dangerous robber was aware that he was riding along this lonely track through the bush with all this money about him, and when he got to one part of the road he felt so frightened that he thought he was not trusting God as a Christian should.

He wanted a little quiet, so he got off his horse and stood by it, with his eyes shaded against it, praying for faith and courage not to be afraid of bushrangers or robbers, and to be guarded against them. He prayed till he felt calm enough to ride on, and then he mounted his horse and reached the town in safety with the money which he had in charge.

Some time later he was once more called to visit a man on a sick bed, and he recognized him as the robber of whom he had been so afraid in his ride. This man told him that he felt he could not die without confessing that on that day he had followed him, intending to rob and murder him, but could get no opportunity.

"Why did you not do it when I got off my horse?" asked the clergyman in surprise.

"I could not then," said the bushranger. "There were too many of you."

"What do you mean?" asked the clergyman. "I was quite alone in the bush, standing with my head resting against my horse's side for a long time. You could have killed me then."

"You were not alone," said the bushranger. "I saw you standing as you describe, but there was a man on each side of you."

Certainly there had been no other men with the clergyman in that hour of terror when he cried to God, but it is just possible that God really opened the robber's eyes and showed him his angels guarding his servant as he went on his dangerous duty, as Elisha's servant's eyes were opened to see celestial guardians around his master.

Whatever may be the explanation, God did send his angels to frighten away the robber, and by so doing be saved him from a great crime as well as the good clergyman from death.—*The Mission Worker*

Are they not all ministering spirits, sent forth to minister for them who shall be heirs of salvation?—Hebrews 1: 14.

Dr. Charles Cullis—the man that believed God

In 1862, a Christian physician in the city of Boston first recorded his desire to open a private hospital, or home, for those consumptives who were excluded from the public hospital on the ground that they were incurable. His professional income was

REMARKABLE ANSWERS TO PRAYER

already wholly consecrated to the Lord, but it was not at all sufficient to justify such an undertaking, and his only hope was that if his desire was prompted by the Holy Spirit, God would provide the way for its fulfillment.

Nearly two years later, as his biographer tells us, "the burden of the possible and yet impossible work grew so heavy that he began to pray in that alternative manner by which in after years he was accustomed to seek the settlement of difficult questions: 'Oh Lord, if this thought is from thee, give me the means to realize it, and if not, I pray thee take it out of my mind.' On the evening of that very day a trifling sum of money was given him, unsolicited, by a friend who knew of his plan for a consumptive's home." Such was the beginning of a work for God that has justly ranked Dr. Charles Cullis among the greatest men of faith the world has ever known.

Of the miracles of grace manifested in answer to the prayers of this devoted servant of God, we can only make a few brief statements. In September, 1864, he opened his first consumptive's home. Within twelve months, by the purchase of a second building, the capacity of the home was doubled and all bills were paid. Constant proofs had been given, both temporal and spiritual, that this servant of God had not trusted in vain. The amount of money received during the first year was $5,916.28.

The second year was in many respects one of trial. His faith was at times severely tested, but eighty-eight patients were cared for, souls were converted, and the total receipts given in answer to the prayer of faith were $8,293.10.

During the third year a children's orphanage was added to the work. At the end of the fifth year the work included five departments, the Consumptive's Home, the Orphanage, the Deaconess' House with its training school for nurses, the Willard Street Tract Depository and the Willard Street Chapel. In his summary of the report of the home for this year Dr. Cullis wrote, "The Lord has given, in answer to prayer, in cash during the year, $13,360.45. For the Home, since the commencement of the work, $47,627.85," and adds, "We still trust that every death has been in Christ. Regarding one case only, we cannot express ourselves with certainty, as this patient entered in a dying state, and in about thirty-six hours passed away. During this time he was too feeble to do more than to say he would ask for pardon through the blood of Jesus."

How severely at times his faith was tested is shown in the following item early in the sixth year: "This noon I had but twenty cents in the world, belonging to myself or any branch of the work. Money was needed to purchase groceries for supper. I asked the Lord to send the amount in season. At three o'clock a messenger from the Home called for the needed money. Just at the same moment, the mail arrived. The last letter opened contained a check for ten dollars from Dover, New Hampshire. Truly 'they that trust in the Lord shall not be confounded!' " Yet the same year he contracted for Grove Hall property, and agreed to pay $90,000.00 for it, in order that he might give his great household of suffering ones what the city could not afford them—abundant liberty and light and air.

Thus the work grew upon his hands, and in the introduction to the report of the seventeenth year of this work, are these memorable words: "For seventeen years I have believed! The Word has been true to me. My God faileth never. The promises stand out upon the firmament of his Word as the stars in the blue above. They shed their light as truly as the stars but, like them, they are only seen by those who look up. The promises are revealed to those who are 'looking unto Jesus.' "

In the same year of the work the entire amount of money received in response to simple faith in God reached and passed the sum of half a million of dollars. At the end of the twentieth year, two thousand seven hundred and seven consumptives had been cared for, the grand total of receipts was $621,960.36 and the value of real estate held in trust for the work at home and abroad, over and above the mortgages upon it, was not far from $300,000.00. Almost a thousand souls had in the Home found pardon and peace in the Saviour. Nor have we even mentioned the millions of tracts and books circulated, the home and foreign missions established, the Cancer Home, the Spinal Home, the Boydton Institute, and other departments of this great work.

How many thousand Christian hearts have been strengthened, how many of the Lord's children have been healed of disease? How many souls saved, how many believers baptized with the Spirit in our own and other lands, as a direct result of the devotion of this servant of God? Only the heavenly records can show. All this in answer to prayer! And yet the record is not finished, for though Dr. Cullis has gone from labor to reward, the different departments of the work which he established still prosper and his mighty influence still lives and the power of his life is still felt all over the Christian world. And when at the last great day all that has been accomplished by his life is made known, will not the answer of the redeemed in glory be, "All this in answer to prayer."

The Lord will provide

Some years since when we were living in Grand Rapids and were trying to pay for our little home there, our heart was burdened because of a payment of one hundred dollars that would be due in a few days. We were at the time laboring in revival work in the southern part of the state, were in very close circumstances and from the human standpoint could see no way of deliverance. But as we took the matter to the Lord in prayer we were greatly helped of the Spirit and received the evidence that God would supply the money needed to make the payment on the home, and wrote to wife that we had the evidence beyond the possibility of a doubt that the money was coming. And it came from a brother in Texas whom we had never seen but once or twice, $25.00 from another brother in the Lord, and the balance in smaller amounts from different sources. Nor is this by any means the only case in which God has helped us in a time of especial need. Even now we have great reason to praise him that in a time of such severe and general financial depression he has so greatly prospered us in the circulation of this book and for the evidence we have had that the book is proving a blessing and encouragement to thousands of hearts.

We also wish to record to the glory of God his great mercy in healing our wife of consumption in January last (1894). About a year before her father died of the same disease. She cared for him during part of his last illness and from that time her own strength steadily failed until she was entirely unable to work. Her lungs pained her constantly, her life was evidently rapidly wasting away, and aside from the power of God to deliver she had no hope of living more than a few months. We, too, felt that in God was our only hope of deliverance.

On the evening of January 15 we attended prayer meeting and then received the assurance of God's willingness to heal her. On our return we said to her, "If you will walk in the light God will heal you not many days hence."

Little more was said but a few minutes after she remarked to a friend who was visiting us, "My lungs certainly feel different." Early the next morning we were each led out to pray for the work to be done and were enabled by faith to claim victory. The same moment the difference in her breathing was clearly observable. Her lungs felt as if having received new life and she rapidly gained strength.

The same morning she was healed she felt clearly called to go out in evangelistic work in answer to a call that had come from friends not knowing of her illness. In about two weeks she started. Before her healing she had only attended public service once in about two months and then in great weariness, but while absent from home she preached every night for five weeks, without exception or difficulty with her lungs, and saw over fifty souls gloriously converted to God.

Truly our God is the Lord, and he is able and willing to help his children in every time of need. . .

If YOU ENJOYED *Touching Incidents and Remarkable Answers to Prayer* by S.B. Shaw, you will be blessed by G.C. Bevington's *Modern Miracles Through Prayer and Faith* (Original title: *Remarkable Incidents and Modern Miracles Through Prayer and Faith*) available from

Schmul Publishing Company, PO Box 716, Salem, OH 44460 or by calling 800-SPBOOKS (800-772-6657).

Ask for our current Book List...